Suicide in America

Also by Herbert Hendin

Suicide and Scandinavia
The Age of Sensation
Black Suicide
Psychoanalysis and Social Research
Living High
Wounds of War

Suicide in America

NEW AND EXPANDED EDITION

Herbert Hendin, M.D.

W. W. NORTON & COMPANY

NEW YORK · LONDON

The text of this book is composed in Electra,
with the display set in Optima and Deepdene.
Composition and Manufacturing by The Maple-Vail Book Manufacturing Group.

Library of Congress Cataloging-in-Publication Data

Hendin, Herbert.
Suicide in America / Herbert Hendin. — New and expanded ed.
p.   cm.
Includes bibliographical references and index.
1. Suicide—United States.   I. Title.
HV6548.U5H44   1995
362.2'8'0973—dc20   94-20554

ISBN 0-393-03688-X

W. W. Norton & Company, Inc., 500 Fifth Avenue, New York, N.Y. 10110
W. W. Norton & Company Ltd., 10 Coptic Street, London WC1A 1PU

1 2 3 4 5 6 7 8 9 0

To my friends and colleagues
at the American Suicide Foundation

Contents

Acknowledgments

SINCE THE FIRST EDITION OF this book was written I had the good fortune to be involved with the formation and development of the American Suicide Foundation, an organization dedicated to suicide prevention through research and education. The foundation has funded over a hundred and twenty investigators studying suicide in the six years of its existence in projects ranging from the neurobiological to the psychosocial.

My work for the foundation enables me to keep in touch with the work of a new generation of investigators who are advancing our progress in understanding and preventing suicide. It has also given me the privilege of working with distinguished senior investigators who are on the Scientific Advisory Committee of the American Suicide Foundation and who participate in reviewing grants, site visits, writing articles, and giving lectures on behalf of the foundation.

Many of them contributed indirectly to the material contained in this book. One of them—Dr. Alan Lipschitz, Associate Director of Research for the foundation—read and made helpful suggestions for the improvement of new material included in this edition.

National Institute of Mental Health grants (07207, 14633, 20818, and 32769) made it possible for me to do most of the studies on which this book is based.

The following journals gave me permission to use material

from articles of mine that they had published: the *American Journal of Psychiatry*, the *Archives of General Psychiatry*, the *Journal of Nervous and Mental Disease*, *American Journal of Psychotherapy*, *Suicide and Life-Threatening Behavior*, and *Issues in Law and Medicine*.

Kabi Hartman typed and corrected the many versions of the revised manuscript.

My editor at Norton, Carol Houck Smith, made valuable suggestions for rewriting that improved the quality of both the original version and the revised edition.

My wife, Josephine Hendin, an invaluable participant in all that I write, was particularly helpful with suggestions for organizing the first and last chapters, which were written for this revised edition.

Suicide in America

Introduction

WHEN I WAS STUDYING THE problem of suicide in the Scandinavian countries, some Danish psychiatrists who felt defensive about their country's high suicide rate as compared to that of Norway offered me a simple explanation. Since more Norwegians emigrate to the U.S. than Danes, the psychiatrists thought it likely that the unhappy Norwegians came to America and became part of *our* suicide statistics. This is not the case, however. The U.S. Bureau of Vital Statistics has kept figures on suicide among immigrants, which show that first-generation immigrants to this country from Denmark and Sweden have the same high suicide rates—compared to immigrants from Norway—as in their respective countries. In fact, the figures show a general correspondence in the suicide rate of first-generation immigrants to their country of origin—higher for the German-Americans, lower for Irish-Americans, etc. After the first generation the rates became indistinguishable from the American rate.[1]

The Scandinavian study was my first powerful encounter with the effect of culture on character in influencing suicide. Subsequent studies of suicide in this country, ranging from blacks in Harlem to college students and to suicide among Vietnam veterans, have persuaded me that without a psychosocial perspective we are limited in our ability to understand and to prevent suicide.[2]

The dramatic rise in suicide among the young (described in Chapter 2) cannot be explained solely by a genetic change, a change in neurobiology, or by the fact that we see or diagnose depression more frequently among the young. A psychosocial perspective is also critical in understanding treatment for the violent suicidal patient in contrast to the one who will never hurt anyone but himself, the difference in treating the young and the old, as well as understanding suicidal motivation in various cultures and subcultures.

One cannot write informatively about suicide without describing suicidal patients in detail. Epidemiological trends provide a valuable context in which to view the individual case, but without a picture of an elderly woman who is suicidal, or a young black who is both violent and suicidal, or a college student who has been preoccupied with suicide since childhood, even the professional reader will remain removed from and unable to understand—let alone treat—the suicidal patient.

The need for a psychosocial perspective that can include the individual patient was further brought home to me at a grand rounds lecture on suicide at a major medical school soon after the original publication of this book. A psychiatric resident asked me whether it was important to understand *why* someone wanted to kill himself since all that seemed necessary was to ascertain symptoms, make a diagnosis, and treat the patient with appropriate medication. Although the question was naive and symptomatic of the problems we face in educating today's psychiatrists with regard to suicidal patients, at the time it was understandable, given developments over the previous decade in both diagnostic classification and psychopharmacology.

Progress in the past ten years has made such a question more inappropriate today. Since the vast majority of patients with depression, manic depression, alcoholism, schizophrenia, or organic psychosis—conditions most frequently associated with suicide—are not suicidal, in recent years we have begun to separate the factors within any diagnosis that distinguish suicidal patients from those who are not, and to identify lethal factors that cross traditional diagnostic boundaries. Clinical, biological, genetic, and psychodynamic studies have all moved forward from this starting point. It will be helpful in dealing with the perspective on suicide addressed by this book to review some of these advances.

CLINICAL ADVANCES

A major clinical contribution to distinguishing between depressed patients who are suicidal and those who are not was made by Aaron Beck and his colleagues at the University of Pennsylvania.[3] They found that the seriousness of suicidal intent was related less to the degree of depression than with one particular aspect of depression—hopelessness about the future. High suicidal intent was observed in patients who showed minimal depression but whose expectations for the future were slight.

Subsequently, the Beck group reported that of 207 patients who were followed after being hospitalized while contemplating suicide, 89 ranked high on a measure of hopelessness utilized by the group. In the subsequent five years, 14 of the 207 patients committed suicide; 13 of them were from the group of 89 who ranked high on the measure of hopelessness.[4]

The diagnoses given the patients who ranked high on hopelessness cut across a wide spectrum. Half were diagnosed as having some form of depression, about a quarter were given a diagnosis of schizophrenia, and the rest were given diagnoses of personality disorders, neuroses, or other syndromes.

Recent work has begun to distinguish schizophrenic patients

who are suicidal from those who are not. Among schizophrenic patients, despite the occasional dramatic psychotic suicide, the greatest risk for suicide occurs during nonpsychotic depressed phases of the illness. Although nearly all of the suicidal schizophrenic patients appear depressed, it is possible to distinguish the most vulnerable among them. Young male patients with chronic relapsing illness, good educational backgrounds, and high performance expectations are most at risk. Their painful awareness of illness and fear of further mental disintegration lead to hopelessness about the future and suicide.[5]

PSYCHOBIOLOGY OF SUICIDE

Neurobiologists have also increasingly come to view suicidal behavior as a separate syndrome which is more frequent in psychiatric disorders but that has features that transcend any particular diagnosis. Evidence for this conclusion has come from several sources: despite new effective treatments for specific psychiatric disorders, there has not been a reduction in the suicide rate; suicide occurs across a wide variety of psychiatric diagnoses; and biochemical findings suggest that there are abnormalities specific to suicidal behavior rather than to a particular psychiatric diagnosis.[6]

The most dramatic such finding came when Marie Åsberg and her colleagues at the Karolinska Institute discovered in the mid-1970s that patients who had attempted or committed suicide had low cerebrospinal fluid levels of a metabolite of serotonin—a substance that transmits nerve impulses across synapses.[7] Although the Åsberg finding was originally the outgrowth of a study of depressed patients, low levels of the metabolite 5-hydroxyindoleacetic acid (5-HIAA), were observed in suicidal patients who were not clinically depressed but had a variety of disorders[8] ranging from borderline and antisocial personality disorders to schizophrenia. Low levels of 5-HIAA were also found in violent criminals, murderers, and attempted murderers who committed their crimes in an impulsive manner, and in arsonists, another group of criminals with poor impulse control. This has led researchers to see a common factor of poor impulse control and inability to regulate aggression as factors in suicidal behavior. Biological markers of suicide are being seen as related to variations in individual tolerance for adversity and in the capacity to restrain impulses and find solutions to problems.

Further support for this theory derives from the fact that levels of 5-HIAA appear to be low in patients at risk regardless of when the suicide attempt was made.[9] This suggests that the response is an enduring trait that might perhaps be genetically transmitted rather than a temporary state dependent on depression or psychological crisis.

Researchers caution that the correlation between low levels of 5-HIAA and suicide does not necessarily indicate a causal relationship—both may result from a common, as yet unrecognized cause. Nevertheless, there is hope that our ability to influence serotonin levels may prove therapeutic in preventing suicide.

For the time being the predictive capacity of low 5-HIAA levels in suicidal patients permits us to identify and concentrate treatment efforts on those at risk. In one study, Åsberg et al. have shown that among patients who attempt suicide, those with low cerebrospinal fluid levels of 5-HIAA, regardless of their diagnoses, have more than a 20 percent chance of killing themselves within a year.[10] As Åsberg points out, this is a stronger predictor of mortality than most of what we have in medicine.

Post-mortem brain research has supported the biochemical findings. Decreases in the levels of serotonin and 5-HIAA have been consistently observed in the brains of suicide victims. There is anatomical evidence in suicide victims of an increase in the number of serotonin receptor cells, an increase that would serve to reduce serotonin levels. These changes are independent of psychiatric diagnosis and seem specific to certain regions of the brain (the brain stem and other subcortical areas including the hypothalamus) that influence the likelihood of suicidal behavior.[11]

GENETIC FACTORS

Considerable evidence from studies of the families of suicides, twins, and of adoptees and their families indicates a genetic factor in major affective disorders, particularly of the bipolar type. Geneticists have asked the same question as clinical researchers—can the factors responsible for suicide be separated from those responsible for depression?

In studies carried out in the 1940s, Franz Kallman and his associates found no pairs of twins where both had committed suicide, and thus rejected the possibility of a hereditary factor in suicide.[12] This view went more or less unchallenged for twenty years until studies conducted in Denmark[13] with larger samples showed that, while there was no case where both *fraternal* twins committed suicide, in 20 percent of the cases involving *identical* twins, if one twin was a suicide, the other also died by suicide. The higher incidence of depressive disorders among the suicidal pairs led most geneticists to assume that the findings reflected the severity of the depressive disorder and only indirectly a predisposition to suicide.

There is a significantly higher rate of suicidal behavior in the families of patients who committed suicide than in the relatives of those who did not. Most of these studies indicate a high incidence of depressive episodes in patients with a family history of suicide, further supporting the linkage between a family history of depression and suicide.[14]

Another Danish study comparing the incidence of suicide in the biological and adoptive relations of adoptees who killed themselves also found a higher incidence of suicide in the biological relatives of the suicides, although the incidence of suicide was highest when the adoptee had had an affective disorder. Analysis of the Danish data, however, also indicated that suicidal adoptees who had no psychiatric history were more likely to have relatives who had no psychiatric history and were nonsuicidal. This finding led the authors to suggest the possibility of a genetic factor independent of such conditions as affective disorder and alcoholism which are frequently associated with suicide.[15]

A more recent study of the Amish population linked suicide and affective disorder over a one hundred-year period. The vast majority (92 percent) of the 26 suicides were diagnosed as having a major affective disorder and the suicides occurred in multigenerational families with a high frequency of affective disorders. The clustering of the suicides in four family trees, however, suggested that there might be genetic factors for suicide apart from those for affective disorders.[16]

The Danish and Amish studies as well as subsequent work[17] support the conclusion that there are genetic factors involved in suicide independent of those related to depression. It appears that such a genetic factor will likely be related to an inability to control impulsive behavior, with depression, other mental illness, or environmental stress serving as a trigger mechanism.[18]

PSYCHODYNAMIC DEVELOPMENTS

As used in contemporary psychiatry, psychodynamics deals with the quality of interpersonal relations, recurrent conflict patterns, and ultimately the meaning of actions and experiences. Such meaning is refined by the psychosocial context in which suicide occurs, but it is also understood through its affective and cognitive components, both of which have been more clearly defined in the last decade.

Although suicide is often described imprecisely as an escape, patients usually commit or contemplate suicide to escape from an intolerable affective state. In addition to hopelessness, some of the emotions that predominate in suicidal patients are desperation, rage, and guilt. The nature and intensity of these emotions help us to distinguish patients who are suicidal from those who are not.[19]

In the past decade it has become clear that the interrelation of rage, violence, and suicide first observed among seriously suicidal young urban blacks is not limited to that population. About 30 percent of violent individuals have histories of self-destructive behavior, while about 10 to 20 percent of suicidal persons have histories of violent behavior.[20] In psychological autopsies of young suicide victims, most of whom were white, almost half of them had histories of aggressive and antisocial behavior, a much higher rate than that of older age groups. Only one-fourth had histories of major depressive disorder, a much lower rate than in older populations.[21]

Despair is the word clinicians have used to convey the emotional state that distinguishes suicidal patients from those who are depressed but not suicidal. Despair has been described as developing from aloneness, murderous hate, and self-contempt[22] or, more generally, as resulting from the individual's "inability to maintain or envision any human connections of significance."[23]

Experience, however, with patients seen a few days prior to their suicide suggests an affective state closer to *desperation* than to hopelessness or despair. Many patients who feel despair or are hopeless about the future are resigned to their situation. Desperation implies not only hopelessness about change but also that life is impossible without such change. Anxiety and urgency are an integral part of desperation. The importance of these affective elements is confirmed by Jan Fawcett and his co-workers in Chicago; these researchers demonstrated that among patients with major affective disorder, anxiety is a stronger predictor of short-term risk for suicide than is hopelessness. [24]

The study of suicide and post-traumatic stress disorder (PTSD) in Vietnam veterans has helped to clarify our understanding of guilt as related to suicide. In a study I directed of 100 veterans with PTSD, 19 attempted suicide and 15 more were preoccupied with suicide. Guilt over actions in combat, usually the killing of civilians—and most often while feeling out of control—was the variable best able to explain their suicidal behavior. [25]

These actions took place when the men were, on average, 19 years of age, but their guilt persisted and fueled their suicide attempts and actual suicide. Their nightmares were often filled with images of punishment that reflected their actions in Vietnam.

In the vast majority of suicidal veterans, the actions committed understandably led to post-service guilt, self-hatred, and nightmares of punishment. The experience of a forward artillery spotter was typical. After seeing friends killed in combat, he called for artillery fire on a village he knew to be friendly, and through his binoculars watched as an old woman with betel nut stains on her teeth was blown up by a shell. At the time he laughed, but later he could not believe he had become so callous. In his recurring nightmare, he is captured, tied to a pole, and spat on by the villagers, led by the old woman with the stained teeth.

In a few cases, however, the combat actions were equivocal and some were related to guilt over surviving while close friends had not. One veteran, for example, shot and killed a woman who advanced toward his patrol and did not heed his order to stop. Although she turned out to be wired with explosives, the veteran ruminated over whether he could have stopped her by firing a warning shot or wounding her in the legs. Subsequently, his closest friend, who had extended his tour in Vietnam so they could return home together, was killed. The survivor's suicide attempts were related to dreams that linked his guilt over both deaths. Such veterans tended to feel they had no right to be enjoying what their dead friends could never enjoy—satisfactory work and good personal relations—and they acted in ways that sabotaged their own success.

The cognitive (perceptual) component of the meaning of suicide helps clarify the affective (emotional) aspects of the suicidal act. For example, the guilt of veterans over their combat actions complements their view of suicide as a deserved punishment. As Otto Kernberg aptly points out, "In clinical practice the question is not the patient's general feeling of 'hopelessness,' but what, concretely, the patient is hopeless about."[26]

Cognition generally refers to conscious ideation, whereas *meaning* includes both conscious and unconscious affects and perceptions. The meanings of suicide can be usefully organized around the conscious and unconscious meanings given to death by the suicidal patient.[27]

We have learned that suicidal patients give a special meaning to death, using death in their adaptation to life. Critical is their actual or fantasized use of their own death in an effort to control others or to maintain an illusory control over their own lives. Some of the common meanings given to death as described in this book are: death as reunion; death as rebirth; death as retaliatory abandonment; death as revenge; and death as self-punishment or atonement. We see suicide as revenge and as self-punishment somewhat differently from the way we did ten years ago.

In Freud's formulation, suicide expresses a repressed wish to kill an ambivalently regarded lost love object, and thus it was ultimately an act of revenge.[28] The mechanism was seen as primarily unconscious. Now we see the striking presence of conscious hostility when young people use suicide as an expression of revenge toward their parents. Such youngsters usually feel overwhelmed by murderous feelings toward their parents, and are even fearful of acting on them. Their feelings may be conscious or expressed in dreams. The act of suicide may be precipitated by some immediate frustration followed by an impulsive response, but invariably a history reveals a youngster who—even if seeming to be functioning well—cannot cope with murderous rage toward parents.

A middle-class girl of 15 who was doing well in school, was well-liked by her many friends, and was said by her parents to have shown no evidence of problems, shot herself in the head with her father's gun after a fight with her parents over their refusal to allow her to go to an amusement park. Sessions with the parents after her death revealed long-standing problems between the girl and her mother. After the suicide, her grandmother revealed that the young woman had said that she dreamed she had killed her mother; shortly before killing herself, she told a friend that suicide would be a way of getting back at her parents.[29]

In the early psychodynamic formulation of suicide, guilt over hatred of an incorporated lost love object was seen as underlying the need for self-punishment. In destroying himself or herself *and* the object, the individual accomplished atonement as well as revenge.

Our later understanding of narcissistic pathology has modified that view. In a classic paper on suicide, Elizabeth Kilpatrick wrote, "When we understand narcissism not as love of the self, but as love of the idealized image of the self, we become aware of the gravity of self-hate and alienation which needs to be present."[30] She pointed out that the unconscious idealized self-image is often accompanied by its counterpart, a despised self-image. Contemporary psychodynamic theory, with its emphasis on the importance of "splitting" as a mechanism of defense, has increasingly seen suicide as an attempt by the superego—with which the good self is identified—to eliminate the bad self.[31] Loss, self-hatred, and failure are directly and inextricably entwined for such suicidal individuals.

Common in psychiatric practice today are young people who feel they have failed to meet their own and their families' social, academic, and vocational aspirations and who feel they fall short of matching the achievements of their siblings and peers. Their lives are filled with a sense of failure and humiliation, their dreams frequently center on "having missed the boat," and their suicide is often an expression of self-hatred and a need for punishment.[32]

Typical was a 20-year-old patient who committed suicide after he recorded this dream in his diary: "I was back at high school and saw familiar faces. I felt embarrassed and humiliated. They were going on with life. I tried to be incognito but was spotted." In a similar vein he wrote, "When I think of myself as a recovering patient, I am more patient with myself and more willing to change things. When I compare myself to my potential, I mourn."[33]

All of the psychodynamic meanings ascribed to death by suicidal patients can be conceptualized as responses to loss, separation, or abandonment.[34]

- Rebirth and reunion fantasies may be attempts to undo or deny such a loss.
- Becoming the one who leaves is one way to avoid the feeling of having been left.

- Feelings of rage that are repressed, suppressed, or expressed may derive from the experience of loss.
- Self-punishment may express guilt at having been responsible for a loss and the fantasy of rapprochement through atonement.
- Numbness or deadness and the insistence that one is already psychologically dead may reflect determination not to live without the lost object.

For most suicidal patients a rejection of life usually includes a rejection of the parents from whom it originated. Anyone so doing is likely to feel in a deep way that he or she was abandoned first. In that sense, although we see a wider range of psychodynamics involving suicide than did Freud, his insight into the relationship of abandonment, loss, and suicide has perhaps the most meaning and has stood the test of time.

THERAPEUTIC CONSIDERATIONS

The need to use one's death to express desperation, rage, or guilt reflects, among other things, difficulty in using less extreme forms of communication. Understanding and conveying to the patient what it is that he or she is hoping to express by dying can provide crucial relief and can reduce the short-term risk of suicide.[35]

The affective states and their accompanying death fantasies are often activated by trauma and seem in part an attempt to resolve an intolerable emotional state through use of a fantasized or inappropriate attachment to someone. The patient's own unique pattern of affect, cognition, and meaning is most dramatic immediately before or after a suicide attempt, during what is referred to as a suicidal crisis or episode.[36] The same combination of psychodynamic factors is present in suicidal patients during the chronic phases of their illness and it is a central element of the individual's psychic life.

For example, grandiose fantasies revolving around conquering or controlling death, immortality, and identification with an important political or religious figure are common among suicidal patients. Such grandiosity usually reflects disturbances in self-esteem and identity formation that occur early in childhood.[37] The fears of disintegration or loss of identity that often derive from such developmental disturbances are frequent in borderline or schizophrenic patients who become suicidal; in suicidal veterans with post-traumatic stress disorder; and in enraged suicidal patients regardless of diagnosis. Although the acute threat of disintegration remits as the suicidal crisis is resolved, the underlying identity problems remain, as does the fantasy of resolving them through suicide.[38]

Understanding what is known of the psychodynamics of suicide is valuable and critical in treating suicidal patients. Patients who committed suicide and who had not received appropriate psychotropic medication or had not been hospitalized when necessary have long been a concern. Today an equally common concern involves suicidal patients, in or out of hospitals, who are receiving appropriate medication but inadequate psychotherapy. The example of the patient who kills himself after his depression has lifted in response to medication serves as a reminder that elements other than depression are involved in suicide. The best treatment today focuses on the interactive roles that diagnosis, medication, and psychotherapy play in the treatment of those who are suicidal. If the psychotherapy of such patients is to be effective, it must be guided by a knowledge of the psychodynamics of suicide.

SOCIAL FACTORS

Although many major factors, such as the stress on family ties and the spread of alcohol and drug abuse among the young, are explored within this study, there are four important social currents that have moved to the forefront of social concern in the past decade: the alarming increase in the number of firearms purchased in America; increased awareness of how potentially self-destructive people are affected by media representation of suicide; the realization that disproportionate numbers of creative people are subject to affective illness, substance abuse, and suicide; and the gathering force of the movement to legalize assisted suicide and euthanasia.

That violence became an overwhelming issue over the last decade is underlined by the fact that access to firearms is now being viewed as a major public health problem. The Centers for Disease Control (CDC) has announced that it is developing a multifaceted National Plan for Injury Control, recommending reduced access to lethal weapons and applying public health approaches, such as are used to deal with epidemics of infectious disease. Just as government attempts to reduce motor vehicle fatalities by raising the drinking age, requiring seatbelts, and educating the public about the dangers of driving while using drugs or alcohol succeeded in reducing driving fatalities, so the CDC hopes legislative efforts to control firearms will help prevent avoidable injury, including suicide.

While some who are seriously suicidal will likely find an alternative method, those who are most vulnerable to impulsive suicide are clearly the most affected by the availability of guns. C. Everett Koop, former U.S. surgeon general, and George D. Lundberg subtitled their editorial in the *Journal of the American Medical Association* (June 10, 1992), "Time to Bite the Bullet Back." They point out that the dramatic increase in suicide among children and adolescents in the United States is "almost solely due to firearms."[39]

There has also been a steady rise in the use of guns as a method of suicide by adult women and men. Since in 1994 almost 60 percent of the over 30,000 suicides in the United States each year involve guns, and since guns are responsible for even more deaths by suicide than there are by homicide, research in the past decade has closely examined the relation between firearms and suicide. The suicide rate has been found to be higher in those parts of the country where people own guns, particularly handguns. States with more restrictive gun laws have lower rates of firearm suicides, and, although they have higher rates by other means, their suicide rate is lower overall. Studies have also found that the suicide rate falls in the years after new laws restrict handgun ownership.[40]

Although three-quarters of gun owners keep guns at least partly for protection, and one-fifth give self-defense at home as the major reason for having a gun, a study by Arthur Kellermann and his co-workers of gun deaths at home found that there were 43 suicides, criminal homicides, or accidental gunshot deaths involving a gun for every case of homicide for self-protection. Of 398 consecutive gun deaths occurring in homes where firearms were kept, only 2 of those killed (.5 percent) were intruders; 12 (3 percent) were accidental gunshot deaths; 50 (12.6 percent) were homicides, primarily adults in the home killing each other during a quarrel; and in 333 cases (83.2 percent) the guns were used by an adolescent or adult to kill him- or herself.[41]

But it should not be assumed that the presence of a gun in the home is associated with psychiatric illness; it is not. Suicide victims from homes where guns are kept have psychiatric disorders less often than did suicide victims from homes without guns.[42] This indicates that even in the absence of clear psychiatric illness, suicide is greatly facilitated by having a readily available firearm.

Fewer than 10 percent of suicides buy guns with the specific intent of killing themselves. Fewer still buy them within the weeks preceding their death, meaning that a waiting period to delay gun ownership is only a first step toward gun control, not likely in itself to reduce suicide. A high percentage of those who survive suicide attempts with guns indicate that their attempts were impulsive and were often made under the influence of alcohol. A strong association has been demonstrated between firearm suicide and intoxication at the time of death.[43]

A comparative study of regions with and without gun control measures indicated that such measures are likely to be most effective in reducing youth suicide.[44] The presence of a gun in the home and a previous suicide attempt have been shown to be the two strongest predictors of adolescent suicide. Attempts at storing the gun in a safe place were relatively ineffective; the decisive factor was the presence of the gun in the home.

The importance of guns in youth suicide is not surprising since impulsive suicide attempts are common among the young and the availability of a gun makes it more likely that such an attempt will be fatal. Gun accessibility makes it possible for impulsive persons to act on suicidal impulses. Since the greatest increase in suicide has occurred among young people, restricting and licensing gun access offers a possible concrete way of reducing suicide, especially among the young.

The current public discussion of the role of the media in encouraging violence is bringing to a wider audience what researchers into suicide have long been discussing. In the past two decades, prominent news coverage of a suicide has been found to increase suicidal behavior, particularly among young people, within the area of the coverage.[45] The size of the increase has been related to the celebrity of the suicide victim and the amount of publicity given to the story. Further confirmation of media influence on suicide has come from research examining the *decrease* in suicide in cities where there have been extended newspaper blackouts. Just after Marilyn Monroe's death, the notes of a number of suicides linked their own deaths to her presumed suicide. Subsequent studies documented a significant rise in suicides in both the U.S. and England in the month following Monroe's death. After John Lennon was murdered, several suicides linked their death to his. A sense of sharing the tragic death or suicide of someone famous, or of identifying suicide with a cause, may enable vulnerable persons to feel their deaths have meaning.

Certain features in media coverage are likely to encourage imitative suicide: detailed depictions of methods employed; minimization or lack of presentation of the physical consequences of an attempt; lack of coverage of the victim's mental health problems; simplistic rationales, such as low marks in school or "pressure"; emphasis on the victim's engaging qualities; mention of the "rewards" associated with the suicide (getting even, gaining attention); and where no mention is made of models of effective treatment.[46]

Recent evidence is confirming the long-held suspicion that there is a clinical link, with important psychosocial implications, between creativity and mental illness. Work by Nancy Andreasen established that the association was specifically between creativity and affective illness and more particularly between creativity and bipolar (manic depressive) disorder.

Eighty percent of a sample of 30 writers studied by Andreasen at the Iowa Writers' Workshop had suffered from affective disorder compared to 30 percent of a matched control sample whose occupations ranged from lawyers to hospital administrators and social workers. Forty-three percent of the writers had suffered from bipolar disorder in comparison with 10 percent of the controls.[47]

Andreasen also looked at patterns of creativity among the family members and first-degree relatives of the writers and the control group. Using a somewhat larger sample (over 100 relatives of both the writers and the control group) substantial creative achievements—such as writing novels, dancing in a major company, performing as a concert artist, or making a major scientific contribution—were significantly more present in the relatives of writers than in the controls. The fact that the creativity was not just literary but was expressed in diverse areas such as art, music, dance, or mathematics indicated that whatever is transmitted in families is a general factor that predisposes to creativity rather than to a specific gift of a verbal nature. The variability in creativity also suggested the possibility of some form of genetic transmission since, if social learning were the sole factor involved, one would expect a preponderance of literary creativity in the families of writers. [48]

Other studies have confirmed an elevated rate of mood disorder in the artistically gifted. University of Tennessee psychiatrist Dr. Hagop Akiskal and his wife, Kareen, undertook an extensive psychiatric interview study of 30 award-winning European writers, poets, painters, and sculptors. Their study found that 50 percent of the writers and artists had suffered from a major depressive episode. [49] Another study by the Akiskals, in collaboration with David Evans of Memphis State University, showed similar findings in blues musicians. [50]

Dr. Kay Jamison, of Johns Hopkins University, studied 47 eminent British writers and artists to broaden understanding of the creative process. She linked the intense productive and creative episodes experienced by the group members with the symptoms described in DSM III as typical of hypomania—enthusiasm, energy, self-confidence, speed of mental association, euphoria, and less need for sleep. The elevation in mood often preceded the creative periods rather than being the result of them.

Jamison recognizes that it is unclear whether the symptoms

seen in the creative group and in hypomania are etiologically related syndromes or patterns of behavior that are similar in expression but causally unrelated. Moreover, Jamison describes a greater ability to concentrate as present in over 60 percent of the writers and artists during creative episodes while distractibility is a more usual symptom of manic and hypomanic behavior.

What Jamison has done, perhaps more comprehensively than anyone else, is to document the frequency with which famous poets, writers, composers, musicians, and artists have suffered from depression or manic-depressive illness, often complicated by alcoholism, while detailing the frequent family histories of such disorders among their close relatives. She powerfully describes the personal anguish endured by so many of those who are creative while experiencing affective disorders. For example, Byron, Keats, Shelley, Tennyson, and Coleridge were among the poets suffering from depressive illness. Among modern American poets, John Berryman, Hart Crane, Vachel Lindsey, Sylvia Plath, and Anne Sexton were suicides.[52]

A social factor of potentially greater importance for the treatment of suicidal patients and the prevention of suicide is the movement to legalize assisted suicide and euthanasia. The likelihood of increased suicide among the elderly, the ill, those frightened by illness, and the depressed of all ages if euthanasia and assisted suicide should be legalized, is great. The prospect of such legalization has warranted rewriting and expanding the last chapter of this book, drawing on the experience of the Netherlands, where there is acceptance and de facto, if not formal, legalization of euthanasia.

The recent legal acceptance by the Dutch of assisted suicide for suicidal patients who are mentally, but not physically, ill implies that physician-assisted suicide can be a treatment for suicidal patients. It appears to confirm the fears of a "slippery slope" that moves from assisted suicide to euthanasia, from assisted suicide and euthanasia for the physically ill to those who are mentally ill, and from voluntary to involuntary euthanasia. A recent Dutch government commissioned report on the subject documenting the alarming frequency of involuntary euthanasia further confirms such fears.[53]

Despite the more than 30,000 deaths a year to suicide, the hundreds of thousands of suicide attempts each year, the millions who have lost someone due to suicide, and the tens of millions who suffer from crippling mental illnesses that may end in suicide, until recently there was no organized effort by concerned citizens and professionals for research, education, and treatment programs to prevent suicide. The unfortunate blame attached to suicide extended to survivors, so that those most motivated to insist that society address the problem of suicide felt they had to suffer in silence.

This attitude is changing because of an alarming increase in the rate of youth suicide. Between 1955 and 1980 the suicide rate among young men aged 15–24 tripled, while the rate for young women in the same age group more than doubled. The rate increase coincided with the coming of age of the "baby boom" generation. The absolute number of suicides in that age group went from a few hundred a year—suicide among 15 to 24 year olds was an uncommon event when I was a psychiatric resident (1950–52)—to 5,000 per year, or one-sixth of the total suicides in the population. No society could afford to see this happening to its young people. Nor could the anguish of so many parents and siblings be contained any longer.

Survivors of suicide began to form support groups to cope with their loss and get on with their lives. Many of them want to be involved in the effort to fund the research, education, and treatment programs that would help others avoid a similar tragedy. Such efforts also give meaning to their personal loss.

In 1987, scientists, survivors, business and community leaders, and volunteers united to form the American Suicide Foundation. This joint effort to fund the research and treatment needed to prevent suicide while educating the public to understand suicide as a medical problem has had impressive initial success that augurs well for future progress.

1. A Psychosocial Perspective

SUICIDE SEEMS SUCH AN individual and personal act whose consequences are tragic to a relatively small group of family, colleagues, and friends that it is easy to lose sight of its social dimension. But suicide, like crime, drug abuse, and alcoholism, arouses a social concern that extends beyond the affected individual and his or her immediate family because it seems to threaten values that most communities have believed essential for survival. We tend to be mildly amused at the classical Greeks, who asked the would-be suicide to first secure permission from the state, but that attitude reflected an awareness that suicide has social or antisocial implications.

The feelings individuals have about life—what they live for and whether there are conditions under which they would prefer not to live—involve a delicate balance of the personal and the cultural. Both the motives for suicide and its frequency have varied from culture to culture. Some primitive cultures have suicide rates that are higher than our own; in others, suicide appears to be virtually unknown. Suicidal people from different cultures may share a common denominator of unhappiness, but what makes them unhappy, how they perceive themselves, and why they want to die are matters largely dictated by the time and place in which they live.

Suicide among the Japanese or the Eskimos differs in meaning, motive, and significance from suicide in the United States, and this is not hard for most people to imagine. It probably also comes as no great surprise that suicide among young urban blacks and suicide among white college students in the United States show striking differences. Yet only in recent years have researchers become aware of other equally predictable motivational differences in suicide, such as those based on age and on sex.

Given the mixture of personal and social forces that so evidently contribute to suicide, how is it that the study of suicide has been so lacking in psychosocial perspective? Part of the answer lies in the limitations of the two men who contributed most to our understanding of suicide—Emile Durkheim and Sigmund Freud. Their work, important in itself, had a continuing and pervasive impact on subsequent work in the field.

Freud gave us our first important psychodynamic insight into suicide, although he did not deal directly with the problem of suicide and described in detail the suicide attempt of only one patient. What he did see, however, and in large numbers, was depressed patients. In "Mourning and Melancholia" (1917) Freud stated that the self-hatred observed in depression originated in anger toward a love object that the individual turned back on himself.[1] He regarded suicide as the ultimate form of this phenomenon, and when he returned to the subject in a 1920 paper, he expressed doubt that suicide could take place without the repressed desire to kill someone else.[2] This concept of suicide as a kind of inverted murder was extremely important although, unfortunately, some overworked it in an effort to explain all suicide.

Freud made his observations on depression long before he came to the conclusion that anger or aggression could be nonerotic in origin. At the time when he wrote "Mourning and Melancholia," he held the view that all aggression had to have a sexual origin. Hence this article is filled with a complex attempt to explain anger and self-directed anger in sexual terms. Ten years later Freud expressed surprise at his having "overlooked the universality of non-erotic aggression."[3] Since he never rewrote his earlier report, the extraneous libidinal explanations for the existence of anger remained unaltered. The basic psychological truth contained in the 1917 paper also remains—namely, that anger toward a lost love object can become self-directed, can lead to depression, and can be a motivating force in suicide.

Freud also recognized that an ambivalent, narcissistic quality characterized relationships that terminated in severe depression. Because early psychoanalytic theory and interest were too instinct-oriented to focus on the role of such affective interactions, little was done with this observation. Contemporary psychoanalytic efforts to include the variations in the ways individuals relate affectively to each other are leading to a reemphasis on this aspect of Freud's insight.

His instinctual frame of reference led Freud in 1920 to see aggression as the manifestation of a death instinct.[4] The death instinct violated too many basic observations of biologists and psychologists for it to be accepted by them or by more than a small minority of psychoanalysts. By 1922 John Dewey had already given his analysis of the misconceptions that arose from elevating a phenomenon to a cause by attributing it to an instinct.[5] "Instinct psychology" soon lost much of its influence in the field of psychology, although it held on longer in psychoanalysis. Gregory Zilboorg probably spoke for a majority of psychoanalysts, however, when he wrote in 1937, "To say that the death instinct gains the upper hand over the life instinct is merely an elaborate way of stating that man does die or kill himself."[6]

Freud also saw little need for systematically considering the problems of social structure that we now see as an important determinant of behavior. His theoretical perspective stressed the immutable and universal context of human drives rather than the changing and culturally relative nature of institutions and practices. It is understandable that Freud's orientation did not lead him to a concern with the psychological impact of the social institutions of particular cultures or with such psychosocial questions as why suicide was very high in one country and very low in another. Nor would his instinctual frame of reference have enabled him to adequately resolve such questions had they arisen. Biologically speaking, the differences between Englishmen and Germans or between Norwegians and Swedes are not very important, and Freud assumed he was dealing with psychological evolution much as Darwin had dealt with biological evolution. Understandably under the influence of the evolutionary anthropology of his day, Freud saw the psychological life of primitive man as "a well-preserved picture of an early stage of our own development."[7] This approach made study of the culture as a unit unnecessary, and Freud had little interest in the comparative anthropology that developed during his lifetime.

Subsequent contributions to the psychodynamics of suicide were made within Freud's frame of reference. Most notably, Karl Menninger, in *Man against Himself* (1938), deepened our understanding of the relation between suicide and other forms of self-destructive behavior such as severe alcoholism.[8] Without a frame of reference that made it possible to deal with social or cultural forces in a meaningful way, however, suicide in psychoanalytic work remained in a social and cultural vacuum.

Most students of suicide have had to turn to the French sociologist Emile Durkheim and to the subsequent elaboration of his work in attempting to fill that vacuum. There is much to be learned from Durkheim, but anyone who expects to find in his work or that of his followers the psychosocial perspective missing in Freud will be disappointed.

In *Suicide,* first published in 1897, Durkheim defined the vulnerable population with regard to suicide and provided a theoretical framework to explain this vulnerability.[9] He saw rising suicide rates in the Western world as a function of the failure of state, church, and family to remain the forces for social integration that they had been prior to the industrial revolution. Vulnerability to suicide, in his view, existed in people who were not integrated into any religious, communal, or family group. Even more vulnerable were individuals who had suffered a disruption in their previous pattern of social integration. The single, widowed, and divorced, for example, then as now, were observed to have generally higher suicide rates than married people. Why some who were single, widowed, or divorced were suicidal when most were not was of little interest to Durkheim. His sense that "social facts must be studied as things, as realities external to the individual" made the psychology of suicide seem irrelevant.

Durkheim's social categories were used to explain the variation in the rate of suicide from country to country. Catholic countries had low suicide rates, and that was in line with his observations that Catholicism forbade divorce and was a more cohesive religion than Protestantism. Subsequent extension of Durkheim's work eventually highlighted some of its weaknesses. It did not explain why Austria, a predominantly Catholic country, had one of the world's highest suicide rates. Nor did it adequately explain the Scandinavian phenomenon of strikingly high suicide rates in Denmark and in Sweden alongside the low rate in Norway. These particular limitations of Durkheim's theory are not surprising, since it rested on putting people into categories, based on age, sex, religion, or marital status, that had no reference to culture *per se* and left no room for what it meant to be Austrian or Swedish or Japanese or French.

Most work on suicide has become an unsynthesized mixture of Durkheim and Freud. Social statistical profiles of the vulnerable have substituted for psychological understanding of suicide. We are thus told over and over by investigators in different cities and in different countries that elderly white men living alone in inner cities have the highest suicide rates. We seldom find discussions of what distinguishes those who are suicidal from those who are not, let alone of the differences in motivation for suicide of elderly Swedes and elderly Americans. Most such work devotes only a single section to the motivation for suicide, uses Freud's dynamic formulation as the organizing point, and deals with all groups in a potpourri.

It has been evident for several decades that a truly psychosocial approach, not an amalgam of Freud and Durkheim, but an approach that includes the examination of the psychodynamics of suicide of individuals in differing social groups, is required for any deeper understanding of the significance of suicide in a society. My work has attempted to move in that direction.

The psychosocial perspective adopted for this book aims at understanding how psychic, social, and cultural factors are interwoven to produce suicidal behavior in Americans from very different backgrounds. The organizing issue of a psychosocial frame of reference must be the connection between psychic and social conditions. It seeks to understand how cultural and social conditions and institutions influence the individual's values and aspirations, while providing the opportunities and possibilities for individual adaptation. Social factors operating through the family have a powerful effect on the individual's early experiences and adaptive capacities, causing certain psychodynamic configurations to develop and shaping their manifestations.

The motives for suicide are dependent on cultural expectations, on the degree to which an individual does or does not incorporate them, and on one's personal capacity to fulfill them. For example, a Marquesan woman raised to see herself primarily as a courtesan might kill herself over her failure to hold her men, but she would not punish herself for what she felt or did not feel toward her children. Women in our culture who are disturbed or guilty about an absence of maternal feeling toward their children may become suicidal, but not all women regard such feeling as something they must have.

It is consistent with a psychosocial perspective that the motivation for suicide cannot be treated as a single subject in a single chapter. The search for one formula that can encompass all groups has led psychiatrists and sociologists to such generalizations as "social isolation" that explain little and take us not much further than did Durkheim. It would seem self-evident, for example, that the motives for suicide of the young are different from those of the old. Older suicides are usually concerned with the stresses characteristic of the latter part of life, young suicides most often with not allowing life to begin. The young and the old will be the subjects of separate chapters in this book, and, within each, differences in the motives of women and men will be compared and contrasted.

No single fact about suicide has aroused more attention than the dramatic rise in the suicide rate of young people over the past four decades. In this country the rate has more than doubled among young women 15–24 and more than tripled among young men in the same age group. Young people of both sexes in this age group now constitute one-sixth of the over 30,000 suicides in the United States each year. Who these young people are, what motivates them to end their lives, and whether the rising trend in young suicides will continue are questions that we will be addressing.

Although the suicide rate among older people has been relatively stable, it is the older white population in the United States that has the highest suicide rate. White men over 50, for example, who make up 10 percent of the United States population, are responsible for 30 percent of all suicides. We will look at the lives of older men and older women who are suicidal to explore the relation of suicide in older people both to lifelong emotional problems and to the crises frequently related to growing old: loss of loved ones, decline in physical, emotional, and mental capacity, and economic hardship.

Having examined the different patterns of suicide associated with growth and age, we will turn to a discussion of three clinical and social conditions that have been correlated with suicide: violence, alcohol abuse, and more questionably, homosexuality. All of these phenomena reflect certain social and cultural stresses. Although some cultures may express stress in one way rather than another—illustrated by the traditionally high suicide and low homicide rates in Denmark and Sweden—such indicators of stress often rise or fall together. In our young population, for example, the rise in suicide of the past twenty-five years has been accompanied by an equally dramatic rise in violent crime and in drug and alcohol abuse.

Suicidal individuals are also far more likely than otherwise comparable nonsuicidal ones to be alcoholic. Alcohol is therefore often simplistically seen as causing suicide in ways that are psychologically misleading. A man may drown his sorrows in alcohol for years before he decides to drown himself. He may even drink himself to death. Both the drinking and the suicide can be responses to the same despair. Moreover, early life disturbances in individuals who later become suicidal or alcoholic lead to a vulnerability that often does not appear to be specifically directed to only one form of psychopathology.

Violence has a more direct connection with suicide, whether in the murderer who kills himself, in the young black whose suicide is an attempt to control his violence, or in the mother who murders her child as part of her own suicide. The role of violence, homosexuality, and drug and alcohol abuse in suicide will be discussed in detail.

Next, we will explore some significant clinical considerations regarding suicide, focusing in particular on the relation between methods and motives and on the problems of psychotherapy with suicidal patients. The way in which an individual chooses to kill himself has much to tell us about the motivation for suicide. Whom the individual chooses to find his or her body and what he or she writes in a suicide note are usually informative. For some suicides, only a particular method—such as hanging or jumping—will do, and that method has specific personal meaning for the individual. The method is also influenced by psychosocial considerations. Among young urban blacks, there is a strikingly high incidence of suicide by jumping from buildings. There is an equally striking frequency of the use of firearms by women, as well as men, in the South. The relation between method and motive in suicide will be the subject of a separate chapter. The neglected subject of psychotherapy with the suicidal patient will be examined. There exist many misconceptions about the treatment of the suicidal individual and considerable harm can result from misguided approaches. Treatment problems presented by young suicidal people and by older ones are very different, but with psychosocial understanding treatment of the suicidal individual can be effective.

Social attitudes and social policy toward suicide must be understood in the context in which they occur. A psychosocial exploration of suicide will be of use in defining what a reasonable social policy toward suicide in this country should be. Social policy that does not rest on psychosocial knowledge is left to the mercy of those who want to ignore, advocate, or punish in a parochial way that serves the interests of society poorly. The last section of the book explores social policy in dealing with suicide,

including suicide prevention measures, institutional commitment of suicidal patients, and the individual's "right to suicide."

Until relatively recently, Western cultures tried to prevent suicide by attaching social shame to the memory of the deceased,
threatening punishment in an afterlife, mutilating the corpse,
denying proper burial, and imposing fines and imprisonment on
anyone who survived an attempt. The question of whether the
sanctions were justified on religious grounds—based on the individual's rejection of God—or on secular ones—based on his failure to meet his obligation to the state—was less critical than the
attitude toward suicide that all such sanctions reflected.

According to English common law, suicide was a felony. The
suicide was not to be buried in consecrated ground, but custom
and practice went further: As recently as 1823, a suicide's body
was buried at midnight at a crossroad with a stake driven through
the body and a stone placed over the face. In time, suicides came
to be treated less harshly, but suicide remained a felony and
attempted suicide a misdemeanor in England until 1961, when
both laws were abolished.

The United States never adopted the English common law
with regard to suicide. The leading American case, the 1903 Illinois case of *Burnett* v. *People*, states, "We have never seen fit to
define what character of burial our citizens shall enjoy; we have
never regarded the English law as to suicide as applicable to the
spirit of our institutions."[10] The 1908 Texas case of *Sanders* v.
State declared directly, "Whatever may have been the law in
England . . . so far as our law is concerned, the suicide is inno-
cent of criminality."[11] And in the few states in which suicide was
regarded as criminal, punishment was not carried out.

Commitment of the mentally ill, including the suicidal, to
asylums became common practice in the United States only after
1820. Social reformers and directors of mental hospitals viewed
asylums as the enlightened answer to the problem of mental ill-

ness. Short-term cures were envisioned in an atmosphere free from the aspirations and pressures of American life. Confusing discharge with cure, leading American physicians in the last century who both helped to create and were caught up in the enthusiasm about the asylum claimed that the institutions they ran were curing 100 percent of their patients.[12] Since much was being accomplished for the patient, little concern was given to legal safeguards to protect patients who might not have wanted to be confined.

As the asylum came to be seen as a failed institution that not only did not help most psychiatric patients but often abused them instead, concern with providing legal protection for those to be committed grew apace with concern for improved conditions within the asylum.[13] By the beginning of this century, most states had passed laws protecting the civil rights of patients for whom involuntary incarceration was proposed. In virtually every state law, however, the danger of suicide was identified as one of the important justifications of commitment.

Is it justifiable to keep someone locked up just because he is potentially suicidal? If so, how long should the confinement last? Does it help? What legal safeguards should a patient have to see that his rights are protected? Current involuntary commitment procedures with particular reference to the suicidal, as well as recent efforts to reform these procedures, will be discussed in detail in a separate chapter.

In this century, suicide has continued to be considered an expression of mental illness. As society has felt an increasing moral obligation to prevent the individual from harming himself, suicide prevention has been seen more and more as the task of psychologists, psychiatrists, and mental health paraprofessionals. Suicide prevention organizations, composed primarily of lay volunteers who encourage suicidal people to deal with their problems in some other way, have developed in the U.S. and other countries. We will examine the results of these efforts as part of a discussion of suicide prevention in this country.

Civil libertarians criticize the labeling of suicidal behavior as mental illness. They point out that we are classifying as illness a host of behaviors that were formerly considered immoral, sinful, or criminal—certain types of sexual behavior and drug and alcohol abuse as well as suicide. They have been joined by euthanasia advocates who have expanded their call for a painless death for the terminally ill into a claim for the "right to suicide." In the last chapter, we will discuss the psychosocial issues raised by those who argue that suicide is a purely personal matter. We will also try to indicate how psychosocial knowledge of suicide can help translate social concern into something more effective and more humane than coercion or laissez-faire.

The perspective that underlies our treatment of suicide is clinical and psychodynamic; it should be distinguished from what is currently being called social psychiatry. Social psychiatry has increasingly tended to view emotional illness as a function of such factors as class, sex, or race, at the expense of clinical, intrapsychic, and developmental factors. Economic determinism, sexism, or racism, however, are not adequate to explain the enormous variation in the ability of people to deal with the problems of class, sex, or race.

The psychology of a considerable number of any group must be examined to understand the actual impact of caste or class on the character and adaptation of the rich or poor. For example, Oscar Lewis gave us an illuminating picture of the "culture of poverty" in his work with Puerto Rican families.[14] Yet anyone who has worked with poor Hispanic, poor white, and poor black families quickly becomes familiar with the wide differences among those groups, as well as with the significant variations within each of the individual and family responses to the fact of poverty.

How can such differences be elucidated? Unstructured psycho-dynamic interviews utilizing free associations, dreams and fanta-sies, reactions to the interviewer, and the challenging of defenses enable us to get a portrait that is deeper than that obtainable in any other way. Psychodynamic interviewing allows us to uncover the meanings of suicide—its significance to the individual's emo-tional adaptation to life, and what he hopes to gain by dying. A psychodynamic approach makes possible an understanding of the role of depression in suicide, the impact of intimacy or the lack or loss of it on an individual's desire for life, and the meaning of being a man or a woman, a child or a parent or both, when contemplating suicide. A better understanding of the organiza-tion of personality makes it possible to understand in a deeper way the meaning of suicide for the individual.

Suicidal patients often hold up an exaggerating mirror to the problems of their culture or social group. For example, suicide among young blacks in the ghetto is often the outgrowth of a devastating struggle to deal with the conscious rage and conscious murderous impulses that are an integral part of ghetto life. The study of suicide in this population can illustrate how psychosocial circumstance and personal tragedy converge in suicide.

Suicide may be part of the possibilities of every culture and every individual. But the dominant psychodynamic patterns that emerge and the ways they are expressed are to a very significant extent molded by the culture in which the act takes place. Although the potential for the act is a cultural universal, the par-ticular nature of the act is to a large extent culturally determined and relative. In the chapters that follow, we shall try to show how differing shared cultural and subcultural experiences operate to shape the psychodynamics of suicide. The differences in ways of coping with love and loss, life and death, make clear that suicide has much to tell us about how we live.

Youth and Age

2. Suicide among the Young

IN THE UNITED STATES from 1955 to 1980, the suicide rate among young people aged 15–24 rose markedly, and has remained high since. Among young women the rate more than doubled, going from 2 to 4.3 / 100,000; among young men the rate more than tripled, going from 6.3 to 20.2 / 100,000. The U.S. now ranks among the highest countries in the world in the suicide rate of its young men, surpassing Japan and Sweden, countries long identified with the problem of suicide.*

Until relatively recently, suicides among young men and women made up less than 5 percent of the total. Since the rate increase has coincided with a marked increase in the percentage of young people in the population, suicides in the 15–24 age group now constitute almost one-sixth of the more than 30,000 suicides in the country each year. Young men aged 15–24 now account for over 20 percent of the more than 23,000 male suicides a year; young women of the same ages are responsible for about 11 percent of the approximately 7,000 female suicides a year.

The accompanying graph, comparing suicide rates among

*The Division of Vital Statistics of the National Center for Health Statistics is the source of most of the statistical data on suicide used in this book. The Bureau of the Census of the U.S. Department of Commerce is the source of the U.S. population figures and projections. The World Health Organization is the source of the suicide data for all other countries.

young men in the United States throughout this century with the suicide rates among the population as a whole, shows how significant a change has taken place. The trend among young women parallels that among men, but the suicide rates are at much lower levels.

Changes in the quality of family life, changes in the intensity of competitive pressures for success, and demographic changes that are related to both competitive pressures and the nature of the family have been seen as primarily responsible for the rise in the suicide rates among young people. A study of the young who are suicidal cannot definitively resolve the question of the relative importance of these factors, but by providing a picture of who these young people are and what they are like, it can give us some necessary guidelines for understanding the problem.

There has been considerable concern about the increase in the suicide rate of college students. Studies indicate, however, that this increase is related to the rise in suicide among 15–24 year olds in general, and the rate is not greater for college students.[1] Student suicide rates are also no higher at institutions where academic standards are more stringent.[2] Even so, the death of young, bright people by suicide is particularly tragic, and since the rate of suicide in this age group continues to be high, suicide among college students must engage our attention.

Some of the most widely known and quoted studies have been epidemiological and retrospective. Psychiatrists and psychologists at major universities—Harvard, Yale, and the University of California at Berkeley are the sites of three of the best-known studies—have tabulated all the suicides committed by students at their universities over periods of ten to fifteen years and examined whatever information or records were available.[3]

Some general facts emerge from this work. The majority of the undergraduate suicides were doing better than average in their

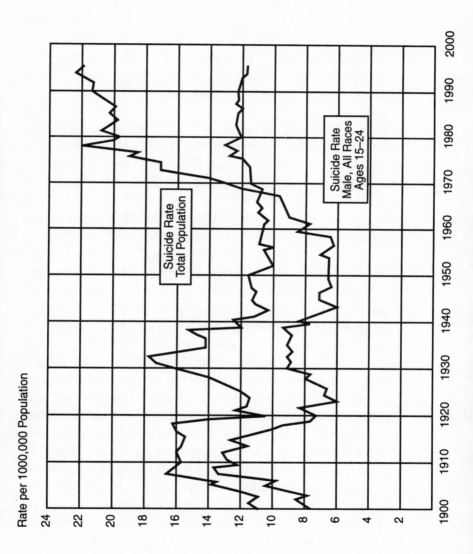

U. S. SUICIDE RATES TOTAL POPULATION and MALES 15–24

Rate per 1000,000 Population

Suicide Rate
Total Population

Suicide Rate
Male, All Races
Ages 15–24

studies, but most had done more poorly than usual in the most recent marking period. Most of them had not sought psychiatric help; those who had did not talk of suicide and were generally not recognized as suicidal. Most, however, had given some warning of their intentions to a friend or teacher. Most were reputed by friends, teachers, and parents to have been troubled by or dissatisfied with their scholastic achievements.

Although all of the studies stress the importance of academic pressure and frustration in the suicide of these young people, Richard Seiden, in summarizing the study he conducted at the University of California at Berkeley, goes even further. After concluding that increasing "pressure on the student to achieve and maintain" is responsible for student suicides, he predicts that such pressure is going to lead to a rising suicide rate among this population. He goes on to say that "the situation ominously resembles a suicidal problem which prevails among the youth of Japan . . . [where] there are tremendous pressures to attend college, and those students who fail to gain entrance frequently turn to suicide as a solution to their dilemmas."[4]

Since the study is based on the retrospective examinations of the records of students who are dead, the evidence on which the opinion rests may be questionable, but its conclusion is shared by many who have seen students who are preoccupied with or have attempted suicide and have survived. A University of Michigan study of students who were judged to be suicidal when seen at a mental hygiene unit listed anxiety over work, including anxiety over examinations, as by far the most common precipitating cause of the preoccupation with suicide.[5] Even more significant, a "tendency to worry," about academic work in particular, was considered to be a primary psychological factor underlying the student's vulnerability to suicide.

Mathew Ross, in surveying British and American studies of

college suicide, speculated that for those "students who have internalized high parental standards and who experience extraordinary academic pressures, academic failure, real or threatened, may signify a loss of parental love. When they fail academically, they cannot face the concomitant loss of parental love."[6]

My own experience with such students has been that they have felt for a long time that they failed to win parental love. In general, they do not come from families that have instilled in them high parental standards for achievement. Most of them have incorporated an emotional lifelessness that characterized their relationship with their parents. Most have learned to use school work in a defensive withdrawal from their families and from the world outside. Often this adaptation is encouraged by their families, who find it easier to deal with the fewer demands of an emotionally muted child.

During a five-year study of suicide, depression, and crisis in college students, I had the opportunity of knowing and studying fifty seriously suicidal students.[7] We saw the students an average of fifteen to twenty times over several months, and we were also able to learn what happened to most of them over the subsequent few years. Many of them had initially been referred to us following suicide attempts that were attributed to concern over academic achievement. In all such cases the psychodynamic picture of the student that emerged was quite different from the one that the original referral evaluation gave.

One freshman told me that, after having studied hard all term, his poor scholastic performance had caused his depression and was a sign of his bad luck. But he turned out to have been thinking of suicide for years; in high school he had compiled a list of reasons why he could not kill himself. He enumerated these to me in the mechanical manner he usually adopted. First, things were so bad that they could only get better. Second, no one had a right to take his own life. Third, his parents had made a great investment in his education, and it would cost a lot to bury him. Fourth, his parents would blame themselves. Fifth, they would be devastated and would miss him. Since his arrival at college, he had acquired a sixth reason—his friends would feel very bad if he did it. He had been able to resist his suicidal preoccupations during his lonely high school years, but after a few months of college and close association with roommates, his need to kill himself became overwhelming. The challenge to his past isolation and deadness that his new friendships presented appeared to be impelling him toward suicide.

He wanted to hold on to his depression far more than he realized. He saw himself as always having been on "the losing side of the law of averages." He would deliberately test his luck, and after a college mixer at which he met no one, he rode the subways and stood for a long time at one station in Harlem in a challenge to fate to see whether he would be mugged. He considered it a bad omen that two of his favorite professional football teams lost on the day after his preoccupation with suicide had led to his admission to a hospital. During the time I saw him, after his favorite team had won its crucial game, he dreamt that in the last minute they lost.

He saw defeat as preferable to victory, but for the most part he sought an impregnability that prevented both. He had a recurring fantasy in which he was a medieval citadel under attack. He drew a map to illustrate the deployment of his protective armies. It indicated areas in different colors to mark his social, academic, spiritual, and emotional defenses. Most of his forces were concentrated in the academic realm. His map of barricades was a powerful symbol of his emotional state. He felt that he would survive only as long as his defenses held.

He saw life as war and himself as the ultimate weapon. It was easier for him to see danger as an outside attack than to see his own destructiveness. After an incident in which his roommates had disappointed him, he dreamed that he was an executioner who had to decide whether people should live or die. He condemned them to death, and "some kind of angel came and killed them all." He saw himself as the angel of death. His suicidal preoccupations and his depression masked his potential for rage. At times he pictured himself as sitting on a time bomb that was "getting ready to explode." When I questioned him about the anger and destructiveness suggested by the image, he was quick to tell me that the most that would happen was that he would "quietly and nonviolently" kill himself.

His need to hide his anger was bound up with his need not to blame his parents for his problems. He insisted that he had had little relationship to them, that he liked them from afar but was always irritated with them when at home. The few incidents of his childhood that he related cast his mother in the role of dampener of his or his father's pleasure or excitement. He found it difficult to depict his father or his mother, other than to indicate that his father was away a lot and that his mother ruled the house. He felt he and his parents had never been able to talk about anything, but he expressed no anger or bitterness over this. His suicide note conveyed the quality of his family life.

In a note addressed to both his parents, he wrote that by the time they read it he would be dead and that they were not responsible for his act. (In suicide notes, dealt with in a later chapter, such statements specifically freeing particular people of blame or responsibility are usually to be read psychologically as meaning the opposite.) He added that he was depressed and could see nothing coming out of his life. He went on to dispose of his possessions, leaving his tapes and tape recording equipment to his mother and requesting that his favorite tape be buried with him. From beginning to end, his note was about communication through or after death. He told his parents that it was too late to reach him but went on to leave them equipment that permitted him to speak to them, like the angel of death he dreamed he was, as a disembodied voice from beyond the grave. In asking to be buried with the tape of melancholy songs he played again and again as accompaniment to his suicidal thoughts, he was asking almost literally to be cemented for all eternity in his unhappy, isolated relationship with his mother. It was not surprising that the stories he made up in response to TAT cards contained the repetitive theme of a parent's affection for a dead son.

Far from being destroyed by any push toward academic success, such students used school as a barricade. "Work," as this young man put it, was his "main defensive army." Nor were the parents of these students more achievement oriented than most. They were merely most comfortable with children who were quietly engaged in school work. Often, as in the next case, they opposed work their children found exciting. In any event, dull demanding mental labor was often the nexus of suicidal students' existence. Such work was an end in itself. It did not tend to lead to success or any pleasurable sense of achievement, but rather functioned as another link in the chain of emotional deadness that bound them to their parents.

Another student, a college senior, serious and intellectual in manner, took thirty sleeping pills for problems she saw as purely scholastic. She told of writing a paper for a history teacher who thought well of her, and of not following his suggestions for the direction the paper should take. She felt the paper had turned out badly and would lose her his good opinion. She had been disappointed when someone told her about a paper that presented good evidence against her point of view in her senior thesis. She said she had taken a difficult math course, knew she was doing poorly, but would not take a pass-fail, because that was "too easy," and was now afraid she would get an "F" which would mar her record. Finally, she said she was depressed because her adviser was unresponsive.

Her feelings about her work both reflected and disguised her feelings about her life and its problems on a far deeper level. Her sense that she would disappoint someone whose good opinion she wanted if she followed her own inclinations, her difficulty in pursuing these inclinations in the face of opposition, and her need to make her performance in school a test of her worth were all evident in her family situation.

Her father had made a fortune in business despite a sixth-grade education. He still led what she described as a working-class life-style. Disappointed that she was not a boy, he felt she could "at least marry an engineer who could fit into his firm." He had no interest in her education, ignored her considerable academic success, suggested that she study dressmaking, and offered to buy a shop for her. Yet his opinion was important to her, and she knew that the life she wanted and an academic career would only take her further away from him. She described her mother as hysterical, unable to tolerate criticism or suggestions, and given to falling apart under pressure. Her mother had told her to do whatever her father wanted.

Since she was 12 or 13, she felt she was simply marking time to get away from her parents. She thought college would allow her to shape a new life for herself, yet she had difficulty in going away to college. Once there, she felt that her life was a sham, that her girlfriends did not know who she really was, and that she had made a failure of her opportunity. She felt she had no option but to go back home to the situation and the life she detested. She had had virtually no social life in the year before she was seen; she commented that she did not enjoy dating, because she did not want people to see how depressed, weak, and unable to cope with life she really was. The lack of involvement with a man, of course, kept her tied to her parents. She had narrowed her life to her school work, feeling that if she could do it well, she would have the confidence to handle the rest of her life. In the process, school had become a life-or-death test of her worth.

Yet this young woman was clearly drawn to failure. On the verge of graduating, she saw herself as having lost out. Going on to graduate school would represent a further break with her parents, and despite her excellent marks and the encouragement of her teachers, she had not applied. She now adopted the attitude that it was too late to try. How "hung up" she felt in emotional deadness was reflected in a recurrent dream she had before her suicide attempt. She dreamed a dead cat was suspended by its hind paws from a clothesline. Her associations made clear that the cat was herself.

During the course of my seeing this patient, her maternal grandmother died. The night before the funeral, she dreamed her father was on the operating table, and a doctor massaged his heart unnecessarily because he thought it had stopped, when actually it was still beating. She related the image of the heart to herself and was afraid that I had the impression that there was less life in her than there really was.

She spoke of her identification with her father and his lack of emotional expression, sensitivity, or responsiveness. He never let her kiss him until she was 18 and was "too big" to push away. She was struck by his failure to try to comfort her mother at the grandmother's funeral. In her drive and ambition, she also seemed to resemble her father, but these were not qualities that won her his love or the support of her mother. Although she fought against it, she also incorporated her mother's tendency to collapse under pressure.

Her suicide attempt was the radical expression of her fear that she would indeed be able to graduate successfully and might begin to make her own life. Her sense of failure, her feeling that her choices were an unhappy return to her family or suicide, expressed how much deadness constituted a persistent bond with her parents and a defense against life. Her suicide attempt managed to fuse, in the act itself and in her perception of its motive, her father's ambition and emotional numbness with her mother's habit of collapse.

This young woman and the previously discussed young man were typical of suicidal students who used intense concentration on academic work as the means for dealing with existence. The meaning they gave to their work served to conceal their deeper personal conflict over living or dying, their sense that they had no right to live. Like the young man who saw his academic life as a defensive army, these students used the continued deployment of uninteresting and methodical work in the service of a withdrawal from either satisfaction or rage. Their withdrawal signified for them a holding on to the past and strengthened the tie of numbness they had forged in their relations with their family.

Some of these students continued to use the contact with their parents to control their own enthusiasm and to insure their lifelessness. Elated by a new relationship, excited by school, they would call their parents when they were feeling best, knowing that their parents' lack of response would squelch their mood. One student recalled that when she was happiest she had the impulse to "throw herself in front of a train" or call her mother, equating the destructive power of each with a wry seriousness. For these students, being happy meant giving up the past; giving up sadness meant relinquishing the most secure part of themselves.

Paradoxically, the most seriously suicidal students waited for college to escape from what they regarded as an unbearable home situation, only to discover that they became severely depressed and suicidal when they did get to college. Graduating from college, which symbolized a further break with the past, often exacerbated the situation.

One might assume that concentration on academic performance, as compensation for a lack of proficiency in other areas, causes a vulnerability to real or imagined failures that is responsible for suicide. It is achievement more than failure, however, that threatens these young people. They usually find it easier to discuss the concrete reality of their school work than their feelings about themselves in any broader sense. Listening less literally to what they say about their school performance, one learns that it is their life that they are grading poorly and considering a failure.

If separation from parents arouses a particular sense of loss and abandonment in potentially suicidal young men and women, what of those young people who actually lose a parent through death during adolescence? There is evidence to indicate that the actual death of a parent is significant in producing suicidal young people in or out of college. Gregory Zilboorg, as far back as 1936, reported on the greater frequency of parental death in the history of young people who became suicidal. He stressed their "ambivalent identification" with a lost loved object. He tried to date the vulnerable period, suggesting that when a boy or girl lost a father, mother, or sibling at a time when he or she was at the height of the Oedipal complex or the transition to puberty, there was a danger of suicide.[8]

A group at the University of Washington, in studying 114 actual suicides and 121 attempted suicides, found that the death of a parent had been a significantly more frequent occurrence in the childhood or adolescence of the actual suicides than in that of the attempted suicides.[9] They concluded that an inability to come to terms with the parent's death—i.e., "an unresolved object loss" in childhood—leads to an inability to sustain object loss in later life.

In regard to the loss of a parent by separation or divorce, the findings have been less conclusive. Several investigators have reported that the incidence of the absence of a parent or the loss of him or her by death was higher in suicidal than in nonsuicidal persons.[10] Others have found no greater incidence of broken homes in a group of youngsters who attempted suicide than in a control group.[11] The Harvard study of student suicide discovered a statistically significant correlation between suicide and the death of a parent, but not between divorce of the parents and the subsequent incidence of suicide among students.

Part of the inconsistency in such studies stems from the variation in how a "broken home" is perceived, depending on the young person's past and current relationships with his parents. Jerry Jacobs and Joseph Teicher, among the few researchers whose work reflects an awareness of this fact, point out that the young people who had attempted suicide were more apt to be alienated from their parents than a nonsuicidal control group, regardless of whether or not they came from a "broken home."[12] Furthermore, it seems that it is not the loss of a love object *per se* that is so distressing but the loss of love—i.e., the reciprocal intimacy, spontaneity, and closeness that one experiences in a "primary relationship." Their finding is in keeping with my own experience that the nature of the relationship with the parents prior to any separation or loss—and with a remaining parent subsequently—is the critical factor.

I have found this to be equally true of the seriously suicidal young people who became so after the death of a parent.

Although significant numbers of young suicidal people have lost a parent, the overwhelming majority of young people who have lost a parent are not suicidal. Working with those who are makes clear that the crucial factor is the quality of feeling that flowed between the youngster and the parent while the parent was alive. When emotional deadness bound these young men and women and their parents, it preceded the parents' death; the situation was similar to that of the young suicidal people described earlier whose parents were alive. Members of both groups were pulled toward their own death primarily by this bond, which defined their relationship with their parents. It continued to control their lives, often in an intensified way, if their parents died.

I have seen, for example, a number of young men whose suicide attempts were related to their mother's death during their adolescence: all had long histories of sad and depressing relations with their mother. One young man who became overtly suicidal only after his mother's death perceived his relation to her when she was alive as requiring his own emotional death. When he said with a flat, depressed intensity, "I don't think life should be lived if it isn't worth living for its own sake" and "No one should stay alive for anyone else's sake," it was clear that he felt he had lived or not lived for his mother's sake, not his own.

This young man, who killed himself four years later, was referred for evaluation following a serious suicide attempt that he barely survived. He had been preoccupied with suicide since he had left home to go to college, and had made previous suicide attempts. Neatly groomed and casually dressed, he seemed distinctly fearful as he nervously touched his bushy beard and mustache and spoke in a lifeless, mechanical manner. He said he tried to have the least possible contact with people and had only the few friends he had made in high school. And while he shared an apartment with two other young men, he said they merely lived together and did not "socialize."

He tried to protect himself against letting me know or reach him, and attempted to stop any observation or interpretation of his behavior by quickly saying, "It is possible." Insisting on the futility of talking and on the futility of his life, he said that he could stand back and listen to our conversation and that it was like a grade Z movie. Standing back and listening while grading himself and others were characteristic ways in which he defended himself against involvement. His insistence that nothing could change his life suggested a determination to see to it that nothing did.

He had one close relationship with a woman with whom he lived for six months, which he described as the liveliest, happiest, and most spontaneous period of his life. Nevertheless, when the time came for her to leave for Europe, where she had planned to live, he made no attempt to persuade her to stay and did not seriously consider going with her.

When he had met this young woman, his mother was dying of cancer. He suspected that her imminent death had made him more willing to become involved. During the six months after his mother had died and his girlfriend had left, he made four suicide attempts. While he felt they had more to do with his girlfriend than his mother, he insisted that he was not bothered by missing his girlfriend, but by his lack of control over the situation. The need to deny her importance to him and the pain of losing her and his mother were further expressions of his use of deadness as a defense.

He attributed the origins of his lifeless, isolated existence to being the only child of an "overbearing" mother and to having a father who was "removed and out of things." One of his earliest memories vividly dramatizes his family situation. When he was about seven, his father was away for a day and his mother was going to a bridal shower. He does not recall what he was doing, but feels he must have "been playing in a way my mother didn't like." His mother screamed at him that she would not go to the shower because of him. Now he thinks she was looking for an excuse not to go. Nonetheless, the situation conveys not only her use of the role of martyr, but also her message to him that if he was playful, mischievous, or alive, she would not live or enjoy anything.

He saw his mother as refusing to let him grow up. She would not let him have a door to his room and insisted on her right to open his mail. She seemed to have been particularly fearful of his involvement with girls. He felt his mother tried to live her life through him. As he spoke, it was clear he thought he had performed and lived for his mother at the expense of living his own life. Yet he had felt lost and "out of control" when he went off to college and felt depressed and cut off without his mother. It was in this period, which had preceded her illness, that he first became preoccupied with thoughts of suicide.

Nothing outside of his family had much deep, living reality for him. He never dreamed of being in his current apartment; in all his dreams he was in the home where he had grown up with his parents. After our first session, he dreamed of a lively, outgoing boy whom he had known as a child and whom he associated with fun. He saw himself as rarely capable of having fun and enjoyed himself only when he had had a couple of drinks or smoked pot. He associated fun with separating from his mother, which he was clearly afraid to do. He said, "What's the use of talking about her? She's dead and I'm alive." Psychologically speaking, the reverse seemed truer.

Discussing his situation made him feel more alive but also aroused alarm at the feelings that were opening up. After our second session he had the following dream:

He was near school, and strong wind currents from basement vents were blowing him around. He was blown into a teacher who wore glasses, and the glasses were knocked off and the lenses fell out. He was then swept into a second collision, but this time he stepped on the glasses and broke them. Then there was an explosion in one building; he could see a crack in the wall, and everything calmed down.

The two collisions suggested to him his two meetings with me, as did the fact that I wore glasses. He felt that he had learned a great deal from the sessions, but discussing his mother had been unsettling. In his dream, while making sure I could see no more, he portrayed his anger as an alien and destructive force beyond his control. He felt that making a break with his mother would be akin to an enormous explosion. He believed, however, that only through such an explosive break would he find the peace suggested in that dream.

He was also concerned about the possibility of losing his father, who had had a heart attack a few months earlier. His father had remarried and seemed much happier than when his mother had been alive. His fear that his father would die and leave him alone stimulated dreams in which he and not his father had the heart attack. He felt he was saying, "Better me than you." This powerfully represented his feeling that one life can be sacrificed in order to keep another intact.

He had seen his "death" as a way of keeping his mother alive. He acknowledged at times that he had wished she would die, thinking her death might liberate him. He became tearful in relating how her death had liberated his father but not him. His numbness minimized the distinction between living and dying and created a middle state in which he figuratively did keep his mother alive through his own emotional death. Suicide represented a dramatization of this process.

His suicide attempt was not simply a journey toward reunion with a lost love object. His whole life had been a death tie to an object both needed and hated. In not living, he kept his mother alive, atoned for his rage toward her, and preserved their past relationship. What overwhelmed him was not only her loss but the fact that her loss constituted an invitation to life—an invitation that his father could accept but that he could not.

The most seriously suicidal young people were those whose absorption and preoccupation with their own extinction formed an integral, ongoing part of their adaptation. They were drawn to death as a way of life. They saw their relationships with their parents as dependent on their emotional, if not physical, death and became tied to their parents in a kind of death knot. For these suicidal students, depression often served the triple function of prolonging the tie with parents, shielding them from the intensity of their own fury, and warding off the excitement of the new life that was opening up before them. Coming to college, graduating, becoming seriously involved with another person, and enjoying an independent existence had the power to free them. Suicide and suicidal longings were often the means of recapturing the protective deadness of a depression that seemed to be slipping away. The meaning of suicide and depression often lay in the young person's encounter with experiences that challenged his capacity for adult separation from his parents, a separation for which he felt ill prepared.

Suicide for love, the wish to die when love and need are not requited, has traditionally been considered a cause of suicide attempts by young people in late adolescence or the early twenties. Moreover, suicide in response to rejection suggests a strong desire for love, life, and involvement, and unbearable disappointment over the frustration of such needs. It would seem to be quite different from the deathly tie to parents and the resistance to involvement that have been described.

Yet relationships that lead to disappointment and suicide often have death, disappointment, and depression built into them. The "I won't live without you" message to an unwilling partner is a restatement of earlier disappointments relived with and through a lover who remains aloof.

Who attempts suicide over rejection? Suicide attempts by young men over rejection by a woman seem to be much less frequent than romantic literature would suggest. Young women, in response to the failure of a relationship, frequently make attempts, which are usually not serious but which are rather designed to revive an affair that was ending.

What I found remarkable, however, was the young women I saw who made serious suicide attempts in the throes of disappointment in love without being aware that they had been hurt by men, and without connecting their depression to the painful experiences they were having with men. Their attempts were more serious almost in proportion to the degree to which they were aware of, or needed to deny, the source of their pain.

One attractive, friendly girl, more poised than her 18 years would suggest, said she had no idea why she made a suicide attempt with twenty-five sleeping pills after she had been drinking heavily at a party. When questioned, she could say only that she felt her life was too boring. A dream provided the first evidence of what was troubling her. She was in a car with a man who was driving fast in order to elude another man who was pursuing them. They had to abandon their car because they had a flat tire, and they started running. The man caught up with them and shot her dead.

In speaking of her dream, she described her relationship with an older fellow of about 30 whom she had seen for a year and whom she called a dangerous driver. He had hurt her very deeply by his rejection of her, and the "flat tire" after the fast ride was clearly an image for her disappointment and depression. He had stood her up the preceding New Year's Eve without explanation; all spring and summer he dated friends of hers and lied to her, telling her he had not seen anyone else. She recalled being depressed during those months but did not connect her feeling to anything that had happened in her relationship with him.

She is too removed from the pain to be in touch with her anger toward him. In her dream someone else is out to get them, but it is only she who is killed. She does to herself what she feels he did to her. A suicide attempt or suicidal thoughts in the context of heavy drinking permitted her to act on her despair without clearly or consciously recognizing it. Her behavior was consistent with her early life, during which she had attempted to protect herself from the pain of an unhappy childhood with parents who fought constantly—a father who drank heavily and a mother who both restricted and rejected her.

Although she was in love with her boyfriend, she insisted she was not bothered by his not loving her, saying that she knew he was "not the loving type." In fact she felt bitterly rejected by him and could not confront herself or him with her feelings. Her heavy drinking, her suicide attempt and suicidal thoughts, and most of all her inability to know why she wanted to die powerfully reflected her attempt to ward off knowledge of her own emotions. Her belief that she wanted to die because her life was boring is belied by her actual story—it was because her life had become so full of the possibility of intense pain and rejection that she clung to the sense of boredom, had the impulse to deaden her awareness with liquor, and felt the desire to end it.

This young woman and many like her try to blot out how hurt and angry they feel in their current relationships, but they do so even more with the pain and disappointment of their early lives with their families. Their present attachments should seemingly serve to separate them from painful and rejecting pasts, but in fact by reliving their earlier disappointments they remain tied to them.

The life-or-death meaning that suicidal young people give their relationships derives from their need to recapitulate and relive the intense unhappiness they have known with their parents. Students whose suicide attempts were precipitated by rejection serve to underline, not refute, the degree to which deadness and detachment can become an integral part of an individual's adaptation. Suicide is almost a way of life for such young people, who, having deadened their enthusiasm, their hope, and their freedom, finally attempt to kill themselves.

Studies of suicidal young people of high school age yield a picture rather different from the one given by studies of college students. Among suicidal young people in high school, provocative and defiant behavior toward parents, delinquency, drug abuse, and little interest in school are usual. These youngsters seem to be seeking experience, even if it is often of a self-destructive nature. Their drug abuse and reckless driving can be fatal, often posing more of a danger to their lives than their actual suicide attempts.

These youngsters seem sociable rather than withdrawn. They need to be around other people and are often uncomfortable if they have to spend time alone. Yet their social contacts are shallow, and they become quite uneasy at the possibility of intimacy. Their rebellious behavior with their parents tends to mask that they, too, are depressed and that they fear separating from their families despite their unhappiness with them.

Most of the suicidal youngsters fitting the above description do not go to college, while most suicidal college students do not have a history of such behavior when in high school. By the very fact of making it to college, suicidal college students indicate that some degree of self-discipline, at least in the academic area, has been possible for them. As we have seen, for many of them school work is an integral part of their adaptation.

College-age students appear to conform to the general population in their ratio of attempts to actual suicides—estimated to be about 10 to 1. In the high school population we see a ratio of attempted suicides to actual suicides of between 100 to 200 to 1. Although all attempts are an indication of a troubled adolescent who needs help, with most such adolescents the suicidal behavior seems to be limited to this particular period of life.

More observations have been made on the families of suicidal high school youngsters than on those of suicidal college students. Several studies have described parental attitudes of resentment, hostility, and rejection going back to the childhood of youngsters who became suicidal.[13] They have observed both mothers and children struggling against an awareness of the maternal demand that the child did not exist.

Joseph Sabbath, in discussing suicidal high school youngsters, writes of the "expendable child," a depressed, provocative child who becomes so much of a disturbance in the family that the parents indicate that they wish he or she were out of the family.[14] They are apt to ignore his or her suicidal threats or gestures. Sabbath discusses several such cases. One young man had an angry, ambivalent relationship with his father, who ignored his frequent car accidents. He was killed in what was suspected to have been a purposeful car crash. Sabbath concludes that the young man "carried out his father's wishes for him to be seriously injured or dead." In another case, a 15-year-old girl provoked her mother by continually lying and stealing. Her mother frequently told her to "drop dead." Of her suicide attempt, Sabbath says, "She tried to comply with her mother's wish to be rid of her and for her to die."

Teicher and Jacobs see adolescence as an "escalation stage" of the earlier problems between child and parents.[15] The efforts of the parents to control their children's behavior and contain their own ambivalent feelings begin to fail. The child's provocativeness, mood changes, and secretiveness shut the parents out. Estrangement grows, ordinary communication breaks down, and another form of communication comes through—a nonverbal message that the adolescent is no longer wanted, that his parents wish to be rid of him.

My own experience suggests that although adolescence may bring such communication out into the open, the message has often been conveyed much earlier. One young woman of 15, seen only after a suicide attempt, had a history of school failure, lying, petty stealing for many years, drug abuse, and almost continual fights with her parents. Her 16-year-old sister was considered to be a model child. Only after a number of visits with each of the family members did it become evident that the younger sister had been a problem for the family literally since her birth. She was born in a period when the father was often away from home and her mother was tense, irritable, and insomniac. The mother saw her second child as tense, unable to sleep, and over-demanding. The parents took a trip when their youngest daughter was a baby. Only after they were in the cab starting for the airport did they recall that they had left her behind. The parents related this event as a funny family story, insensitive to the fact that for their daughter it summed up where she stood in the family. Her provocative, defiant behavior made it impossible for them now to forget her existence. Her suicide attempt was a reflection of the pain that lay behind her behavior.

We need much more study of the quality of family interaction that produces the suicidal child. One pattern that I have observed frequently with seriously suicidal youngsters and their families is somewhat more specific than their merely being unwanted or

unloved children. Unlike many parents of delinquent children
who are not suicidal, these parents do not convey a sense of "I
don't want you, go out and stay out of my way." Rather, they
seem to want the child's presence, but without emotional
involvement. They want him to be there and not there at the
same time—to be under their control and to fulfill parental
expectations, though as parents they have given him little incen-
tive to do so. The youngster may incorporate parental expectations in a mechanical manner but derives little pleasure or
satisfaction from fulfilling them. At the same time, he does not
feel free to act in ways that would separate him from his parents.
The youngster is left with a sense of being unhappily tied to parents, as represented in the dream of the young woman who saw
herself as a dead cat hanging on a clothesline.

Whether suicidal youngsters retreat into their rooms or their
books or become provocative and defiant, they share a pain, frustration, and anger that most often come from disturbed family
relationships. Since we seem to be seeing unhappy families,
absent parents, and unwanted children in increasing numbers, a
case could be made for the pessimistic predictions that the suicide
rates among young high school and college students will continue to rise.

The trend of growing suicide among young people was evident
through the quiet of the fifties, the affluence and activism of the
sixties, the rise of the drug culture in the early seventies, and the
economic problems seen later in that decade. The persistence of
the trend through varying socioeconomic conditions has
strengthened the assumption that the problem is rooted in the
diminishing cohesion of the family.

A somewhat different perspective on both the family and suicide among the young is provided by a demographic view of the

problem. The rise in the suicide rate among the young in the 1960s and 1970s, for example, took place at a time when there was a dramatic increase both in the number and the percentage of young people in the population. It coincided with the coming to adulthood of the youngsters who were born in the post-World War II baby boom. One might think that this should affect the numbers of suicides in this age group, but not the rate; yet the population percentage of the young and their suicide rate seem to be related.

Demographers relate the stress on any birth cohort to the size of the cohort.[16] To paraphrase and summarize the work of Richard Easterlin, one of the leading exponents of the theory: A generation born in a baby boom is liable to be adversely affected when it reaches adulthood.[17] The young people face difficult odds in competing with each other for a limited number of new (and challenging) positions. Young adults will be hesitant to marry and will be under pressure to put off having children, and women will often combine a job with the care of children. Marital stress will be high and divorce frequent. Psychological stress among young adults will be comparatively severe, and suicide, crime, and feelings of alienation will be high. The situation is very different when smaller cohorts enter the labor force. Then there are too few entrants to efficiently fill new openings and old slots, producing increased competition among employers for the new arrivals. Long-term trends show that in such a situation young people are under less stress, marry earlier, and have more children.

The suicide rate in the 15–24 age group has in fact gone up and down with the percentage of 15- to 24-year-olds in the population. The accompanying graph, going back to 1900, indicates how closely the suicide rate conforms to the changing percentage of this age group.

The rate tends to be lowest when the percentage of 15- to 24-year-olds is lowest, and highest when the percentage of 15- to 24-year-olds is highest. The graph shows that the highest rates of suicide among those aged 15–24 occurred at the beginning of the century and in the last twenty-five years, when the percentage of 15- to 24-year-olds in the population stood at its highest levels.

Since the mid-1950s we have been experiencing a decline in the birth rate so that by the late 1980s there was a significant drop in the percentage of the population in the 15–24 age group. If the correlation observed between the population percentage of the young and their suicide rate continues to hold, we expect a drop in the latter, but so far that has not taken place.

The problem faced by social and behavioral scientists is how to integrate individual data and demographic data in a meaningful way. For example, demographers postulate that adults forming families evaluate their relative economic status by comparing their immediate situation and prospects with those that prevailed when they were teens in their parents' households. As cohort size increases, the relatively worse economic conditions of young adults cause them to postpone marriage and childbirth. Although the theory fits the social pattern well, study of the individuals involved in such decisions has not supported it in any significant way. The actual operative dynamics may, of course, be more complex than the theory implies.

The individual data in the case of seriously suicidal college-age people do not indicate that either economic or job concerns—or even concerns with academic performance that are related to the future ability to obtain a good job or be admitted to a desirable professional school—were major precipitating factors in suicide. Douglas Gurak, of Fordham University, a demographic expert to whom I presented the suicide and population data, offered the following explanatory hypothesis:

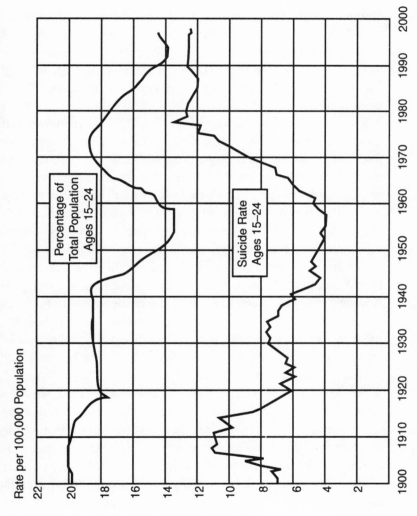

15–24 YEAR OLDS: PERCENTAGE of TOTAL POPULATION and SUICIDE RATE

Rate per 100,000 Population

Percentage of
Total Population
Ages 15–24

Suicide Rate
Ages 15–24

The delay in marriage associated with the tightened job market and the increased relative size of the young adult cohort mean that the formation of new familial ties that have been shown to counter suicidal tendencies become less of a factor at this crucial point of the life cycle. Moreover, although getting a job may not itself be a conscious problem, the decrease in planning for or forming new familial ties may be an intervening fact, brought about partly by the impact of age structure as youth enters the labor market.

The poorer outlook for success and growth may manifest itself more in a sense of the meaninglessness of life than in economic insecurity. Getting a job may not appear to be the problem, but doing something meaningful may. Popular culture may even deemphasize "making it" as new (nonfamilial) life-styles emerge along with an extended transitional period between adolescence and adulthood. When there was no surplus of young adults, more attention was given to, and more emphasis placed on the importance of, the new cohort. Rapid advancement of a small cohort creates a milieu in which things appear more meaningful. Among the large cohort, individual articulation need not refer to economic pressures or to insecurity or concern with "making it." Individuals may rather be more concerned with the meaning-lessness of life and perceive fewer social constraints on suicide.[18]

Gurak's hypothesis is consistent with clinical observation. It is not so easy, however, to find clinical support for Easterlin's contention that psychosocial changes in the role of women are not affecting the trends he describes. Easterlin believes that the pressure for large families will reassert itself when the members of the smaller cohort formed by the children of today's young adults reach adulthood. He sees sex role changes as too insignifi-cant to be likely to influence the cycles he postulates. Most of those changes take place among educated women, and he does not believe that the relatively small number of them in the job market will significantly dampen the next baby boom.

In a study of college students conducted over twenty years ago, we already found that the young women were far less committed to a marriage with children than their mothers had been—a finding in keeping with demographic predictions for their cohort. Yet most of them trace their attitudes to their mothers, who were educated women from a small age cohort but who had found motherhood difficult or unsatisfying. This dissatisfaction was communicated either directly or indirectly to their daughters, with the implicit message not to make the same investment in marriage and children that the mothers had. Many of these young college women, even if uncertain of what they wanted to be, knew that they did not want to lead lives like those of their mothers.

It seems likely that in the 1950s and 1960s many women were having children that they found they did not really want at a time when other options seemed a possibility—if not for them at least for their daughters. Their daughters, as a group, are having fewer children. Young women today who do not want children seem aware of that fact before they have them, and they act on that recognition. The culture today seems more accepting of a woman's decision not to have more than one child or not to have any at all. It is certainly possible that fewer unwanted children today may contribute to a lower suicide rate tomorrow. And although a change in the daughters' attitudes could be said simply to reflect the cyclical change, the mothers' attitudes toward their daughters suggest the possibility of more basic and enduring changes.

Although Easterlin acknowledges that factors ranging from the energy crisis to illegal immigration could affect the labor market and interfere with the cycles he has observed, he believes that such problems will be resolved without significant impact on the age structure effect. Since he presents no evidence to support the latter contentions, one at times gets the impression that he is too eager to dismiss economic and psychosocial considerations that may alter the population-stress relationship.

Contemporary demographic theory has added a new dimension to the problem of situating individual pathology in the context of multiple changing social forces. Even if Easterlin exaggerates the long-term unchanging cyclical effects of the population-stress relationship, and even if we understand only dimly how it operates, the evidence is convincing that its effects will slow the rapid increase we have seen in the suicide rates among young men and probably even cause those rates to drop. This does not mean we should take a sanguine attitude toward the alarmingly high levels we are witnessing in every barometer of psychosocial stress among the young—crime and drug and alcohol abuse as well as suicide. Quite the opposite; it suggests that we should concentrate on the problems we have without making the nihilistic assumption that the problems will continue to grow geometrically in ways that we cannot control.

3. Suicide among Older People

DESPITE THE FACT THAT the suicide rate in the United States rises consistently and markedly with age, suicide among older people has received little public attention and relatively little attention from clinicians and researchers. This neglect stems in part from the mistaken assumption that little can be done to treat older people who are suicidal, an assumption that is related to and reflects our general neglect of the mental health of older people. In addition, since the suicide rate among older people, although high, has been relatively constant, it has not created the sudden alarm accompanying the dramatic increase in youthful suicide.

A look at current demographic statistics makes evident the relation between suicide and age. Persons over the age of 50, while making up 26 percent of the total United States population, account for approximately 39 percent of the total deaths by suicide each year. This pattern is seen somewhat more clearly when one considers only whites over 50, who make up about 23 percent of the population and account for over 37 percent of all suicides. Even more striking is the fact that white men over the age of 50, who constitute about 10 percent of the total population, are responsible for 33 percent of the annual deaths by suicide.

These figures indicate that it is the pattern of white male suicides that primarily determines the relation between suicide and age. Indeed, in the United States today almost three-quarters of the suicides among people over 50 are by men, and 96 percent of these male suicides are by white men. *

There is good indication that in coming years, as the large post-World War II birth cohort moves into the over-50 age group, suicide will become a still more significant problem among older persons. Demographic evidence suggests that a large birth cohort manifests increased stress throughout life and high suicide rates at every age level. As the stresses of age—including physical infirmity and the loss of loved ones—operate on the vulnerable cohort, it is quite likely that the already high suicide rate among this group will become even higher.

Not only is suicide significantly more prevalent among older persons, but the suicidal act itself reflects important differences between old and young. In particular, the ratio of attempted to actual suicides shifts quite markedly among older persons. Among the population as a whole, the ratio of attempted suicides to actual suicides has been estimated to be 10 to 1; among the young (15–24), it has been estimated to be 100 to 1; and among those over 55, it has been estimated to be 1 to 1.

In the 1973 American Psychiatric Association report *Mental Illness in Later Life*, the authors state, "When an old person attempts suicide he almost fully intends to die."[1] They attribute

---

* For black men, the highest suicide rates are reached by urban males in the 20–34 age group (for reasons to be discussed in Chapter 4), and a subsequent rise in the later age brackets barely reaches the level of the earlier peak. The level reached by older black men, about 10 per 100,000, is also relatively low when compared with that for white men in our culture.

The suicide rate for women, however, does rise steadily with increasing age, reaching its highest levels over a sustained period between the ages of 45 and 65, and then declining slightly thereafter. Although the high point is strikingly low when compared with that reached by older men—about 12 per 100,000 for women as contrasted with close to 50 per 100,000 for men—that rate is still more than double the rate for young women.

survival to accidental factors or poor planning and emphasize the infrequency of the manipulative suicide attempts seen in the younger groups. A Canadian study reports that the usually important distinction between suicide attempts designed for secondary gain and genuine efforts to end life has less relevance for an aged population whose manipulative suicidal gestures are rare compared with their serious suicide attempts. [2]

Such statements are somewhat extreme. If the one-to-one ratio of attempted to actual suicides that has been projected for older people were true, there would be no more than six or seven thousand older patients scattered throughout the country who survived suicide attempts each year, and such cases would be even harder to find than they are. Older suicidal individuals, in my own experience, often made recent attempts that were not serious before the serious attempts that resulted in their current hospitalization. More often than with younger patients, the nonserious attempts were followed in a relatively short time by attempts that were potentially lethal.

The word *manipulative* is nowhere used more pejoratively than with regard to suicide. More important, it is used incorrectly to imply that a suicide attempt is not serious. It should be kept in mind that fatal suicide attempts are often made by people who are hoping to influence or manipulate the feelings of other people even though they will not be around to witness the success or failure of their efforts.

In the case of older people who are suicidal, there are often grown children as well as siblings or marital partners whom the patient wishes to influence, control, or force to assume a more protective role. The demands of the patient are often impossible to meet, the patient is often uncompromising with regard to them, and suicide attempts that are not serious are often followed by attempts that are.

In dealing with the social psychology of suicide among older people, contemporary behavioral scientists have rediscovered and revised the work of the French sociologist Emile Durkheim. "Disruptions in social relations" have replaced Durkheim's "anomie" as a presumed cause of suicide in the elderly. Social isolation has replaced his "egoistic" suicide.

Peter Sainsbury, in the monograph *Suicide in London*, which influenced a generation of British and American psychiatrists, found evidence for the hypothesis derived from Durkheim "that where social mobility and social isolation are pronounced, community life will be unstable, without order or purpose, and that this will be reflected to a greater or lesser degree in the suicide rates."[3] Combining Durkheim's concepts with a social-psychiatric approach, he examined the suicide rates of London boroughs having different psychosocial characteristics.

With regard to suicide among older people, he found that "suicides were living alone to a significantly greater degree than the population at risk."[4] Moreover, suicides aged 60 or over were found to be living alone to a significantly greater extent than either middle-aged or young suicides.

Although living alone is often seen as synonymous with loneliness, studies have shown that they cannot be equated. Approximately 25 percent of the people over 65 in the United States live alone. An extensive 1968 study of the subject found that people who have been single all their lives complain less of loneliness than married, widowed, or divorced individuals.[5] Its authors conclude that loss is more closely related to loneliness than is social isolation. Such awareness has led some behavioral scientists to use the term *social desolation* rather than social isolation to convey the more critical factor of subjective distress. In either case, as researchers have pointed out, we need reported studies of the frequency of subjectively experienced loneliness among persons who have attempted or committed suicide.[6]

Some of the predisposing factors Sainsbury found of importance to older suicides in London—physical illness, lack of employment, and bereavement—have been confirmed as significant by studies of suicide among the elderly in this country as well. The sociocultural differences between England and the United States, are too great, however, for Sainbury's statistics or the interpretation of their significance to be simply applied to the United States population.

Sainsbury and his followers have helped bring Durkheim's work into the mainstream of contemporary psychiatry. In the process, they have not addressed the deficiencies in his work that were long evident to sociologists. Durkheim made us aware of vulnerable groups with regard to suicide, such as widows and widowers, those whose social status has declined, and those who are not integrated into any social group. Since, as indicated in Chapter 1, individual psychology was of little interest to Durkheim, his work did not address such questions as why only a small percentage of widows are suicidal. Nor, unfortunately, have such questions been of sufficient interest to contemporary psychologists and psychiatrists.

A great deal of attention has also been focused on the psychiatric diagnosis of older suicides. A group at Washington University stressed in its 1956 study that "every elderly patient who attempted suicide had a clinically diagnosable (evident) psychiatric illness prior to his attempt."[7] They reported that 89 percent of those patients had a psychotic illness, acute or chronic brain syndrome, or psychotic depression. They quoted a study done in Scotland as showing a similar diagnostic picture. The Scotch authors, however, had pointed out that "the diagnosis of an abnormal type of mental reaction is not a sufficient explanation of a suicide attempt."[8] And indeed it is not.

Although older depressed patients show substantially higher suicide rates than do other psychiatric patients, depression is not the *sine qua non* of suicide even in this age group. Studies have demonstrated that about 40 percent of the older individuals who kill themselves do not exhibit the clinical or psychodynamic features of depression—psychomotor retardation, loss of appetite, insomnia, dreams of oral frustration—described in work going back to Bleuler, Freud, Abraham, and Rado. Depression is a common occurrence in an elderly population, and the vast majority of elderly patients with recurrent or chronic histories of depression are not suicidal.

Establishing the presence or absence of depression is but a preliminary to trying to understand why some depressed patients are suicidal while others are not. Some of the limitations of Freud's important insights into suicide stem from the fact that his observations were primarily based on depressed rather than suicidal patients.

A Yale University study distinguished suicidal patients from depressed patients who have not attempted suicide on the basis of the fact that more open hostility was manifested by the suicidal patients during the interviewing process.[9] We have referred to the work of Beck and his colleagues, who found that the seriousness of suicidal intent correlated less with the degree of depression than with one particular aspect of depression—negative expectations about the future.[10] High suicidal intent was observed in patients who showed minimal depression but whose expectations for the future were slight. Although the Beck study provides no satisfactory explanation of the source of such hopelessness about the future, that study and the one at Yale supply further evidence that more than depression is needed to explain suicide.

The diagnoses of an acute or chronic brain syndrome and of chronic schizophrenia are also often used to explain suicide in older people. Here, too, the vast majority of patients with either condition are not suicidal. Two case illustrations to be presented in this chapter indicate some sources of susceptibility that seem to contribute to such patients becoming a danger for suicide.

Vulnerability to suicide cannot be explained simply by relating it to the inevitable problems of growing old. To be sure, older people increasingly confront illness, the loss of people to whom they had been close, and the declining ability to master and control the circumstances of life. The individual's capacity to deal with such events, however, depends on the meaning and personal significance that they have for him. The objective stress, a person's subjective distortions of that stress, and his adaptive-protective capacity to deal with both the objective and subjective factors are involved.

We have already noted the striking variation in suicide rates between older men and women and between older blacks and whites, as well as the different age peaks in suicide for men and women. These findings suggest that even for groups, psychosocial differences regarding the problems age brings are more critical than the reality of aging itself.

We have reached a point of diminishing returns, however, in defining vulnerable groups among older people. There has been a dearth of information concerning the lives of people who become seriously suicidal late in life. Our own studies are just beginning, but they suggest that the vulnerability of older people to suicide is a function of demonstrable lifelong problems in dealing with such issues as attachment to others and performance in work or in family life. The elderly must face these issues with greater frequency and finality, as the following cases illustrate.

The first two are representative of the seriously suicidal older women we are seeing. At various times both women were diagnosed as suffering from psychotic depressions, but their stories reveal that we can learn much more about their particular vulnerability to disruptions in relationships, loneliness, or social isolation if we do not regard the diagnosis as an explanation for their suicidal behavior.

Mrs. M., a 64-year-old widow, had spent most of the last two years in hospitals because she had become depressed and suicidal following her husband's death. He had died suddenly as she greeted him at the door when he came home from work. After having made several less severe suicide attempts during the course of a year, Mrs. M. was discovered comatose following an almost fatal suicide attempt with fifty .1 gram barbiturate capsules. In a psychiatric hospital, she did not respond to medication or psychotherapy, had only short periods of response to shock, and at times was virtually nonfunctional. She hated the hospital, speaking of it as a form of punishment.

When first seen, Mrs. M. appeared depressed, dependent, and helpless. She was most immediately concerned that her son, who had come from another state after her suicide attempt, would be leaving again. She talked of feeling abandoned by him and by her daughter, both of whom were involved with and concerned about her. She complained of weakness, lack of energy, and loss of memory. At first, her memory difficulty seemed attributable to the shock treatment she had received during the course of her hospitalization, but eventually it seemed more related to her way of shutting out things around her in an exclusive concentration on being cared for and not being alone.

Her fury toward her son and daughter for not doing enough for her came out in a session in which they were all together. She was enraged, out of control, pleading and supplicating in her attempt to persuade her son to stay another month. She reproached her children, coerced them, and yelled at them, revealing a side of her personality that she had not shown in the sessions with me. After her son did leave, she became more depressed and withdrawn.

Mrs. M.'s younger sister and brother described her as a coercively dependent and hypochondriacal person since childhood. They attributed these traits to excessive parental solicitousness about her needs and her health, stemming from an overreaction to the death of an older sibling, a boy of five, when the patient was two.

Mrs. M., saw herself as someone who had never been alone. She went directly from her parents' home to her first marriage. When that ended, she went back home with her children and lived for ten years with her parents. This arrangement continued until at the age of 37 she married for the second time. This marriage had lasted for twenty-four years at the time of her husband's sudden death.

She evidently functioned well with her daughter and first husband for the first six years of their marriage but stopped functioning in any effective way as a wife and mother shortly after the birth of her second child. She later attributed this to some medication she took for anemia. She said that this "shot her nerves" and that she was therefore unable to care for her children or her husband, a situation that led to divorce. She was almost delusional in insisting that this medication was the source of all her difficulties; this belief seemed necessary in order for her to avoid accepting full responsibility for neglecting her husband and children.

The son and daughter when young were raised by their grandparents, with whom they and their mother lived. Her daughter felt she had never had a mother until her mother remarried. By that time the daughter was grown and away at college. Both children said that their mother changed totally after her remarriage. Although the marriage had a neurotic quarrelsome quality, she functioned well both as a mother and as a wife. She had a hypochondriacal streak, however, that expressed itself in her going to bed virtually every winter for weeks at a time.

Mrs. M. says that she was very grateful to her second husband, who she felt had changed her life. He had adopted her children, and they had become very fond of him. However, he had stopped their sexual life approximately seven or eight years before he died, claiming he could not help it but never giving her any satisfactory explanation.

Apart from talking of her husband indirectly through her emphasis on her current helplessness and panic at being alone, Mrs. M. seldom spoke of him in terms of missing him as a person or of good times they had together. She expressed more direct grief in discussing the loss of her parents. What affect she expressed toward her husband was positive but focused mainly on his kindness to her, her parents, her sisters, and people in distress. It was easier to get a three dimensional picture of her husband, and the quality of her interaction with him, from her children than from Mrs. M.

Mrs. M. saw her mother as strong and her father as always available to help her with her problems. When her first marriage broke up, they were available to care for her and her children. She agreed that had they still been alive, she would not have had as intense a reaction to the death of her husband by the second marriage. In one of her recent dreams she was in a restaurant with her mother. Her mother disappeared and then so did every-one else, and she was panicky at being alone.

She had transferred many of her dependency needs to her hus-band. They were almost never separated, except for brief periods. A symbiotic quality in their relationship is suggested by the imag-ery she used in saying that when he died she felt "as if I had been connected to him, as if my veins were now being separated from his."

When Mrs. M. was away from the hospital, she was extremely anxious if someone was not with her. She complained of "silence" in her head, of feeling that nobody was in the room if she was there alone, feelings that were close to depersonalization. At times she felt as though her head had been split open by someone with an axe.

The nature of Mrs. M.'s relation to her husband and her parents, her virtual abandonment of her children after the breakup of her first marriage, and the rage and even hatred she currently expressed toward her children (and her sister and brother) if they did not gratify all of her desires suggested her long-lasting problems in relating to and caring for others. In this respect, Mrs. M. exemplified in an almost classical manner what psychoanalysts going back to Freud and Abraham referred to as the narcissistic quality of those who react to loss with depression and suicide. From childhood to age 60, Mrs. M. had managed to find someone to gratify her primitive dependent needs. Her husband's death and the fact that her parents were now also dead and that her children could not be coerced into abandoning their own lives to gratify her wishes meant that her former adaptation was no longer possible. Although she used the threat of suicide in an attempt to force her son and her daughter to care for her, she was genuinely and seriously suicidal. She saw having no one to care for her as an unbearable condition from which death provided some relief. *

The reaction to the loss of a husband or wife is a natural focus in dealing with suicide among older people. The reaction to the death of parents of the elderly is often overlooked, because it has often occurred many years earlier and is presumed to have little to do with the patient's current difficulties. Yet people often become suicidal in their fifties and sixties after the death of a parent who may be 70 or 80 years old. More striking is the fact

---

* The outcome of therapy with this woman and in the other cases to be considered in this chapter will be discussed in Chapters 8 and 11.

that most of the elderly suicides have unresolved difficulties in accepting the death of a parent or parents, even if these deaths occurred many years earlier. In such cases the difficulties may not precipitate the suicide, but they are a psychological barometer of the difficulties that potential suicides will experience later in life.

Mrs. C., an Austrian by birth, had more reason than most to remain fixated on the death of her mother and sister, whom she lost in the holocaust. Immigrants to the United States from countries like Austria and Germany that have high suicide rates tend to mirror the suicide rates of their country of origin; evidence is accumulating that rates are even higher for those who survived the holocaust while losing close members of their families.

Mrs. C. was 65 years old when she made an almost fatal suicide attempt, in which she slashed her arms after sealing her kitchen and turning on the gas. She was saved because a neighbor smelled the gas. She had made a suicide attempt by swallowing pills some months earlier—an attempt that she believed had not been intended to be fatal and that had led her husband to be more attentive for a few weeks. Now, however, she felt worn out, lost, useless, and a burden to her husband. She wanted to die and was sorry she had been rescued. She also added that she wished to join her mother and sister, who had been killed in a Nazi concentration camp. She left a suicide note that was partly a reproach to her husband and partly a reflection of her desire to die by gas, as her mother and sister had.

She said she was tired of forty years of a wasted life in a marriage in which her husband was never present when she needed him. For the past twenty years they had lived in separate rooms, having little to say to each other. He would read the paper during breakfast, they would both go to work, and after dinner he would leave to "take a walk for the evening."

She denied suspecting that he had been involved with other women during this period. Yet she had stopped having sexual relations with him because of these walks. And he confirmed that liaisons with other women had been a major reason for his being out of the house.

They had married in England during World War II, had a child, and then been separated for a few years while he fought with the Dutch underground in Europe. They had come to the United States in 1950. In the beginning of the marriage, she had seen him as loving and gentle, but things were different when they were reunited after the war. Some of the problems centered on their son. She saw her husband as uninvolved with him; he felt she was a mother to her son more than a wife to him.

She had also been troubled by, and had undoubtedly troubled him with her concern over, his lack of ambition. He had worked as a real estate agent and she as a lab technician. She had not been happy in her work but was involved in it, and her frustration with him and her need for more from him had increased after she had stopped working four years earlier. He, on the other hand, attributed all their difficulties to her depressive episodes, which had begun in the 1950s and increased in frequency in recent years.

In response to a question as to why she had stayed with her husband if she had been so unhappy with him, Mrs. C. spoke of her childhood, telling first about her father, who was killed in World War I, when she was two, while her mother was pregnant with her sister. Her mother and the two daughters went to live in a household headed by her mother's bachelor brother, an Austrian newspaper publisher, and by the patient's grandmother. Her mother was something of a servant in the household, and although they were treated well, they were all conscious of the need not to offend her uncle and her grandmother. She seemed to be indicating that her fear of being uncared for and abandoned had a long history.

She had strong interests in dancing, which she pursued covertly since her uncle disapproved, and somewhat less interest in medicine, which she pursued with his blessing. She was close to finishing medical school when she left for England at the last possible opportunity to get out of what had become Nazi dominated Austria. (Her father had been Catholic, but her mother's family was Jewish.)

She tried to persuade her mother and sister to join her, but her mother would not leave her brother (who would not have been allowed to leave), and her sister would not leave her mother. All three eventually died in the gas chambers of Nazi concentration camps.

Mrs. C. told me that she was frequently preoccupied with the question of why she was spared when her mother and sister died. She felt that maybe God spared her in order to punish her—that she was destined to live an unhappy life ending up in suicide. She had had one dream years earlier that she regarded as the most significant dream of her life;

Her sister, dressed as a monk, was behind barbed wire and was trying to hand her a letter. She never learned what was in the letter. The monk's outfit suggested death to her; the barbed wire, the concentration camp. The letter appeared to be a message from her sister, perhaps an answer to the question she had always wanted resolved—why she lived and they died. What she appeared to need and had never received from her sister was permission to enjoy her life—permission that would free her from her sense that she had no right to live or was destined to live unhappily.

Her son, with whom she was close and who was fond of her, lived with his family in Arizona, and the possibility of living with him was open to her. She had called him a week before the suicide attempt, and he thinks in retrospect she might have hoped he would make that suggestion. On the other hand, she had come out alone for indefinite visits before and each time had wished to return home after a relatively short time.

She had one dream shortly after her admission to the hospital in which she was mixing together some makeup that she felt would do very good things for her skin. She related the dream to her preoccupation with the aging process and its effects on her appearance. She also mentioned a frequent dream in which she was young and dancing at a studio in Vienna. She had little personal preparation in dealing with aging, since her father, mother, and sister had all died before becoming old or sick. Dreams and fantasies of being young were, of course, no substitute for seeking some solution to her current dilemma.

Mrs. C. was at least figuratively a widow because of the way in which she had been emotionally abandoned by her husband. Her vulnerability to abandonment had an individual and personal history, however, beginning with her father's death and the family's dependence on her uncle and grandmother and culminating in the loss of her mother and sister. All of these circumstances combined to make her feel that she could not shape her life, whether in finding work she liked or in leaving a husband who made her unhappy.

Suicide attempts in response to abandonment and loss are seen in older people of both sexes. The next patient had many hospital admissions and made his almost fatal suicide attempt while he was a hospitalized patient. The large number of suicides each year among hospitalized patients or those who have recently been discharged is a sobering reminder of the ineffectiveness of hospitalization as a suicide preventive. In the case of this patient, the diagnosis of schizophrenia appeared regularly on his hospital chart as an explanation for his suicide and actually served to prevent an understanding of the basis for his vulnerability.

Mr. E., a 55-year-old white man, had initially been admitted to the hospital following threats to his wife that he would jump out the window because of her indifference and abuse. While on pass as a patient, he had jumped from a nearby railway bridge, head first to the tracks below. He sustained multiple fractures of his legs, broke several vertebrae, and suffered severe injuries that he barely survived.

Although he had hospital admissions going back twenty-five years, had been diagnosed as schizophrenic, and was at times rambling and circumstantial in his speech, he was sufficiently coherent to provide a strong indication that his suicide attempts were closely connected with separations from or the loss of people he cared for. He first became suicidal while serving on a ship in the Pacific during World War II. He was homesick, felt he was treated badly by his shipmates, and often thought of jumping overboard. Once, when the ship was docked, he deliberately swam into shark infested waters, leaving it to chance whether he would survive.

After the war he married twice, became quickly dependent on both wives, but appeared to have little ability to relate to either of them in anything but a dependent manner. Each time he chose a wife who used and exploited him in ways that he subsequently compared to earlier treatment by his mother.

In his first marriage, which took place shortly after he returned from the service, his wife was unfaithful and left him. He could not get her out of his mind for many years, drank heavily, and attempted suicide again. During this period he lived with his ailing and aged mother.

He remarried in his forties. He had numerous hospitalizations during this marriage; they centered on difficulties with his wife.

He said his wife dominated him, refused him sexually for years, went out nights, gave him menial chores to do, and hit him on occasion. He became suicidal when his mother died and again when his marriage was terminating.

Mr. E.'s vulnerability to separations, loss, and suicide had a long history. His father had had a head injury in an accident on his job as a truck driver, when Mr. E. was a child of almost three. A combination of physical and emotional problems caused the father to stay home without working for the next few years. When Mr. E. was five, his father was confined to a psychiatric hospital and three years later killed himself by jumping from a window of the hospital. Mr. E. attributed his father's suicide to his helplessness and hopelessness.

There were seven children in the family. Mr. E. felt that he was being used by the family, including his mother, to do the unpleasant chores no one else wanted to do. He had a resentful dependent relationship with her, based on his being her "good son." He wrote to her daily while in the service and became terribly upset when she did not reply. His mother stayed with him and his wife during much of his second marriage. Her death, when he was 52, contributed both to a worsening of his marriage and to his becoming increasingly disturbed and suicidal.

His suicide attempts reflected a mixture of his sense of abandonment and his rage toward his wife over her mistreatment of him. It was hard for him to discuss any subject without returning to his anger toward her. He felt persecuted by her, and suicide seemed to be the only sure way for him to be free of his tormentor.

His threats to jump out the window and his nearly fatal jump from the railroad bridge suggested some identification with his father's situation and suicide. He talked of not wanting to end up like his father. He frequently said that people always demanded that he "jump to their tune" or jump when they asked him to do something. Jumping from the bridge appeared to dramatize his feeling of how far he felt he had been pushed by his mother and most recently by his wife.

Although suicide attempts in response to loss or abandonment appear in both sexes, suicide as a response to an inability to tolerate loss of mastery and control originating in work situations is seen predominantly in men. Many authors have pointed to the fact that the greatest number of male suicides occur right after the retirement age of 65. The steady rise in suicide with age among men suggests increasing anxiety over the decline in the capacity for mastery, as a result of the physical, the emotional, or the social limitations that age imposes. It also suggests that men may tolerate less well than women the dependency on others that age often requires.

Mr. N., a 60-year-old man, had been a well-functioning college professor of sociology until a stroke left him almost completely paralyzed on the left side. He was depressed, enraged, and unable to tolerate the decline in his physical and mental abilities. He told me, "When you came out to see me, I watched you like a hawk. You can move your left arm and left leg, and envy and anger just swells up in me." Although Mr. N. had some difficulty in recalling recent events and trouble with numbers and figures, he was perceptive and intelligent and could, despite his depression, cooperate in being interviewed.

He had recently been hospitalized following a suicide attempt with sleeping pills. He had asked his wife for a loaded gun (he is a gun collector), but the family had hidden his bullets. She was afraid that in his current anger with her children (from a prior marriage) he might do harm to them as well as himself. After his paralysis, suicide was always in the back of his mind. He imagined that he would shoot himself in the heart; if he shot himself in the head, he feared, he might survive with even more brain damage.

Mr. N. had been married three times. His first marriage lasted twenty years, and his last two marriages were to women considerably younger than himself whom he met as students in his classes. He had met his current wife in a summer session class two years earlier. They were extremely happy together and married at the end of the summer. A few months later he had his first stroke, which did not result in any permanent loss of function but which was followed six months later by the more serious stroke that left him partially paralyzed. He recovered sufficiently and insisted on resuming teaching that summer. Four days before the end of the summer session, he had a third stroke, which while not severe forced him to give up his job. Since his second stroke he had acted irritably toward his wife's children, although he had a good relationship with them previously. He was aware of being enraged at their ability to come and go as they pleased, in contrast with his own incapacity. He also became critical of everything his wife did, resenting being so dependent on her. He became increasingly possessive of her, was annoyed by the time she spent with her children, and insisted that she choose between them and him.

Although the change in his behavior seems understandable considering his circumstances, his past life had made him particularly vulnerable to what had happened. He had grown up feeling he wanted to be a "warrior" and as an adolescent had taken paramilitary training during his summer vacations. Being a warrior was associated with a need for self-sufficiency that was fostered by a sense of his mother's indifference to him. He spoke with some feeling as he related that she did not come to his graduations and did not give him a party when he returned from the service. Whatever affection he received came from his grandmother, with whom he spent the summers, and from his father, who was somewhat passive and withdrawn.

He enlisted in the army during World War II and served as a captain. He was a strict disciplinarian who often blew up at his men, but he was proud of not having lost anyone in his unit.

Mr. N. said of himself: "I was driven to achieve because I had been a captain in the army and I couldn't be a nothing anymore. I couldn't make the transition from being God himself to being nothing. Are you familiar with the absolute authority a company commander has?"

He went on to take a degree in sociology, marrying during that period. His marriage was unhappy, and he pictured his wife as ungiving and uncooperative. They had many fights over money, he frequently discontinued her charge accounts, and further fights resulted. On several occasions he hit her. He did not leave her, however, until he met in one of his classes the woman who was to become his second wife. She eventually left him for someone else.

He had one child in his first marriage, a daughter, whom he considered "a perfect girl" till she became a rebellious adolescent. He sent her to live with his mother during her high school years, and they have been estranged ever since.

A great deal of his self-esteem was bound up with his teaching. He was considered the best teacher in his department, frequently received ovations for his performance, and was nominated several times for special teaching awards. His wife confirmed that the majority of his students would say that he was the best teacher they had ever had.

He had a recurrent dream during the last five years. He was teaching a class, then began to move his arms as if they were wings, and rose to the top of the room; he flew around the room and then out the window and over some tall trees. He finally became afraid of the height. From his talking about the dream, it was clear that he did get "high" on teaching and on the administration and awe of his students and was fearful of falling from that position.

His present wife had treated him with similar awe and respect. Indeed she continued to do so. His own self-esteem was so tied to receiving admiration for his performance, knowledge, and ability to control situations that he could not imagine that his wife would continue to love him in his partly disabled condition. As a result, he became increasingly critical of her in a manner that was bound to push her away.

He described himself by saying, "I used to say I was like Lou Gehrig, invincible; anyway, I couldn't envision anything bringing me down, no problem, no disability—and, boy, was I full of crap." He spoke poignantly of the difficulty he now had turning the pages of a book with one hand while holding it with the other. His frustration had been aggravated by the tendency of some of the hospital staff to treat him in a dehumanized way because of his incapacity.

The preoccupation with his decline had been a major factor contributing to his mood. He went from talking of suicide to saying, "I was always quick and alert, I would have all these details straight, but, you know, I can't even subtract now. A guy with a Ph.D. that can't even add or subtract or multiply." When he gave good advice to some other patients on his ward and I said something complimentary, he immediately responded with "I'm not as sharp as I was." The need to compare himself with what he was and to deflate his current activities by contrasting them with past abilities was a recurrent theme.

Mr. N.'s case makes clear how intertwined are the need for mastery and the vulnerability to object loss in older suicidal patients. In response to a sense of loss or abandonment by his mother, he used intellectual performance and control of work and personal relations to attempt to bolster his self-esteem. He described himself as someone who trusted logic but had no use for emotion. When his sense of mastery and control were threatened, whether by an adolescent daughter or by his strokes, he had few other adaptive resources to fall back on. After his stroke he became more fearful of losing his wife, more possessive, controlling, and demanding with her, and more resentful of his dependence. Suicide was partially an attempt to reinstate control over a situation that had become intolerable for him.

The existential issues raised by age and by differences in the responses of older men and older women appear to have the distinctive coloration of Western experience, which stresses the values of marriage, motherhood, and relationships with others for women, and those of competence and authority for men. The suicide rate among women reaches its peak at the time when menopause, the end of longstanding marriages through death or divorce, and the loneliness caused by children leaving home frequently create crises. The steady rise of male suicides with age, the clustering of a large number shortly after the retirement age of 65, seems to link such suicides to psychological issues of mastery and control.

The case evidence suggests, however, that if life—or life in our culture—provides the stress, the vulnerability to a response by suicide usually has a lifelong history. Knowledge of the life of the individual generally changes an impression based simply on the individual's social situation or immediate crisis.

Perhaps the greatest loneliness among the patients here presented was experienced by the Austrian woman who was actually living with her husband. Her inability to leave him was related not only to her guilt over having left her mother and sister, victims of the concentration camps, but to a lifelong sense that her existence and that of her family depended on sufferance—originally her uncle's and now her husband's. The vulnerability of the woman who was suddenly widowed takes on a different meaning when one understands the symbiotic nature of her attachment to her husband, and before him to her parents.

The 55-year-old man whose marriage was breaking up and who was tied to his wife in an angry, dependent, self-destructive manner had been suicidal in situations of separation and loss throughout his life. He had never managed to fully separate himself from an originally angry, dependent tie to his mother. And the man who became suicidal after his stroke was vulnerable because his entire adaptation had necessitated feeling that he could determine the admiration and attention he received by virtue of his personality as a teacher to his class and as a mentor to his wife.

In all of the above cases—and in most other cases seen to date in an ongoing study of suicide in the elderly—financial concerns were a problem to the patient, but they were not decisive in the motivation for suicide. The case sample studied is not yet large enough for us to form definite conclusions on this matter.

It is an assumption that a culture like ours, with a minimal social commitment to the economic and social problems of the aging and with an emphasis on youth and change, would tend most to encourage suicide among older people. But Sweden and Denmark, which have comprehensive social welfare measures for the aged, also have higher rates of suicide among their elderly people than we do.

Since the U.S. Census does not ascertain data on socioeconomic class, we have no reliable national evidence relating suicide to class and economic security. James Weiss, in an analysis of 278 suicides that occurred in New Haven over a fifteen-year period, found that among whites (the number of nonwhite suicides was too small for statistical comparison), members of the lower socioeconomic classes had lower suicide rates than did members of the upper socioeconomic classes, but that among males over 65 the situation was reversed, that is, suicide rates among lower-class males were considerably higher than among upper-class males.[11] Weiss offers no explanation for this phenomenon, but Sainsbury, whose findings were similar, suggests that although the higher social classes retire to more secure circumstances, it is probably more significant that they retire to opportunities for more varied interests and outlets.

Sainsbury also compared the suicide rates for older people in Western nations before and after old age pension plans were introduced in their countries. He found that the incidence of suicide in the later period did not decrease, no matter how comprehensive the provision for the elderly. Such measures make life more pleasant for those who wish to live and should be continued. But my own studies of suicide in Scandinavia, reported elsewhere, would support the conclusion that culture and character are even more critical than economic circumstance in determining suicide in older people.

Psychosocial Correlates

4. Suicide and Violence

VIOLENCE AROUSES OUR sense of outrage; suicide is more likely to arouse our compassion. If only on the basis of our contrasting subjective responses to them, we tend to see suicide and violence toward others as totally different psychological phenomena. The average clinician has a similar perception, because the depressed, sometimes suicidal patients who come to the offices of psychiatrists are seldom violent toward others.

The depressed Viennese patients Freud originally saw and described also were not violent. Yet psychoanalytic observation led Freud to recognize that there was a psychological link between murder and suicide. He saw that depression could originate in anger toward a lost love object that the individual turned back on himself. He observed in such individuals repressed murderous impulses toward the love object and expressed the belief that a repressed desire to kill someone underlay all suicide.

The formulation would seem to link murder and suicide, but its effect was quite the opposite. Instead, a rather simplistic notion came to dominate psychoanalytic thinking on the subject—that the suicide repressed what the murderer expressed. Suicide and homicide were said to reflect "opposite types of adjustment." Behavioral and social scientists, intrigued by the possibility of relating two seemingly radically different ways of dealing with violence, formulated propositions concerning a literal inverse relation between suicide and homicide.

Social groups were presumed to deal with frustration and aggression by either suicide or homicide, and the high homicide and low suicide rates among American blacks were regarded as evidence. So were the low homicide and high suicide rates in Sweden and Denmark. A social theory formulated by Andrew Henry and James Short related homicide to external constraints imposed on people of low social status, leading them to blame others for their frustrations; the absence of such constraints, it claimed, led people of higher social status to blame themselves for their frustration and thus to be prone to suicide.[1]

Experience has invalidated such claims. Although homicide appears primarily in the lower end of the socioeconomic scale, suicide seems to be relatively evenly distributed throughout the scale. Young urban blacks with the highest homicide rates in the country turned out to have high suicide rates as well. Among other cultures there are those like Finland's that rank high in both suicide and homicide, and others like Norway's and Ireland's that rank low in both. In our own culture over the past twenty years, there have occurred striking rises of close to 300 percent in both suicide rates and homicide rates among young white males aged 15–19. In fact, if we take young males as our reference point, the United States now ranks among the highest countries in the world in both suicide and homicide. Finally, taken as a group, individuals who kill themselves have committed homicide at a much higher rate than has the population as a whole, and individuals who have killed others have a much higher suicide rate than has the overall population.

All forms of psychosocial pathology tend to correlate with each other, if only for the simple reason that an individual who is in distress is likely to manifest this distress in more than one way. The early life disturbances seen in individuals who later become suicidal, violent, or alcoholic, lead, as we have indicated earlier, to a vulnerability that often does not appear to be specifically directed to only one form of disorder.

The violent nature of and the relation between suicide and homicide in the United States are concretely dramatized by the fact that guns, the instrument used in slightly over 60 percent of the homicides, are used in about 55 percent of the suicides. What is more important, and only somewhat less concrete, both suicide and homicide involve violent disruptions in family and personal relations that in their totality are violent disruptions of society as well. Our understandable concern about the frightening impersonality of homicide committed in connection with robbery, or even without apparent motive, leads us to forget that in four out of five homicides the victim is a relative, lover, friend, or acquaintance of the murderer. Murder, like suicide, is for the most part a personal or an interpersonal matter: both suicide and homicide usually have destructive consequences to a number of people involved with the perpetrator or the victim.

Among the urban black population, homicide rates are ten times higher than among any other group in the United States; it therefore seems appropriate to begin with suicide and violence in that population. My own study of black suicide in New York City indicated how misinformed we were about the relation between violence toward others and suicide.[2] A detailed statistical study made in the late 1960s, with the help of the New York City Bureau of Vital Statistics, provided a necessary background for the investigation. A breakdown of the New York City figures revealed the then surprising information that, among blacks of both sexes between the ages of 20 and 35, suicide was more of a problem than it was among the white population of the same age. Among black men in New York between the ages of 20 or 35, suicide was twice as frequent as it was among white men of the same age group. Even after corrections were made for the census underestimation of black males in this age group, the suicide rate in New York City was considerably higher among young adult black males than among young adult white males. The distribution pattern of black to white suicides among urban males in the 20–35 age group was confirmed in subsequent studies of other metropolitan centers.

A superficial examination of the national figures without an adequate breakdown of the data had obscured the frequency of suicide among young urban blacks. The high frequency of suicide among older whites had led to the misconception that suicide is a "white" problem, obscuring the fact that among young adults, particularly in urban areas, it is as much or more a "black" problem. Only after the age of 45 does the suicide rate among whites become so much greater than that among blacks of the same age that it causes the white suicide rate to rise to a total level much higher than that of the black rate.

While suicide among young blacks has been obscured or ignored, the high frequency of homicide by blacks has not been similarly neglected. At all ages, the black homicide rate is significantly higher than the white homicide rate, with the overwhelming majority of blacks murdered by other blacks of about the same age. Black homicide, however, reaches a peak at the same 20–35 age period as does black suicide. The high black suicide and homicide rates in the 20–35 age group cannot be attributed merely to the social changes of the sixties and the generation influenced by them, since the pattern goes back to at least 1920.

With both black homicide and black suicide, one is dealing basically with a problem of the ghetto, that is, with the poorest socioeconomic group among the black population. Our study of young black suicides made clear the suicide is often the outgrowth of a devastating struggle to deal with conscious rage and conscious murderous impulses. Study of these young people brings out the close connection between the disastrous individual and social circumstances that culminate in suicide.

Suicidal blacks have a striking history of violence in their childhood. Fathers who were physically violent, many of them dying violent deaths, and mothers who were brutal or left their children in the hands of others who were brutal to them recur in the stories of such patients. For example, one young man who eventually killed himself had been trapped as a boy in a room with his father who engaged in a shoot-out with the police. They had been called because he had been beating his wife. The father, although wounded, continued to fire with what amounted to a small arsenal until he was killed. As a teenager this young man came to admire Hitler's ability to kill millions. He was arrested for violent fights and wrestled with the idea of knifing his mother and brother before attempting suicide. What he found most disturbing about his violent behavior was the loss of control that it represented; he thought he might get kicks from killing if he could do it in a cool, controlled, detached manner.

The mixture of despair and violence and the desire to detach oneself from both are even more tragic among black men in their late twenties and early thirties who have lived long enough to experience fully the bitterness and disappointment of ghetto life. Typical of these was a dark-skinned man of 33 who became acutely suicidal after being fired for drinking on the job, but whose life had been marked by drinking, depression, and sporadic episodes of violence that he felt might make him kill. His worst outbreaks were with policemen: one of his arrests was for throwing two policemen through a window. Because of that episode, he had lost a civil service job as a hospital attendant. After his wife left him, he bought a gun and intended to kill her and her boyfriend, but was talked out of it. He has dreamed of killing his wife and her boyfriend and then killing himself.

Apart from violent episodes, his life consisted of lonely drinking in the hallways of the tenement where he lives or in parks. His childhood was a similar mixture of loneliness and violence. His father, a railroad chef, was robbed and beaten to death when the patient was four. His mother, whose severe beatings he still recalls, died when he was twelve. His brother was in frequent trouble with the police. His sister had a "nervous breakdown," precipitated by having been raped by their older half-brother and becoming pregnant. Spending a lifetime in a climate of violence, being violent himself, and drinking to drown his anger were this man's ways of dealing with the total frustration he felt about his life. He mentioned that he had several friends who drank themselves to death, but he did not seem to be aware that he was following in their footsteps.

The rage and violence that marked the lives of black suicidal men were equally characteristic of black suicidal women. One tall 31-year-old black woman had made two serious suicide attempts after violent fights with male and female friends. In describing one of the fights she said, "I beat her as long as she moved, as long as she moved I kicked her. Blood frightens and excites me."

She had thought of suicide since her Alabama childhood in which "there was not a day without a beating. My mother would make me break a branch, and she'd beat me with it—hit me wherever it landed. I wanted to take her and choke her to death. Wished that I would die or she would." Although she feared the beatings, she reached a point where she did what she wanted, since she was beaten anyway. "My mother," she said, "once told me that she wished I had been born dead or that she had gotten rid of me. The way things worked out, I wished it, too. She was never happy over anything I did." As a child she had recurring nightmares in which someone was about to choke her. These dreams appear to have expressed fears of retaliation for her wish to choke her mother.

She made her first suicide attempt at 21, feeling "disgusted with everything." After this attempt, which followed a violent fight with a girlfriend, she had what proved to be a recurrent nightmare: she saw a very large man who had been dead for a long time.

Her height, her fighting, and her mother's disparaging insistence that she was like her father, who had abandoned the family, all contributed to her masculine self-image. She felt men had an easier time than women, since they could fight and protect themselves better. They were also freer to leave and less liable to be left. She herself had a child that she left with her mother, as her father had left her mother with her. She viewed death as a quiescent state, free from violence and loss of control. Living itself was an act of uncontrolled violence in which the only image of peace was "a big dead man."

Her childhood, hard as it was, was no worse than that of the majority of black suicidal patients I have seen. Often the mother, abandoned by the patient's father, did not actually raise the child herself but gave it to a relative. Rage toward their mothers is the usual source of the violence that is expressed through the teens and the adult years.* As one married woman put it, "My mother never gave a damn about me. If she were dying now, I'd be glad

---

* It should be noted that although the rage of most of the patients has its source in maternal frustration, and although their mothers are blamed by most of them for their misfortunes, their fathers, who have often totally rejected them, are usually allowed to escape criticism or anger. Their mothers have evidently been the source of enough security and gratification to arouse expectations—expectations that they have frustrated or failed to fulfill. Their fathers, in contrast, are often seen as figures of whom nothing is expected.

and I'd spit on her." This woman had used a knife to attack her sister and was violent toward her husband although he was not violent toward her. When he left her for another woman, she jumped from the roof of her five-story tenement, after having first wrestled with the impulse to kill him. Her dreams made clear that his rejection had opened the wounds of the earlier rejection by her mother.

The study of young suicidal blacks in the ghetto makes clear that their consciousness is flooded with angry homicidal impulses. What they find most disturbing is the feeling of being overwhelmed by the loss of control over such impulses, and what they describe seems to be a fear of ego disintegration. Seeing such young people after they have been violent, one is impressed with how often their concern is not about the consequences of their violence but about the feeling that they could not predict or control what they did and that it threatened their capacity to function. Suicide can be a form of control of violent impulses by people who feel torn apart by them.

The culture's overt rejection of black people in the ghetto all too often reinforces feelings of rage and worthlessness that are already present—feelings that that culture, operating through the family, has insidiously helped to produce. In their most repetitive self-images, many of these patients saw themselves as black bugs or black rats. While these images appeared in dreams as symbols linking sexuality, destructiveness, and blackness, it is no accident that the symbols originate in the most despised and unwanted living things in the Harlem tenements—rats and roaches.

Regardless of the origin of their frustration and rage, these black patients feel trapped at an early age in an unalterable life situation—trapped by lack of education and job opportunities, by unwanted children or families, and by the destructive effects of the ghetto on their own personalities. As one man put it, "There is no place in the world for a fellow like me. I'll always be on the same level. I'll get nowheres."

For most of the suicidal patients, the capacity for love, tenderness, and friendship was crushed at its source in childhood. Many of these young men and women came to life only through acts or fantasies of violence. In merely talking of past fights or brutality, they became far more animated than usual. They saw living itself as an act of violence, and death as the only way to control their rage. Perhaps this explains the long periods of emotional death that punctuated their violent acts or the variety of deaths in life that they used to keep their anger in check. For many young blacks, life seems to be charted on a self-destructive course—whether the route is drugs, crime, homicide, or suicide. Even the young homicide victims often appear not to be "accidental" victims, but to be leading lives that seem destined to end violently.

It is not surprising that suicide becomes a problem for blacks at a relatively early age. A sense of despair, a feeling that life will never be satisfying, confronts many blacks at a far younger age than it does most whites. For most discontented white people, the young adult years contain the hope of a change for the better. The rise in white suicide after 45 reflects, among other things, the waning of such hope that is bound to accompany age. Those blacks in the ghetto who survive past the more dangerous years between 20 and 35 have made some accommodation with life— a compromise that has usually had to include a scaling down of their aspirations.

Culture influences character by a complex psychodynamic process in which culturally induced family patterns play a key role in perpetuating problems. The rage and self-hatred that are integral parts of the black family situation in the ghetto are inseparable from the rage and self-hatred that are the outgrowths of racial discrimination in a society that stimulates the desires of blacks but blocks their fulfillment.

Whether an individual acts on homicidal impulses, tries to drown them in alcohol, "cools" them by emotional detachment, or turns these impulses inward in suicide, the picture that emerges of young black adults struggling with conscious murderous impulses is far different from that which appears from most studies of white suicide. Among young adult blacks there is a direct relation, not an inverse one, between suicide and violence. It rests on the particular black experience in our culture, an experience that generates violence within blacks and presents them with a problem of controlling it. The statistics showing that the high peaks of black homicide and suicide occur during the same 20–35 age period take on more meaning when it is noticed that behind both homicide and suicide is the central common attempt to deal with rage and violence.

The violence of young blacks, whether suicidal or not, is partially an attempt to deal with underlying depression and despair. The violence often seems to be an expression of unacknowledged self-destructive impulses. One youngster was shot in the stomach by a policeman in his first attempt at a bank robbery. Although he used a pistol that was not loaded and could not be fired, his brandishing the gun undoubtedly led to his being shot. His behavior seemed an invitation for this to take place. Had he died, he would have been classified as a homicide victim who was killed in an attempted armed robbery. The formal requirements of our research did not permit us to include him as a case of attempted suicide, but we had the impression that his self-destructiveness was a critical motivation for his behavior—more critical than any serious attempt to acquire sudden wealth.

Marvin Wolfgang, whose 1950s study of homicide in Philadelphia may still be the best American study of the subject, used the term *victim-precipitated homicides* to describe individuals who are violent in ways that provoke fatal retaliation.[3] Victim-precipitated homicide is surprisingly common: 150 of the 588 (26 percent) consecutive homicides in Philadelphia whose records Wolfgang examined fit this description. Black males, who constituted 50 percent of all homicide victims, accounted for 74 percent of the victim-precipitated homicides—i.e., 110 of his 150 cases.

Such victims appear to be willing participants in their own death. Although Wolfgang was primarily describing husbands who used lethal weapons to attack their wives and provoke their wives into murdering them, it seems likely that police or bank guards can be provoked for similar reasons.

Wolfgang related the much higher incidence of victim-precipitated homicide among blacks to the lower social status of blacks. Like Henry and Short, he saw lower-status people as less successful in internalizing the middle-class norms and values of the culture, and thus more prone to aggressive other-directed behavior. That whites who become victim-precipitated homicides also tend to come from the lower socioeconomic levels was believed by Wolfgang to be supportive evidence. So was the fact that blacks and whites who are suicide prone and become victims of the homicides they provoke have a high proportion of prior arrests.

Henry and Short's hypothesis concerning an inverse relation between suicide and homicide based on social class has not stood the test of time. Nowhere is this more evident than in the high suicide and high homicide rates among young urban blacks. In recent years Wolfgang has moved toward a more fruitful emphasis on the culture of violence in which poor people of all races are often raised.[4] As we have seen, however, the problems of blacks involve caste as much as class, so that a poor and violent subculture affects blacks and whites quite differently.

Certainly the shifts between deadness and loss of control, between conscious, overt violence and self-destructive behavior, provide a psychodynamic picture different from that of the depressed white middle-class patients originally described by Freud. Suicide among young blacks illustrates how distinctive psychosocial conditions shape the psychodynamics of suicide.

With some differences, the relation between suicide and violence extends to the white population as well. Unfortunately, we do not have psychosocial studies of whites that are comparable to our study of these problems in blacks. We have some excellent sociological studies, but these suffer from the inevitable limitation that they are based on figures rather than on people. There are a few fine clinical studies, but they exist for the most part in a social vacuum.

A particularly direct connection between suicide and violence is evident in the study of murderers who go on to kill themselves. We do not keep national statistics that would enable us to know the frequency in the United States of murder followed by suicide. Homicides and suicides are recorded separately, and the accumulated national figures provide no way of linking the two. The FBI, which uses police records to collect and publish information about perpetrators rather than about victims, has not as yet undertaken this task. For the time being, we are forced to rely on the specific examinations by individual investigators of police records in given parts of the country. Wolfgang's excellent study in Philadelphia is an example.

Wolfgang found that whites made up one-fourth of all homicide offenders and one-half of the homicide-suicides.[5] Some 8 percent of the homicides involving whites were murder-suicides. Wolfgang's figure of 8 percent provides a suicide rate for white murderers that is almost seven hundred times the U.S. rate; it certainly dramatizes the point that suicide and murder are far from "opposite types of adjustment."

In Wolfgang's study, men (both black and white) accounted for 83 percent of all homicide offenders but for over 90 percent of all homicide-suicides. The suicide occurred very soon after the murder, and the victim was most likely a relative or a lover. The murder was apt to be particularly and excessively violent (characterized by many stab wounds or shots and preceded by beatings). Wolfgang found that ten of fifty-three husbands who killed their wives committed suicide, whereas only one of forty-seven wives did.

Wolfgang hypothesized that husbands were more likely to precipitate their death by beating their wives, and therefore their wives felt less guilty after murdering them than the husbands did after murdering their wives. Since murderers who kill themselves have histories of having been more law abiding (as measured by fewer arrests) than nonsuicidal murderers, he suggested that guilt might have been responsible for the subsequent suicide of murderers.

It is, of course, hard to deduce psychology from a statistical analysis of the records of dead people. And Wolfgang was trying to draw general psychological principles from a sample of female homicide perpetrators who were 85 percent black. These people live in the poorest socioeconomic circumstances, amid greater violence, than their white counterparts. The more heterogeneous sample studied by Donald West in England showed that half of the women who killed their husbands also killed themselves.[6]

Guilt is not as simple an emotion as Wolfgang implies. Among poor white women in our culture, who are less likely to respond to violence with violence, chronic mistreatment often does not alleviate guilt; in fact, guilt may even increase. Paradoxically, people who are abused for a long time come to feel they deserve abuse. In *The Fall* Albert Camus describes individuals who were punished by being kept in four-foot high cages and who eventually felt that innocence consisted of the ability to be able to stand up straight.[7] Most wives who put up with chronic abuse fit this description; few such women kill their husbands. And a sense of righteous anger and injustice among such abused women is as apt to lead them to suicide as to murder. Women with some capacity for dealing with aggression do not tolerate this kind of abuse and will leave rather than kill or kill themselves to stop it.

Suicide following murder has generally been thought of as self-punishment for the crime that has been committed. But what takes place psychologically often seems somewhat the reverse. The man described earlier who bought a gun with the intention of killing his wife, her boyfriend, and then himself felt that his life was already over. Although he blamed his wife and her boyfriend for his "death," it was the decision to end his life that seemed to move him to act on his anger. Even before Freud, Nietzsche recognized that punishment can lead an individual to feel justified in crime.[8] The punishment that leads to crime can be the self-punishment of an intended suicide.

The individual who believes his life is already over, who feels he has nothing to lose, who may welcome or be planning his own death, and who is enraged with others whom he holds responsible for what has happened to him is particularly dangerous because his homicidal impulses are not checked by considerations of self-preservation. Since the individual himself may be unsure whether murder or suicide is his aim, he arouses much greater uncertainty in those who have to deal with him. This uncertainty makes the potential suicide-murderer especially frightening and gives him immense power over us. The possibility, even if remote, that the armed man who holds hostages, or the political assassin, not only may be willing to kill, but may not care if he is killed and may even want to die makes it especially difficult for us to protect ourselves and limits our options in dealing with him.

There have been some studies of individuals who committed homicide and were subsequently seen in prison. Although these studies are too unrepresentative in their sample and too limited in focus to give us any social perspective, they do contain valuable psychological insights.

Among men who murder women, suicidal tendencies are found to have been prevalent before their crime. Projective identification is a common feature among them; they thus attribute to women those aspects of themselves that they hate most, and in killing their victims, they destroy the hated part of themselves. Such mechanism is usually apparent in individuals of marginal integration (borderline personality) who have difficulty in maintaining their ego boundaries.

Franz Alexander has given us perhaps the best description of such a case, involving a young man whose attachment to his dead mother had stopped him from forming serious attachments to women.[9] After his father, from whom he had been estranged, remarried, he rejoined the family and became close to his step-mother. When his father teased him about his interest in his stepmother, he left in a rage and soon after started an affair with a woman who closely resembled his stepmother. This woman came from a wealthy family and was engaged to a man of comparable status whom they both knew she would marry. When she suggested they could remain lovers afterward, he became acutely disturbed and threatened suicide, whereupon she said she wished to die with him. He shot her, intending to kill himself as well, but he did not and called the police instead.

Alexander felt that her suggestion, like his father's remark, stirred up unconscious guilt deriving from his oedipal attachment to his mother. Murder-suicide provided both gratification and self-imposed punishment. In his sweetheart he found the hated, forbidden part of his own wishes, so that in killing her he was destroying his own bad self. For this reason, he presumably felt little guilt afterward.

A real or threatened separation is often the trigger for murder-suicide. T. L. Dorpat suggested that in severely disturbed individuals the threat of such a separation "brings about massive rage and a further regression in an already impaired ego."[10] As we have seen, hatred in such cases may be turned on the self, on the object, or on both, the individual often being unsure whether murder or suicide is the aim. The potential for such mechanism is considered to originate in a state of infantile development in which self and object are not fully differentiated. Suicidal individuals struggling with violence and fear of loss of ego boundaries are probably more vulnerable to regression to a state where such boundaries were not fully developed.

In no case does the question of separation of self and object seem more a part of murder-suicide than in that of a mother who kills her children and herself. In none does murder seem more closely related and perhaps subordinate to suicide. Children under nine are the victims in 5 percent of the homicides in the United States each year. They are most often killed by their mothers, this being the one form of homicide in which women outnumber men.[11] Child murders also form a significant proportion of the total homicides committed by women. A 1968 study of 112 women convicted of homicide in California revealed that 22, or one-fifth, of them had murdered their child.[12]

Although the mother is three or four times more likely than the father to be the perpetrator, the father is often no longer part of the family. A paramour of the mother is next most likely to be the perpetrator, often with the mother's tacit consent. When the father is the perpetrator, he is often seeking revenge and kills both the mother and their children.

Child murder usually takes place in poor families with a history of prior child abuse involving the victim and other siblings.

The assailants show prehomicidal behavior characterized by alcoholism, narcotic abuse, and crime.

For reasons that have been indicated earlier, no national figures are available regarding the frequency with which such homicides are associated with parental suicide. A 1969 review of the published literature on what has come to be called filicide revealed that of eighty-eight women who had committed child murder, 42 percent had done so in connection with their own suicide attempt or suicide.[13] Because the review mixes cases in this country and Europe without distinguishing them, the figure cannot be applied to the United States alone. A Detroit study examined the records of seventy-one individuals found guilty of the murder of preadolescent children.[14] Twelve of the seventy-one (17 percent) killed themselves subsequently. Unfortunately, no information is provided as to the sex or race of the perpetrator. Projecting the Detroit figure of 17 percent as an estimate for the country as a whole is likely to yield a better approximation than the figure of 42 percent obtained when European and American cases are lumped together.

How critical cultural differences are in such matters is illustrated by Saverio Siciliano's survey of all homicide in Denmark over a period of twenty years.[15] He found that 35 percent of the killers were women, almost one-half of whom killed themselves later. He found that 59 percent of those who killed their children subsequently committed suicide. He concluded that the most common type of homicide in Denmark was committed by a woman in the 25–40 age group, with one or two children under 12, who out of despair and depression, gassed them and herself. This does not mean that child murder is common in Denmark. It rather indicates that homicide is extremely uncommon and that many of the small number of victims are children killed by their mother in connection with her suicide.

In the course of a study of suicide in Denmark, I saw many

women who were acutely suicidal over guilt related to their inability to love or care for their children. [16] To a degree that is striking to foreigners, including Norwegians and Swedes, Danish women are expected to be maternal and protective toward children. The inability to meet these expectations contributes to the women's being suicidal. In a macabre way, the murder-suicides express the Danish mother's sense that she must be totally responsible for her child and provide for its future wants. That she takes her children with her in death reflects not merely her inability to love them in life but also her inability to think of any other protector for her children but herself.

Child murder followed by suicide is not common in the black population. Among black suicidal women, we saw many, however, who were troubled by the knowledge they had neglected or abandoned their children. Several, like the woman described earlier, had given their children to their own mothers to raise. The availability of such an alternative in the black subculture freed these women from the pressure of raising their children and from the need to consider what to do with their children if they killed themselves.

In West's study of murder-suicide in England, half of the victims were children killed by their mothers in connection with the mother's suicide. West was able to trace the history of a selected number of his sample, many of whom had had some contact with social workers or psychiatrists. Finding very little evidence that the suicidal murders were concerned with punishment or anger, he thought that the large number of infanticides, death pacts, and mercy killings pointed to feelings of despair. He believed that murderers who killed themselves resembled suicides more than other murderers, and he concluded that homicidal-suicidal acts were extensions of suicidal acts. Mothers who had spoken to social workers or psychiatrists before their homicide-suicide invariably indicated fears that if their children lived without them they would be neglected or unhappy.

The few case studies in this country of child murder followed by a mother's suicide or suicide attempt tend to classify the mother's motive as altruistic, that is, motivated by the mother's concern for what would happen to the child when the mother was dead. My own clinical experience, although limited to a small number of such cases, suggests that a more complex mixture of attitudes toward children is involved. These attitudes are elaborated in the following case in which murder-suicide involving children seemed likely.

A 36-year-old woman was referred for consultation because of her preoccupation with killing herself and her two daughters, who were nine and three. She had first become suicidal when her husband had left her a few years earlier.

She said she thought of suicide every day. Once she had taken an overdose of pills but said she had not been serious then about killing herself. Now she felt she would drive into the garage with the children and leave on the ignition. She believed that sooner or later she would end her life and her children's lives if she could not feel better about the future.

She did not want her husband to have control of the children, and she felt they were too good for anyone she knew. She described killing them as a result of loving them and being selfish at the same time.

She often thought that she would like to kill her husband with a knife but knew that she would not. Sometimes she imagined that she could punish her husband by leaving him with the responsibility for the children. She believed, however, that killing them would hurt him even more, in a way that her death never could.

The night after I had seen her for the first time, she dreamed that she was making a presentation about justice to a court. Someone told her that it did not matter how well she did, because she could not win. In a second part of the dream, an old man was living in an upstairs room of a house in her town. No one would talk to him or have anything to do with him. She interpreted the court to be family court, where she said there was no justice and where she never won her battles with her husband. The courts made him pay only a minimal amount for the support of the children and did not enforce their decision when he failed to do even that. She felt that no one blamed him sufficiently for what he had done.

She said that she had lost all of her old friends since her marriage broke up. She had dated but without enthusiasm. She realized that she was representing herself as the isolated old man in the room.

What she did not realize was the degree to which her preoccupation with the unfairness of the situation, and with persuading the world how much her husband was to blame, was responsible for her emotional isolation. Her suicide and the death of her children would establish this unfairness, point to how much her husband was at fault, and make her case. At the same time suicide seemed to be the only way of freeing herself from a murderous, destructive attachment to her husband.

Although occasionally she seemed to enjoy her children, she had also discussed with them how sad she was and how often she wished she were dead. They talked together of a man in a neighboring town who killed his four children and then killed himself. Her older daughter said that she could understand how he could feel so bad that he might want to kill himself but that she did not see why he killed the children, since perhaps they did not feel that bad and wanted to live. She thought that the daughter probably sensed her feelings and was telling her that she wanted to live.

She expressed no conscious resentment toward her children and had only praise for them. Some of her recent dreams concerning her children are revealing. In one, a big truck was about to run over her youngest daughter. In another dream a war was going on, and she and her children were captured by Germans. She was shot and killed by them and felt relieved in dying that she would not have to watch the Germans kill her children.

Her anger toward her children, understandable given her situation, was more disturbing in the totality of her need to deny it. Her sense that there was no pain if she did not see her children die reflected the extent of her wish to be free of responsibility for their fate.

In seeing her children as a means of revenge on her husband, or in using their death and her own to dramatize the unfairness of her life, she was unable to see them as having and as being entitled to have a life independent of her. On the surface, killing her children would seem secondary to her suicide, but her anger toward her children and her desire for revenge on her husband constitute an even more critical part of the picture.

As awareness has developed that the relation between suicide and violence can be more direct than was first realized, a number of clinical studies have emerged dealing with the theme of aggression and suicide and claiming to refute Freud's psychodynamic formulation of self-directed rage toward a lost love object as a source of suicide. Most of them have demonstrated that suicidal patients are as openly aggressive as nonsuicidal patients or more so. Depressed suicidal patients in particular have been shown to be more openly belligerent than depressed patients who are not suicidal. Such observations have been used to contradict Freud's formulation, but they have been based on a striking misconception and oversimplification of Freud's work. By incorporating a lost love object, identifying with it, and deciding to kill the object in oneself, the individual may remain protected from an awareness of murderous anger toward the object—but not from anger toward other people or from anger in general. Freud never stated or implied that individuals who were depressed or suicidal had an inability to express anger as a general character trait. Insofar as he characterized them, it was by the nature of their attachment to the lost object, which he saw as a dependent and ambivalent bond.

What Freud described was undoubtedly true for the patients he was seeing and can be confirmed in a number of patients we see today who are also usually not violent. However, such psychodynamics cannot be substantiated in all suicidal patients, and in many cases, as we have seen, quite different and varied psychodynamics seem to be at work. Some individuals or cultures—Denmark's, for example—seem more prone to depression and suicide than to violence and homicide. Such observations were not part of Freud's work.

Suicide and violence toward others show many similarities even when they are not present in the same individual. Hopelessness and desperation are common to both. So are difficulties in dealing with frustration and loss, and in expressing aggression effectively.

It is necessary to understand violence in order to fully understand suicide, and necessary to understand suicide in order to fully understand violence. It is as important to see the suicidal intentions that may be hidden by homicide as to see the homicidal intentions that may be concealed by suicide. Suicide can be used to check homicidal impulses that threaten to overwhelm the individual in ways more frightening than death. Suicidal intentions also may unleash and permit a homicide that would otherwise not take place.

5. Suicide and Homosexuality

Much confusion and misinformation has surrounded the question of whether homosexuals, and particularly young homosexuals, are more vulnerable to suicide than other members of the population. Gay activists have claimed a higher suicide rate among homosexual youth as further evidence of the consequences of discrimination. Those opposed to gays in the military have made the same claims, arguing that suicidal behavior indicates an emotional instability that would undermine order and discipline in the armed forces. [1]

We have no confirmation, however, that there is a greater incidence of homosexuality than might be expected among actual suicides. The comprehensive Robins psychological autopsy study based on data gathered in the late 1950s found no homosexuals among 134 consecutive suicides in St. Louis, of whom 103 were male. [2] If we accept a male homosexual rate of 5 percent in the population, the statistically improbable finding ($p = 0.005$) suggests that the greater concealment of homosexual sexual preference in that time period influenced the result.

A more recent study by Charles Rich et al. concluded that the rate of suicide among homosexuals is not greater than that for heterosexuals. [3] Significantly, all of the homosexuals in the Rich sample were males between 21 and 42 years of age. There were no homosexual suicides beyond the age of 42 among the sample in this study, again suggesting that concealment was a factor. The need for concealment is itself, of course, a reflection of the negative social attitudes toward homosexuality with which gay activists are concerned.

The most recent information comes from David Shaffer and his colleagues at Columbia who did a psychological autopsy study of adolescent suicide, wherein 2.5 percent of the suicides were definitely homosexual, with additional cases that might be, so that the total could be as high as 6 percent.[4] In the uncertain cases, an accurate determination of sexual orientation may have been difficult to obtain from parents. Communication between suicidal adolescents and their parents is notoriously poor, so parental ignorance, denial, or concealment may have been factors.

The lack of reliable information about homosexuality in the general population makes the situation even more difficult to assess. For years Alfred Kinsey's conclusion that gay men make up 10 percent of the population has been accepted, although many considered the estimate high.[5] A recent study indicates that the actual figure may be closer to 2 percent.[6] If this lower estimate is correct, then the Rich figure indicating that 7 percent of young adult suicides were homosexual or the Shaffer figures of 2.5 to 6 percent for adolescents would have a different significance. Based on Kinsey's figures, there was little reason to conclude that homosexuals were disproportionately represented among suicides.

The suicide rate for male homosexuals is likely to increase at least slightly because of AIDS. In New York City and nationwide, the suicide rate of men with AIDS is significantly greater than in men of a corresponding age who do not have the disease.[7] Although we do not know exactly what proportion of the AIDS suicide victims were homosexual, a significant proportion are likely to have been. Since the Rich study was completed before AIDS cases would have had an impact on its figures, and the Shaffer study was limited to 15–19 year olds who would not then have been the population primarily affected, an accurate estimate of the impact of AIDS on the suicide rate for homosexuals has yet to be determined.

Attempted suicide among young homosexuals is another matter. Researchers at Washington University were among the first to find evidence of a link between overt homosexuality and attempted suicide among both male and female homosexuals.[8]

The Washington study and other studies supporting their findings have relied on samples from gay and lesbian student organizations or rap groups and have been criticized for using "convenience samples" that may not be representative.[9] A Harvard study, however, based on a more representative sample, found that in 44 male suicide attempts among all Harvard students from 1963 through 1967, 27 percent had engaged in homosexual activities.[10]

My own work has provided some evidence that homosexuals are overly represented in suicide attempts. In the study of college students referred to in Chapter 2, five of twenty-five, or 20 percent, of the male suicidal students I saw were homosexual.[11] Out of a randomly selected control sample of fifty nonpatient male college students, only four, or 8 percent, were homosexual. Among twenty-five female suicidal patients seen, four, or 16 percent, were homosexual, while not one in the randomly selected control sample of fifty nonpatient females was homosexual. I found no evidence that seriously suicidal homosexuals had suffered more from negative social attitudes or direct discrimination than nonsuicidal homosexuals or that such attitudes are a major factor affecting their suicide attempts.

If further work supports the conclusion that adolescent and

young adult homosexuals have their own distinct pattern regarding attempted suicide and suicide, that is, greater frequency of attempted suicide but no greater frequency of actual suicide, it should not be so surprising. Other groups also have their own distinctive patterns. At all ages women attempt suicide three times more than men, yet men outnumber women among actual suicides 4 to 1. The ratio of suicide attempts among adolescents to actual suicide is about 100 to 1; with adults it is approximately 10 to 1.

In the study of black suicide referred to in the preceding chapter, four out of twelve seriously suicidal black males were homosexuals.[12] This proportion far exceeds the rate of male homosexuality among the entire black population, which, as in the case of the white male population, is now considered to be between 2 and 5 percent. Again this finding suggests a link between suicide and homosexuality within the black male population. Figures for black suicidal women are less conclusive; only one of thirteen such women included in the study was found to be homosexual.

In the study of young blacks who were homosexual and suicidal and in that of white college students with the same problems, I had the opportunity to obtain a psychodynamic picture which revealed something of the nature of the relation between suicide and homosexuality. Among blacks, however, that relation is complicated by the interactive effects of race and violence.

The violence that was part of the adaptation of black suicidal men in general was equally part of the picture of blacks who were homosexual and suicidal. The young man whose father had been violent toward his mother and had been killed in a shoot-out with the police, and whose own violence toward others was an integral part of his problem with suicide, was also homosexual. Fathers who had been violent toward the young men's mothers were common in the history of black suicidal homosexuals. From their fathers' treatment of their mothers they had derived an image of masculinity and male sexuality that was frighteningly violent and to be avoided. In these patients' nightmares they were often running from men who represented their fathers, themselves, or both; fleeing from the father involved a running away from their own masculinity.

The black suicidal homosexuals I studied generally saw their mothers as cold, severe, and rejecting, and as the source of much of their frustration and rage. They tended to blame excessive maternal control and criticism for making them fear women and turning them into homosexuals. Yet they remained attached to their mothers in an angry, dependent way, and serious quarrels with their mothers often precipitated their suicide attempts. One young man, after his mother locked him out of their apartment, roamed the streets for days, before obtaining enough drugs to kill himself.

Another aspect of the mother's role operated to encourage a homosexual adaptation in a boy already frightened by a violent conception of heterosexuality. The black homosexual suicidal subjects were usually uneasy and uncomfortable when discussing relations their mothers had with other men before or after being abandoned by their fathers, and they often saw their mothers as promiscuous or unfaithful.

The father's abandonment and the mother's sexual activity often made her seem an available sexual object, making the need to avoid heterosexuality all the greater. The black homosexual patients' need to protect themselves against temptation and their view of heterosexuality as violent combined to produce a recurring double bind. These men usually tried to handle their relationships with their mothers by identifying with them and remaining attached to them in a dependent, emasculated manner. While they had had sexual relations with women, their attitude toward heterosexuality and their continuing sense of frustrated dependency appeared to make it impossible to maintain such relations.

To have a better basis for comparison, we saw ten black nonpatient homosexuals who were not suicidal and noted how they differed from black suicidal homosexuals. Sons whose fathers were violent or absent and who viewed their mothers as unfaithful or promiscuous were found frequently among black homosexuals who were not suicidal. The homosexuals who were not suicidal were not violent, however. Indeed their homosexuality appeared to have helped them to contain their anger, since in rejecting a male identification, they were rejecting what they saw as the violent aspect of themselves. For the black homosexuals who were suicidal, homosexuality was not sufficient to bind their violence, and suicide often seemed the only way to do so. The preoccupation with maternal abandonment and rejection was central to the lives of the black homosexuals who were also suicidal. These men tended to be much less accepting or forgiving of their mothers than were the homosexuals who were not suicidal.

Three of the four homosexual patients in the black suicide study were most attracted to white partners. The preference for white partners among black homosexuals does not seem restricted to those who are suicidal, since six of the ten nonpatient black homosexuals were involved with and preferred white partners. This interracial pattern of sexual preference was not evident among black suicidal heterosexuals.

Self-hatred directed at being black was, not surprisingly, strongest among the blacks drawn to white males. Their sexual impulses and their black penises in particular were seen as alternately destructive and repulsive. The self-hatred was often repressed and denied. One of the young suicidal homosexuals, who blamed his thick lips for everything from his fear of women to his failure to find work, sought an operation to correct his condition, while denying he connected his lips with being black. He tried to explain his preference for Puerto Rican boys by saying he liked whatever was different.

The idea that an anger-free, purifying whiteness could be incorporated, or that blackness—which was perceived as dirty and violent—could be obliterated, runs through the black homosexual histories. The degradation of blackness, the patient's need to deal with this by feeling he degraded white partners (one black suicidal patient accomplished this literally by defecating on his partner), and the shame and humiliation that accompanied such experiences were recurrent themes.

James Baldwin sensitively and powerfully explores the racial significance of suicide, violence, and male homosexuality in his novel *Another Country*, while at the same time indicating the importance of the white male to the black homosexual.[13] Rufus, the black hero of the book, is filled with self-hatred because he hurts, degrades, and humiliates others through his sexual involvements with them, most significantly a white man and a white woman. Rufus's self-hatred is concentrated on his black penis, which he sees as a venom-producing weapon and ultimately as "his most despised part." In the months before he kills himself, his rage gets out of hand in his beatings of his girlfriend, his fights with strangers, and his threat to kill his best friend with a knife. He recalls his father's rage, and, like many of the subjects in our study, he stays away from his family for over a month prior to his suicide.

The night of his death, while taking the A train, presumably going back to Harlem and his family, he fantasizes the destruction and death of all the passengers. The train stops in Harlem, and Rufus does not get off, realizing in that moment that he will never go home again. In jumping to his death from the George Washington Bridge, he is aware of merging the blackness of his skin and of his life with the water below.

Throughout the book, sexual relations between the black and white male appear to have special redemptive power even for nonhomosexuals. Vivaldo, Rufus's white friend, is guilty of not having loved Rufus sexually the night before he killed himself; he is convinced this would have saved Rufus's life. Eric, the white homosexual, is so glorified in the novel that sex with him—for man or woman, white or black—seems to have almost magical significance.

In *Another Country* and in *The Fire Next Time*, Baldwin shows homosexuality for blacks to be an alternative to drugs, crime, or religiosity in coping with the pain, frustration, and violence of the ghetto.[14] Clinically, one sees that for some blacks homosexuality binds their rage and makes some adaptation possible. For homosexual blacks who are also suicidal, however, the rage and bitterness induced by their sense of overwhelming rejection are expressed both in their homosexual relationships and elsewhere, or contained by depression and suicide.

Because the relation between homosexuality and suicide among blacks is complicated by the interactive effects of race and violence, a definitive picture does not emerge from the relatively small number of cases studied. Among white college students who were homosexual and suicidal the picture is somewhat simpler. The struggle with violence that characterized the blacks was not apparent among the white college students. Among the latter group, homosexual rejection was found to be the usual precipitating event for the suicide attempt.

What suicide can accomplish for the individual in such a situation is suggested by an 18-year-old homosexual white college student who was seen following a serious attempt with sixty barbiturate pills that he barely survived. He dreamed he was working for the United Nations and had an office that occupied the entire floor of the UN building in New York. A friend of his was applying for a position, and the patient was interviewing him and reviewing his qualifications. He told his friend that he did not qualify and could not have the job. During his waking associations to the dream, he revealed that he "had a crush on" the friend. Although he had never tried to become involved sexually with him, the friend may have become alarmed at the intensity of the patient's feelings, and was quite obviously backing out of the relationship. Several months before the suicide attempt, he had more or less broken off with the patient.

What does the young man accomplish in the dream and by the suicide attempt? He gains an illusory control over the situation that involves rejection. In the dream, if there is any rejecting to be done, he is going to do it; by committing suicide, he is the one who leaves or does the rejecting. That he experienced a sense of omnipotence through death is strongly suggested by the important UN post and the large office.

Suicidal homosexuals typically attributed all their unhappiness to rejection, but it was clear that unhappiness and rejection formed intrinsic parts of their relationships. When these students were not being rejected in their homosexual relationships, they were the ones doing the rejecting. Although this pattern also emerged among homosexual students who were not suicidal, homosexual students who were suicidal had abandonment and death at the center of their adaptive history.

The life-or-death, "I can't live without you" quality that suicidal homosexual students gave their relationships appeared to derive from their need to recapitulate and relive the intense unhappiness they had known with their parents, particularly with their mothers. Homosexuality permitted the student to be more alive while not making a break with his mother—i.e., he did not reject her for another woman, and by identifying with her sexually, he did not feel he was giving her up. Bound to his mother in a depressed way, and recapitulating his relationship to her, the homosexual suicidal student found loss and rejection built into each of his relationships.

Bill, a college senior who was homosexual, made a suicide attempt with thirty sleeping pills after a quarrel with Tom, a student with whom he was sexually involved. Quarrels, jealousy, and faultfinding had marked the several stormy months of their relationship. It was usually Bill who felt hurt and neglected by Tom. He became convinced that Tom had lost interest in him and felt he had been "overly friendly" with some other fellows at a New Year's Eve party. Nevertheless, Bill came to life only when discussing the jealousy and arguments that persisted in his relationship with Tom.

In a depressed, inert manner, Bill told me that he had moved from New York to Virginia as a child, when his father went there to sell antiques. His mother helped out in their shop. He described hating Virginia because he felt lonely and isolated, thought the other kids were mean, had no friends, and was not good at sports. He discussed how lonely and uncared for he felt as a child, without relating this feeling to his mother. He did complain, however, that his parents did not know or care what he felt, perhaps because his mother was "too busy with her own depression."

In high school he appeared to have overcome his sadness and isolation for a few years. He was on the basketball team, was active in social organizations, and became president of his class. At this time he actively hated his parents and defied his mother's "strict, puritanical rules" against staying out at night with his friends. Even during this period he would often react to the restrictions placed on him by locking himself in his room.

Bill dated his own chronic depression from the time his mother died of cancer, when he was 18, the summer before he entered college. His sadness in relation to his mother clearly had a much longer history. He saw his mother as having been depressed all of her life. She did not complain in the last painful months when she knew she was dying and seemed to Bill "beautiful and sad." Bill felt he was closer to her during that period and became tearful when discussing this. Bill feared his father, who occasionally drank and physically abused his mother. He was told by a family friend of his mother that she would have left his father had it not been for the children.

Both Bill and his father drank heavily after his mother's death. His father eventually pulled himself together, remarried, and seemed much happier than he had been in his first marriage. Bill never got over the death and attributed to it his insecurity and uneasiness in all his relationships. Since the age of 16 he had been aware of being attracted to both boys and girls; his earliest sexual relationships, however, were with girls. The summer after his first year in college, he was involved with a girl who became serious about him. Bill felt "awful" over his inability to love her and attributed a suicide attempt he made that summer to this. He first became sexually involved with a man after his sophomore year in college. While he fought it at first, he presented himself as accepting and wanting to be homosexual, stating that he was quite open about it and felt no guilt.

Bill's dreams illustrated the object of his guilt and the source of his conflict. The night he took the sleeping pills, he dreamed he was in the home of his first-grade teacher, a woman he did not like. He was trying to destroy the evidence of something he had done, but was unable to do so. The woman called the police, and people were running after him, chasing him. Bill believed the evidence must refer to the empty bottle that contained the pills he had taken. A sense of guilt in relation to the school teacher pervaded the dream. He associated the school teacher both with his mother and with the pain of separation from her when he started school. He was conscious of feeling guilty about not having loved his mother enough. This feeling seemed related to his sense that he was not able to give his mother what it would have taken to bring her out of her depression. He said he must identify with her, since he predicted he will die at 38, which was her age when she died. At the time of his suicide attempt, he recalled, he felt he just wanted to die; later he thought his attempt was directed against Tom. The imagery of his dream suggests, however, that his attempt was even more involved with his feelings toward his mother.

Bill was also aware that his mother's need to constrict him was destructive and punitive. In his brief phase of open rebelliousness in high school, Bill found relief in unleashing his resentment at the damage he felt she had done to him. His earliest memory was of being burned by his mother at three or four when she accidentally dropped scalding water on him. The image was expressive of what he felt did occur in their relationship.

Just as Bill when younger dealt with his resentment against his mother by locking himself in his room, so does he deal with his current life in a self-destructive, punitive way. He had been an excellent student in high school, had one of the highest IQs of all the students tested, but drifted through college and dropped out of school just a few points before graduating.

His past experiences made him particularly vulnerable to rejection, yet it was Tom's aloof, rejecting quality that attracted him. The experience of disapproval and the extension of rejection into his adult, sexual life were what he required to maintain his connection to his mother. Bill's sense of relationships was shaped by his association of closeness and affection with death— the prolonged emotional depression of his mother, and his increasing closeness with her as she died.

In our research, the student suicide problem involved female homosexuals as well. Like the homosexual young men, these students tended to make their relationships a life-or-death matter. They were generally conscious of the pain of rejection, although not of their need to provoke it. Suicidal behavior and the threat of withdrawal often dominated their lives with each other. Typical was the relationship between Sally and Ann; their relationship had survived—perhaps because of—illness, infidelity, and respective suicide attempts.

Sally was a 21-year-old college senior who impulsively jumped seven stories from the window of a hospital, where she had been admitted for a checkup. She shattered the bones of her legs, tore her liver, damaged her jaw, and loosened many of her teeth. When I saw her a few days after she jumped, she told me what happened pleasantly and coherently, despite her pain and immobility.

At first she blamed her jumping on the fact that she had missed a lot of school because of illness. Her recent hospitalization had followed her having been found unconscious by friends who knew she had an epileptic history. She had had occasional seizures since being at school, and since no disturbed EEG pattern was found, she was told that the seizures were "functional." She said she was upset because she had just been reprimanded for missing so many classes, felt she might be dropped from school, and because the hospital did not permit her to attend classes.

As Sally spoke more about her life, it was clear that her difficulties in school were the least of the problems that made her feel "everything in her life was going downhill," a striking expression in view of her jumping. She began to speak of her difficulties with her boyfriend, a homosexual man of 29 with whom she had had her first sexual relationship, but who had rejected her when she had become pregnant. It soon became clear that the boyfriend's rejection was secondary to her rejection by her black female lover, Ann, who had become involved with another young woman.

Sally's relationship with Ann was central to her depression. On an earlier leave of absence from school, recommended because of her seizure difficulty, Sally spoke regularly with Ann on the telephone and became upset when she sensed an emotional distance on Ann's part. She impulsively and severely cut her wrists, which required extensive stitching. Ann had earlier made a suicide attempt because of Sally, motivated by anger when Sally had gone off with friends for a weekend and left her. Sally's first seizure occurred while Ann was in the hospital, following this suicide attempt. Sally felt guilty not only about Ann's attempt but about remaining in school after Ann had flunked out. She was very concerned about losing Ann, and her blackouts—like her suicide attempt—seemed to say she would not accept life or consciousness without Ann.

Sally traced her vulnerability to a feeling of family neglect since childhood. Her father and mother were never affectionate with each other or with their children. Her earliest and most powerful memory was of feeling upset when she was about three, climbing into her mother's lap because she wished to be held, and being pushed away by her mother, who was reading a magazine and who said rather brusquely she had no time for Sally. Sally recalled crying and leaving the room, hurt because all her mother was doing was reading a magazine. She felt this incident had an enormous impact on her, but as she talked about it, it was clear that it was a prototype of less dramatic repetitions of the same experience.

Sally also felt rejected at an early age by her father, who made no effort to conceal his disappointment that he did not have a son. In fact, he treated both Sally and her sister like little boys, buying them guns and refusing to get them dolls which they wanted. She saw him as a rigid taskmaster who spanked his daughters severely with an open buckle for any expression of disobedience or anger. Sally described herself as a shy child, frequently sick and protected by her mother, at least in this regard. Illness was one way she had of getting attention, and although robust in appearance, she continued to have an image of herself as sickly. She seemed surprised, however, that her father had flown to see her in the hospital. When she told him she had not fallen but jumped, he left the room, came back, and never referred to it again.

Sally felt she and Ann had become friends because they shared a common misfortune: each had felt rejected by her mother. Sally's mother died of cancer when Sally was 14, and her father remarried two years later. Ann had been a devoted friend through all Sally's illnesses. Since her jump, Ann had been to see her every day. Sally was planning to live with her when she was discharged from the hospital. Nevertheless, she still did not want to make a permanent commitment to a lesbian life. She dreamed she was living with Ann on Cape Cod and her boyfriend Mark was living nearby. Ethel, who was Ann's music teacher and a very successful singer, was singing at a party Sally was giving for everybody. The mood of the dream was very happy.

Although Sally liked Cape Cod and had lived there previously with Mark, Ann did not and would not go there. In her dream, Sally was not forced to choose between homosexuality and heterosexuality. She had both. Her involvement with both Ann and Mark—each of whom impelled her toward suicidal thoughts and acts—suggested how much she sought to maintain the link of rejection that prevailed with both her mother and her father. Depending so greatly on a woman when she did not want to commit herself to a lesbian life and falling in love with a man whose allegiance was strongly homosexual were dramatizations of the degree to which she expressed her need not to be fulfilled in any relationship, at the same time that she believed she was pursuing affection and sustenance.

Sally's Cape Cod dream also suggested the significance that her seven-story jump had for her. She identified with Ethel, the successful singer, whom she had been told she resembled. Sally also sang, and seemed to feel her suicide attempt had brought her the kind of attention Ethel got through her voice. Ethel was also someone Mark admired and had once been involved with. If Sally's jumping epitomized her sense of "going downhill," it also meant to her the opportunity and attention of a starring role at the Metropolitan Opera. She was willing to be dead in order to be noticed, and Mark, her father, and most of all Ann had responded.

Each of these young women had a mother who had rejected her. In each other they found some extension of the tie of resentment and need that they had experienced with their mothers. It was no surprise that Sally spoke of their bond as one of a "shared misfortune." Both used suicide coercively, to induce remorse or concern from the other. Whatever affection they had for each other, their respective suicide attempts made clear their feeling that someone would care about them only if they were dead or about to die.

Suicidal lesbian students seemed to link affection with loss and death. Their relationships were marked by an alternation between hurting and feeling hurt similar to the seesaw between Sally and Ann. Some lesbian students used suicide attempts to arouse the concern of women whom they had been involved with and who were rejecting them. But if, after the attempt, they succeeded in bringing back the woman, they frequently rejected her. For such students, rejecting or being rejected appeared to serve as necessary brakes on involvement. Commonly, these students saw closeness as inevitably destructive. As one student put it, "All anyone really wants is that you should be dead. People like to have corpses around."

Suicidal male and female homosexual students generally had far more traumatic personal histories than did nonsuicidal homosexuals. One does not see in the suicidal students the overprotective binding by parents that is often found in homosexual histories. Overt rejection, or the loss of a parent through death, and the parental desire for a lifeless child predominate. They use another man or woman to relive their original sense of rejection, and the panic and sense of helplessness in the face of current abandonment are painfully suggestive of their earlier anxieties over abandonment. Crucial to maintaining the bond with their pasts was their image of themselves as lifeless. Long before Bill's mother had died, he had bound himself in an emotional death and depression. Sally's "extinction" had taken place early in life in her relations with both parents. For these students, death and despair were links to their childhoods in a chain they saw as unbreakable.

Unresolved separation anxiety is a common factor in both suicide and homosexuality. In our culture, for homosexuals who are suicidal, the separation anxiety seems to have been produced by maternal rejection or abandonment. This is true of both black and white homosexuals. Suicide is often an attempt to master the anxiety and rage of such rejection. Although overt violence is more characteristic of the black culture, and of the black suicidal homosexual's response, the coercive attempt to use suicide to force a reluctant partner to return is much more characteristic of middle-class white culture and white homosexuals.

Guilt or shame at being homosexual was not a significant element in either case. When guilt was a factor, it stemmed from the destructive nature of the individual's sexual impulses. Several of the homosexuals avoided homosexual experiences as much as possible, because the destructive fantasies they unleashed were intolerable to them. Such destructiveness, whether expressed or not, served to cut off suicidal homosexuals from other people and heightened their sense of estrangement and rejection.

The extreme vulnerability to rejection of suicidal homosexuals may have an important social component as well. With all its sexual and social activity, the "gay life" provides no more than an alienated and isolated existence for many homosexuals. Continuity of relationships between two homosexuals is rare, although many homosexuals spend a lifetime seeking it. For those who do seek it, any relationship that offers that possibility is apt to be intensely overinvested rather quickly. Since such relationships usually lack social or family support, rejection or disappointment signifies not merely abandonment but despair over the inability to escape emotional isolation.

6. Suicide and Alcoholism

STUDIES OF THE DRINKING HISTORIES of suicides have been a major source of information about the relation of alcoholism to suicide.* Virtually all such studies have reported a percentage of alcoholics among suicide victims far higher than the 5 percent of alcoholics usually estimated to be in the general population of the United States. Studies based on coroner's reports or police records of suicide victims in particular cities such as Minneapolis and Philadelphia have reported a 10 percent incidence of alcoholism among suicides.[1] More thorough investigations in St. Louis and in King County, Washington, in which close relatives of the suicide victim were also interviewed shortly after the suicide, found evidence of alcoholism among 28 percent and 31 percent respectively of the suicides.[2] The accuracy of these latter studies is enhanced by their use of widely accepted criteria for establishing the presence of alcoholism.

Attempted suicides also show a high incidence of alcoholism. In the Washington study, for example, an attempted suicide group of 118 patients drawn from consecutive such admissions to a major hospital was compared with the actual suicides. Some 23 percent of the attempted suicides were alcoholic.

---

*Alcoholism is too large a subject to be treated comprehensively in this chapter, which must be confined to the alcohol-suicide relation, which is evident primarily in men over the age of 30. Recent increases in drinking by adolescents have been shown, however, to be correlated with suicide.

Investigators have found further evidence of a connection between alcoholism and suicide by examining the mortality figures of alcoholics and comparing them with mortality figures among the general population. Most of these studies have been done in Europe; they indicate that from 7 to 21 percent of all alcoholics die from suicide in countries where suicide is the cause of death for from 1 to 2 percent of the total population.[3] Frederick Lemere, in one of the only studies of completed suicide among alcoholics in the United States, obtained from non-alcoholic patients a history of the causes of death in five hundred alcoholics to whom his patients were related.[4] Fifty-five, or 11 percent, had committed suicide—yielding a suicide rate at least ten times greater than would be expected among a group of non-alcoholics.

If there is general agreement about the presence of a correlation between alcoholism and suicide, there has been no agreement about its meaning or significance. Some have seen alcoholism and suicide as related because both are the consequences of common underlying causes; others have seen alcoholism as a form of suicide or as a temporary substitute for it; still others see alcoholism, regardless of its cause, as having consequences that lead to suicide.

William Rushing examined the hypothesis that suicide and alcoholism are linked by common underlying factors.[5] He set aside theories suggesting that the links between suicide and alcoholism may be such factors as urbanization, social disorganization, social integration, or common personality traits, on the grounds that measures of these variables are not available. He turned instead to variables he could examine readily, such as age, socioeconomic status, unemployment, and marital status. He found that even when these variables were controlled, the relation between alcoholism and suicide continued to exist. His results did indicate, however, that there were interactive effects. Alcoholism appeared to have a stronger predisposing effect to suicide when accompanied by unemployment; the effects of alcoholism on suicide were more severe for the nonmarried.

Rushing favored a process interpretation of the alcohol-suicide relation in which excessive drinking regardless of cause may lead alcoholics to neglect familial, occupational, or social roles, alienating family, friends, and work associates, so that the alcoholic becomes a social outcast. Citing the accumulated evidence that disruptions in social relations are a precipitant to suicide, he suggests that the alcohol-suicide relation may reflect an association among the variables of excessive drinking, negative social reactions with disruptive social relations, and suicide.

Rushing recognized that since the variables are sequentially related, confirmation of this hypothesis would require longitudinal investigation examining differences in the social reactions to alcoholics (punitive vs. nonpunitive) as well as resulting differences in the alcoholic's behavior (suicidal vs. nonsuicidal). He also acknowledged that antecedent social structure and/or personality attributes may combine with negative social reactions to make suicide more probable. He suggested that a full understanding of the alcohol-suicide relation would require "research in which personality and social structure variables as well as the measures of social response are systematically included in the same research investigation."

Experimental intoxication studies have given support to the impression that intoxication per se may be a crucial factor in the suicide attempts of alcoholics. They have shown that alcoholics experience increasing anxiety and depression with continued heavy drinking. John Tamerin and Jack Mendelson observed the development of severe depression, to suicidal proportions, in alcoholics after two weeks of experimental intoxication.[6]

Clinical studies have identified three groups among intoxicated suicide attempters.[7] In a small group, which may or may not be alcoholic, intoxication facilitates a suicidal impulse. A second group consists of alcoholics, who relatively early in a particular drinking episode, and usually in the context of an argument, make an explosive, aggressive, impulsive suicide attempt. In a third group, closer to that seen in the Tamerin and Mendelson experimental studies, the suicide attempt occurs after a prolonged period of drinking of at least two weeks. This group is usually depressed, guilty, and self-reproachful.

Paul Whitehead examined the presence of suicidal thoughts in a group of 147 male alcoholics and believed his results supported Rushing's hypothesis that alcoholism generated a process that precipitated suicide.[8] Whereas Rushing postulated the negative reactions of significant others, Whitehead attempted to study them. He found that alcoholism preceded suicidal thoughts in his subjects; that breakdowns in their interpersonal relationships occurred largely before the onset of suicidal thoughts; that two-thirds of the suicide group had sought help for difficulties in their relationships with others before the onset of suicidal thoughts; and that almost three-fourths of those who had contemplated suicide reported rejection by friends before the onset of suicidal thoughts. He thought his results supported the proposition that alcoholism led to a breakdown in significant relationships and that the resulting stage of "overindividuation" led to suicide. He also believed his work refuted the proposition that alcoholism and suicide were effects of the same causes.

Whitehead found no evidence, however, of any differences between the alcoholic suicidals and nonsuicidals in their marital status; nor was there a difference in terms of whether or not their wives or in-laws reproached them for their drinking. He does not comment on these findings, which to a considerable degree contradict his results and Rushing's hypothesis.

To clinicians who have worked with alcoholics, the approach of Whitehead and Rushing may seem simplistic. Alcohol is commonly used to withdraw from the responsibilities and commitments of marriage and family life. Both a husband and a wife may attribute their difficulties and quarrels to the man's drinking, and both may blame their breakup on the drinking, but often one who comes to know such couples learns better. Difficulties in relationships and consequent rejection seem to be common to both suicide and alcoholism. The subject's vulnerability to such rejection is another dimension that needs to be examined in both conditions.

Rushing and Whitehead focused on a point late in the life history of the alcoholic—a point at which drinking, the complications it entails, and the response of others begin so to dominate the life of the individual that it becomes harder to establish the earlier symptoms of the process. Something comparable takes place with the heroin addict. Early in the addictive process, it is not hard to establish the difficulties that are leading the individual to use heroin. Later on, when getting and using heroin virtually dominate the life of the individual, everything else is obscured. *

It was Karl Menninger who most coherently presented the view that alcoholism is a form of self-destruction used to avert the greater self-destruction of suicide. Menninger saw early-childhood frustrations with consequent aggression, guilt, and the need for self-punishment as common to both suicide and alcoholism. He emphasized the irony of alcoholic self-destruction "accomplished in spite of and at the same time by means of the

---

* Addicts, too, have a high suicide rate, although the total number of suicides by addicts in the U.S. each year is relatively small compared to suicides by alcoholics. Calvin Frederick found that white male addicts commit suicide more than eight times as frequently as nonaddicted males of the same age; the attempted suicide for white addicts of both sexes was three and a half times greater than that of a matched age sample.[9]

very device used by the sufferer to relieve his pain and avert this feared destruction."[10]

Menninger applied his formulation to every form of psychological illness, from accident proneness to neurosis. Recent extensions to his work by others include overeating and cigarette smoking. Menninger helped to make us forever aware of the varied and subtle forms that self-destructiveness can take. But his formulation contains the seeds of much conceptual confusion.

Part of the difficulty is that Menninger's formulation of childhood frustration, aggression, guilt, and the need for self-punishment is the same for all the forms of self-destructive behavior he described. Such encompassing explanations tend to be so broad and general that they leave us feeling they have explained nothing at all.

More important, the formulation regards all behavior having self-destructive consequences as self-destructively motivated by the need for punishment, whether consciously or unconsciously. Clinical observation does not substantiate such a view. Sometimes the self-destructiveness is incidental to behavior that is otherwise motivated. Nor do all individuals learn self-protectiveness or risk-taking behavior in the same way. Many clinicians follow Menninger's lead in assuming that the need for self-punishment is the motivating cause in all cases involving behavior that has potentially self-destructive consequences, but the burden of proof lies on them.

A group of researchers believe they have support for Menninger's thesis that alcoholism is a form of chronic suicide, from a study in which they found that suicidal thoughts preceded the alcoholic's loss of control over his drinking.[11] Whitehead makes a case for the exact opposite, i.e., that the social complications brought on by alcoholism antedate the preoccupation with suicide. My own experience has indicated that either sequence is possible.

However one interprets the chain of events leading to suicide attempts and suicide in the alcoholic, the evidence that recent interpersonal loss frequently precedes the suicide attempt is convincing. George Murphy and Eli Robins reported in 1967 that one-third of a series of suicides suffering from alcoholism had experienced loss of a close relationship within one year or less of the suicide.[12] The distribution of these losses was strikingly skewed, the majority having occurred in the final six weeks. No such pattern of loss was found among nonalcoholic suicides suffering from depressive illness either within six weeks or within a year.

Murphy and a group of coworkers reported in 1979 on a study that replicated the 1967 study with a group of fifty alcoholic suicides.[13] Some 26 percent had experienced a loss within the final six weeks of their lives. The research group did not include as losses the frequent occasions on which a separation was pending or likely but had not yet taken place. Ernest Palola and his coworkers had found that such losses in alcoholic suicides were commonly due to separation or divorce to which the subject's alcoholism contributed, while in nonalcoholic suicides such losses were due to the death of a loved one.

Because of the frequently made association between depression and suicide and the widely held view that alcoholism is a defense against depression, the Murphy group was surprised to find that depression was not universal among the alcoholic suicides. Eleven of the fifty cases (22 percent) had uncomplicated alcoholism with no evidence of depression, even though five of the eleven had experienced interpersonal loss within six weeks of their suicide. Two-thirds of their cases did give evidence of a depression, but the depression was secondary to other psychiatric or medical illness. Only four had depressive disorders that antedated problem drinking, and these were diagnosed as primary affective disorders with secondary alcoholism.

Aaron Beck and his coworkers had demonstrated a few years earlier that hopelessness in alcoholics is more significant than any other symptom of depression in determining suicidal intent.[14] For Beck, hopelessness is the key factor in all suicide, whether the individual is alcoholic or not. His work has been a valuable corrective to the misconception that depression explains suicide. However, since his formulation is so inclusive, and since he offers little to help us understand the variations in individuals in their sense of hopelessness, the work sheds little light on the specific alcohol-suicide relation.

The capacity to deal with stress in general and with loss in particular seems to be partly a function of vulnerability produced by early life experiences. Our knowledge about what determines whether suicide or alcoholism is seen, or whether both appear, in response to later stress is still rudimentary, but almost every sequence described by the authors mentioned in this chapter can be observed, and efforts to prove the primacy of a particular sequence do not seem particularly fruitful.

Most of the work on the alcohol-suicide relation is based on statistics that provide no grasp of the individual for whom alcoholism and suicide become interrelated responses to stress in general and to loss in particular. The following case illustrations are intended to provide a more personal sense of the individual who is alcoholic and suicidal. They suggest some of the different ways in which alcoholism and suicide can be related and some of the sources of the vulnerability that make both alcoholism and suicide more likely.

A 45-year-old man who built up his own accounting firm came home from work to find that his wife and only son—a boy of 14—had drowned. They had been visiting his wife's parents, and he had asked his in-laws to make sure that his wife and child did not sail alone in a small boat he owned. They had done so anyway, with the result that the boat had overturned in rough water.

Two weeks after their death, this man turned on the ignition of his car in his closed garage with the intent to commit suicide. He would have succeeded if his neighbors had not noticed that no lights went on in the house after he pulled into the garage. They became suspicious and rescued him just in time.

In the ten years that followed the deaths of his wife and son and his suicide attempt, this man progressively became alcoholic. He gave up his business and worked on and off at menial jobs, some of which he lost because of his drinking. Contrary to the popular belief that people drink to forget, he claimed that he did not think of his wife and son except when he was drinking. He had broken off with his in-laws, blaming them for what had occurred. His anger toward them permitted him to avoid facing his anger toward his wife for not listening to him or his own guilt about having bought the boat for his son.

He had a recurrent dream during his drinking episodes. He was on a rooftop (a place where he often drank), and two rats were trying to climb up the drainpipe to reach the roof. He was pushing them down with a stick. His associations indicated that the two rats were his wife and son—rats for having abandoned him, rats because what had happened continued to gnaw away at him.

His mother and father had been regular drinkers, but neither of them had had a problem with alcoholism until his father was killed on his job in a boiler accident shortly before the patient's marriage. His mother then drank heavily and constantly over the next few months, after which she died.

His parents were social people who were out every night, and he had felt abandoned by them as a child. He was their only child, but he said they really should not have had any children.

They were more interested in him when he was a young adult and they could include him in their social activities.

His family background, and his identification with his mother, who drank after she lost her husband, at least partially explain his use of alcohol to deal with his loss. Given the catastrophe that befell him, neither the suicide attempt nor the alcoholism might seem to require much explanation. Yet the majority of people who experience such loss do not react with alcoholism or suicide. His vulnerability was greater because his sense of abandonment by his wife and son was superimposed on his earlier sense of abandonment by his parents.

To say that alcoholism was a way of warding off suicide for this man would be an oversimplification. Alcohol seemed to permit him, in a self-destructive way, to hold on to the emotions engendered by the tragedy that ended the lives of his wife and son. Sober, he managed to avoid thinking of his family or dealing with his loss. It does not seem to be stretching the metaphor of his recurrent dream too far to say that washing his own life down the drain with alcohol was his self-punitive response to what had happened to him.

Despite this man's vulnerability there is no reason to believe that he would have become suicidal or alcoholic without the unforeseen tragedy. The next man was approximately the same age when his wife left him, but his drinking contributed to her leaving. This man's drinking was an expression of his fear that his marriage had gone out of his control. His drinking problem, however, was even more aggravated by their separation.

A successful business executive of 48, he became depressed and suicidal when his wife left him after fifteen years of a marriage that had evidently been deeply frustrating for both of them. He described her as cold, unmovable, sexually frustrating, and unwilling to cooperate in his desire to have children. His wife had complained of his heavy drinking, his abusive, tyrannical behavior, and his lack of interest in her.

Although he had "given up on the marriage" and during an earlier separation, not dictated by his wife, had been happy with another woman, he now found her leaving intolerable. He drank much more, and his drinking and depression began seriously to interfere with his work.

His wife seemed to be satisfied with the life she was making for herself apart from him. He insisted, however, that he could not go on with his own life, because she was behaving irrationally and was destroying her chances for satisfaction and fulfillment.

The unhappy attachment to a woman he feared to lose was rooted in his attachment to an aloof, chronically depressed mother for whose unhappiness he felt responsible. He left home when she became terminally ill, when he was in his thirties, and he married shortly after her death. Just as he saw his mother's unhappiness as reason not to live his own life, so he now insisted that his wife's unhappiness made it impossible for him to meet other women or make a new life for himself.

A dream he had when he was concerned about my leaving for a summer vacation opened up some of the meaning of his wife's leaving him. He dreamed that his father had died, and he was annoyed that his two brothers had not consulted him about the funeral arrangements. The issue of who had control over the circumstances of separation or loss was more critical to him than the loss itself: this turned out to be true with both his wife and me.

His increased drinking reflected his loss of control over the situation. Suicide became a way for him of reexerting control. Drinking, depression, suicide, all meant a refusal to go forward with his life in altered circumstances—circumstances that his character had helped to produce.

The next man comes close to Karl Menninger's picture of

alcoholism used to ward off suicide. A combination of heavy drinking and work appears to have helped this man stay in an unhappy marriage; deprived of both, he became suicidal.

This man was over 60 when he made a suicide attempt in which he slashed his wrists and nearly bled to death. He had been a heavy drinker throughout the thirty years of his marriage, yet despite his substantial daily intake of alcohol, he managed to hold both a day position as an accountant and an evening position with a sports facility. He attributed his drinking to a desire to escape from his unhappiness with his wife, who suffered from recurrent depressive episodes in which she often took to bed for weeks at a time. His heavy work schedule seemed to have a similar purpose of keeping him out of the house.

Most of the time he talked of his wife as a cross that he had to bear. He saw her as someone who was never satisfied and impossible to please. He had thought he might leave her when his daughter went off to college, but he appeared instead to have expressed the wish to leave her by becoming impotent.

He generally did what his wife wanted, becoming openly critical of her only when she would not get out of bed or when she quarreled with his elderly mother, who had lived with them for the past twelve years.

Two years before his suicide attempt, he had to stop drinking because of an almost fatal acute pancreatitis that had been precipitated by his alcohol intake. Both his wife and daughter confirmed that he had been more tense since he had to stop drinking.

Nine months before his attempt, he was forced out of his job because his employer wanted a younger, more productive person. His financial worries were compounded by the fact that his wife became depressed again and had to resume seeing her psychiatrist.

Now that he was out of work and at home, he was more frequently witness to the quarrels between his wife and mother.

Since he virtually sanctified his mother, the situation made him even more dissatisfied with his wife. Since his marriage, his mother had been available to run the house whenever his wife was not functioning. He believed his wife envied his mother's competence and ability, but he was insensitive to his wife's resentment at the way in which he always sided with his mother.

Not working was also intolerable for him. He became preoccupied that termites in a dead tree near his home might have spread to his neighbor's house and his own. He worried that the heating system in his house was failing. He did nothing to correct either situation, and his fears proved unfounded. Although his ideas were close to delusional, they seemed to be an outgrowth of his depression. Their content suggested a projection of his internal feelings of decline, rottenness, and not functioning. When his mood improved, these ideas disappeared.

He described himself as always needing someone to lean on. Before he married at the age of 31, he had lived with his mother. He was unable to cook, run the washing machine, or fix things around the house. If he tried to repair anything, his mother took over and did it for him.

Since his suicide attempt the severed tendons in his right hand made him more dependent on his wife to help him dress and take care of himself. "I eat it up" was the expression he used in describing his reaction to his wife's caring for him, that is, bringing his slippers, buttoning his shirt, or giving him a manicure.

In his sessions with me he never admitted any irritation with his mother but would gently criticize his wife for the problems at home and then try to mute that criticism. In sessions in which I saw him and his wife together, he agreed with her assertion that he became annoyed at the ways in which his mother would tell him what and how to eat and expected him to be always ready to run her errands or do her bidding.

In the hospital, immediately after his suicide attempt, he worried that he would be punished for having secretly kept double medical coverage on his two different jobs. He was afraid that the hospital would retaliate against him and his daughter because she had been critical of the care he received. The one dream he reported in our sessions concerned a feeling that he had done something wrong or bad in the hospital and that the staff would be angry with him.

He had managed a lifelong dependent adaptation as a good son and dutiful husband who did not complain or protest and who kept his dissatisfaction to himself. Both alcohol and work had permitted him to avoid facing how bad he felt about his marriage, himself, and his life. The series of events that befell him undermined this adaptation: the pancreatitis forced him to stop drinking, and the loss of his job thrust him into the difficulties between his wife and mother. He responded as though he were being punished for being bad, and suicide took on the quality of atonement.

The next man would seem to embody features of all of the preceding cases, although the stress of extensive combat in Vietnam was an added factor. His drinking contributed to the breakup of his marriage and the loss of his job. The loss of both his wife and his job contributed to his becoming suicidal. His unhappy attachment to his mother underlay both his drinking and his being suicidal. In his case both alcohol and suicide were related to the punitive self-destructiveness that had become so pervasive in his life.

This 32-year-old divorced, alcoholic combat veteran was hospitalized following an impulsive suicide attempt in which he jumped in front of a truck, which swerved to avoid him but knocked him off the road. This was his fourth suicide attempt since his wife, whom he had married before going to Vietnam, had left him.

During his combat duty in Vietnam, he was under rocket fire almost continually and began to drink to put himself to sleep. After he came home, he began to have frequent nightmares about combat, particularly about a Vietnamese woman he had been forced to kill. He was unable to talk about his war experiences, or much else of what he felt, to his wife and friends. Under the tension of his reactions to combat and the pressure of a family with two children, he began to drink more, to stay out, and to see other women.

After his wife left, he drank even more. He had several hospitalizations because of alcoholism and others because of his suicide attempts. Although he had lived with another woman on and off for two years, he continued to drink heavily, to fight with her, and to mourn the loss of his first wife. Once when drunk he fell through some glass, severed several tendons in his right hand, and could no longer continue his work as a mechanic. He became more suicidal and jumped while drunk onto some railroad tracks, attempting to touch the third rail.

More recently, he felt he could make a new life for himself if he could get back in the service. He had been accepted, but when he showed up for induction intoxicated, he was told to come back the following day. On that day he missed the bus for the return trip. In a mood of frustration and despair, he impulsively jumped in front of the truck, and was hospitalized.

He had cut himself off from friends and family, with the exception of his mother, with whom he maintained a troubled relationship. He saw his mother as playing the role of martyr and saint. She made a point of saying that for the sake of the family she did not see other men after his father left her when the patient was about three. She went to work, and he was actually raised by his grandparents and uncles, with whom they lived.

His mother took his drinking as an affront to her and at times would not have anything to do with him. A dream he had a few days before I first saw him was revealing about his relationship with her and its connection with his suicide:

His mother had died and was lying in a coffin. He picked up her hand and could feel there was still some life in it. Then she was hissing at him, and was out of the coffin chasing him, and he was running away. He tried to pick up something to hit her, but could not. She was like a vampire.

His own manner was so deathlike that several people in the hospital commented on his looking like a walking corpse. His identification with his mother was further highlighted by his concern in the dream with the life in her hand, because the question of how much life there was in his own hand had been critical to him since he crippled it. His mother was also identified with the Vietnamese woman he had killed, because he associated her hissing in the dream with a sound common in the speech of Oriental women.

He had incorporated his mother's critical and punitive attitude toward him. He seemed to blame himself for her unhappiness as well as his own. He saw himself as having hurt his mother, wife, and children, and his vision of himself as destructive merged with his wartime experiences—in his nightmares about the woman he had killed, she turned from Oriental to Occidental.

Most of the patients seemed to feel they deserved punishment for letting down their wives, mothers, or themselves. Guilt as much as abandonment is central to the desire to end their lives.

An inability to separate from a troubled relationship with their mothers is also a feature common to alcoholic-suicidal patients. Since such separation problems appear in alcoholism and suicide when viewed separately, this is perhaps not too surprising.

No one sequence of events is paramount in these cases. The young veteran responded to the traumatic and posttraumatic stress of combat with drinking and emotional withdrawal. His response to the woman he killed in combat is rooted in his guilty self-destructive attachment to his mother. His drinking and withdrawal precipitated the breakup of his marriage, yet he became suicidal primarily in response to the loss of his wife.

Drinking in response to marital problems, which worsened as a consequence and led to separations or divorce followed by even more drinking and suicidal behavior, was observed in several of the cases. And in one of them suicide became an issue only after a life-threatening illness forced the patient to stop drinking and to confront the problems in his marriage.

In the case of the man who suddenly lost his wife and son, suicide was the initial response, but was superseded by alcoholism. Without the sudden accidental loss of his family, he would probably not have become alcoholic or suicidal, yet his vulnerability to abandonment went back to his childhood, and in his drinking he identified with his mother's response to the accidental death of his father.

Alcoholism and/or depression served to help all of these patients stop their lives at a fixed point. They could live without plans for any future. For one man, time was frozen when his wife and son died; for another, when his wife left him; and for another, during his combat experiences. The man who used alcohol and work to avoid facing his unhappy marriage also suspended time, but in a somewhat different way. He managed to live from day to day until circumstances made this impossible and suicide became the resolution of his difficulties. Although suicide was for all of these patients a way of stopping time permanently, all had earlier been making efforts to do the same thing in a less absolute manner.

Clinical
Considerations

7. Method and Motive

THE METHOD EMPLOYED BY the suicide often has much to tell us about the psychosocial meaning of the act. Only a minimal awareness of the relation between method and motive in suicide is reflected, however, in the usual statistical treatment of the subject of the methods used in suicide. From such an approach we can learn that in the United States firearms are the means chosen by more than half of male suicides and by one-third of female suicides. Or that one-third of female suicides ingest toxic substances while only 15 percent of men commit suicide this way. Or that about one-tenth of the suicides of both sexes use the exhaust of motor vehicles. Or that one-seventh of the men and one-eighth of the women who commit suicide do so by hanging. Or, finally, that drowning, jumping, and using cutting instruments all have an incidence among both sexes of less than 5 percent. *

Methods used by attempted suicides are often contrasted with those used by actual suicides. The statistics, rather than serving

---

*Differences in methods by age are not striking and are usually not given. Hanging, however, is slightly more frequent in young men aged 15–19 (20 percent) than it is in the remainder of the male population (12 percent). Firearms are used by more than half of the young women who kill themselves in the 15–24 age group as compared to 31 percent of the rest of the female population. Since there has been no study of these differences, any suggestion as to their meaning or significance would be purely speculative.

as an introduction to the relation between method and motive, are usually presented in order to introduce a discussion of the relative effectiveness of particular methods. We are apt to learn the unsurprising information that jumping from a high building or shooting oneself in the head leaves less to chance than does taking sleeping pills.

Suicidal method, as it relates to motive, includes more than merely the lethal means employed. Of equal importance are the circumstances surrounding the suicide, such as whom, if any-one, the individual informs of his suicidal intentions and what the contents are of any suicide note that is written. Moreover, the relation of method to motive in suicide cannot be understood without reference to the cultural context in which suicide occurs.

I was first impressed with the way in which psychosocial factors play a role in determining the frequency of any particular method of suicide while I was working in Norway, where 15 percent of the suicides are by drowning, although drowning as a method of suicide has a worldwide frequency of between 1 and 2 percent.[1] Norwegians have a fishing, sailing, and shipping tradition that goes back for centuries, and the sea is central to their conscious and unconscious life. It is a major theme and symbol in literature and art, and for most people the sea takes on personal and com-munal significance. Since many Norwegians live and work on the water, it is perhaps not surprising that some of them choose to die in the water as well.

To take another example closer to home, a startlingly high 50 percent of the black suicides in New York are by jumping.[2] Although jumping as a method of suicide is relatively high in New York for whites as well, its surprising frequency among the black population warrants some discussion.

As life in Norway centers on the sea, so life in Harlem and other sections of the city where the black population is concentrated centers on its endless blocks of five-story tenements. So much of life in Harlem is lived in and on top of these tenements that they occupy the conscious and unconscious life of their inhabitants and come to provide a tragic setting for black suicide. Sexual experience, fighting, and drug usage frequently take place on the Harlem rooftops. In this context, it is not surprising that jumping from the top floors or roofs of such buildings is a very common method among black suicides.

One could similarly conclude that the sociocultural acceptance of guns in the U.S. is related to the frequency with which they are used in suicide. Alan Marks and Thomas Abernathy drew on their own studies and those of others to demonstrate that in the South, the area in the country where guns are most accepted as part of the household and where children are often introduced to their use by their parents, firearms are used in suicide by both sexes more frequently than in the rest of the country.[3] They believe that their findings lend support to Raymond Gastil's description of a southern "regional culture of violence," in which weapons, and knowing how to use them, play an important part.[4]

Maurice Taylor and Jerry Wicks believe that social variables such as race, sex, occupation, religion, and income rather than regionalism are the decisive factor in the choice of suicide methods.[5] In studies conducted in Dayton, Cleveland, and Detroit, they found that suicidal black men and women used firearms more frequently than did whites. They also point to such studies as Paul Friedman's 1967 analysis of ninety-three suicides over a seven-year period among New York City policemen. Friedman found that "nine out of every ten individuals in this group killed themselves with revolvers."[6]

In both studies cited above, the researchers conclude that there is no relation between particular methods of suicide and suicide intent. Certainly no simple equation is possible between suicidal methods and suicidal intent. Such an equation might be suggested by our knowledge that firearms are a preferred method of those with high suicide intent, that there are relatively few survivors of suicide attempts with guns, and that a high percentage of those survivors turn out to have had lethal intent. That ingestion of toxic substances, however, often considered to be a nonlethal method of attempting suicide, can be lethal is attested by the one-third of suicidal women and the 15 percent of suicidal men who use them to kill themselves. But, more to the point, tranquilizers and sleeping pills are used in the majority of nonserious suicide attempts by young people, particularly young girls. For people who wish to make a nonlethal attempt, drugs are *the* preferred method; they are also a preferred method of those who make lethal attempts.

If the attempts to understand suicidal methods as a function of social factors have psychological limitations, psychodynamic analysis of suicidal methods has been highly speculative in its attempts to explain individual motivation. In a 1920 paper, "The Psychogenesis of a Case of Homosexuality in a Woman," Freud gave us his only detailed analysis of an actual suicide attempt; it was made by a young Viennese woman who had impulsively thrown herself down a railway embankment.[7] Her actions followed a rebuff by her father when he met her on the street in the company of a woman with whom she was infatuated.

According to Freud's reconstruction of his patient's history, her adolescent fantasy of having a child with her father was crushed when it was her mother whom the father made pregnant when the patient was fifteen. Her disappointments in her relationships with both parents were instrumental in turning her sexual interest toward women. He saw the young woman's suicide attempt as an expression of her feeling that she fell through her father's fault. Freud mentioned that the German word *nieder-kommen* means both "to fall" and "to be delivered of a child." In her suicide attempt, Freud felt, this woman both expressed her desire for her father's child and punished herself for the murderous anger toward her mother that accompanied it.

Freud remarked that the young woman's dreams helped him to reconstruct her psychodynamics. Although he did not actually tell us these dreams, his presentation is persuasive even though he assumed a seriousness to the particular suicide attempt that does not seem warranted either by the minor back sprain the young woman suffered or by her case as he presented it.

Freud's description of the young woman and her family is also typically graphic, so that although he attaches no importance to them, some of the psychosocial outlines emerge. The patient's coquettish mother, the nature of the rivalry between mother and daughter, the strict, authoritarian father, the difference in the family's attitudes toward male and female children, and the sexual imagery of the fallen woman—all bespeak Victorian Europe and particularly Vienna in the early part of the century.

In a footnote to this paper Freud wrote that "the various means of suicide can represent sexual wish fulfillments . . . to poison oneself = to become pregnant; to drown = to bear a child; to throw oneself from a height = to be delivered of a child." Many analysts have taken Freud's footnote as an injunction to give universal symbolic meaning to the method employed in every suicide attempt, with or without psychodynamic evidence.

Sidney Furst and Mortimer Ostow, in a major psychoanalytic article on the subject, suggest that the suicidal method is an expression of a sexual wish and / or punishment for the fantasied crime.[8] Without psychodynamic evidence from case material, they maintain that male homosexuals, if suicidal, will stab or shoot themselves or arrange to be stabbed or shot as an extreme expression of their wish to be attacked by another man's penis. In actuality, stabbing is too infrequent a method of suicide to be significant, and there is no evidence to suggest that homosexuality is a significant factor in victim-precipitated homicide or that homosexuals kill themselves more with guns than do other people. If these writers were correct, homosexuality would presumably be a far more important factor in suicide in the United States than it is elsewhere in the world, since only in the United States are guns the major method of suicide.

Furst and Ostow regard falling from heights as an expression of sexual guilt for "phallic erection under improper circumstances." Since jumping is a method of suicide that is relatively insignificant throughout the country, but quite common in New York, their thesis could presumably be used to justify the view of New York as sinful that is held in some parts of the country. Given the alternative of such unsubstantiated speculation, it is not totally surprising that psychiatry has settled for the safe but sterile statistical approach that has dominated the subject.

The best possibilities for understanding the relation of method to motive in suicide lie between psychoanalytic speculations that are removed from social reality and social correlations that are psychologically barren. Psychodynamic study of the suicidal individual can often provide evidence of the meaning of the choice of a particular method.

For many suicidal individuals, choosing the means of their suicide is integral to their use of suicide as a form of control. For such people the method must be of their choice, be used at their time, and be in keeping with their personalities. If they are hospitalized, they will wait to go home on pass or until discharge in order to execute their intention. One woman who tried many times to kill herself with pills before doing so was being truthful when she told her doctor, who was concerned about her being on a high floor of a hospital, that she could never jump, because she was afraid of heights. And the popular story of the policeman telling the man on the window ledge, "get off or I'll shoot," could conceivably work, provided one were dealing with the right person.

Some suicides use their control over how they choose to die to express their feelings about why they want to die. A prisoner can hang himself because it is the only method of suicide available to him, but hanging is also used to express a variety of suicidal motivations. Some people hang themselves as punishment for their desire to choke others: one patient who did, used to "playfully" choke his wife. For other suicidal individuals, hanging represented how choked and "hung up" they felt. One such young man came from a family that blocked his every independent constructive effort, while constantly holding out hope of what they would do for him in time. No one could have more effectively "hung up" anyone than this family "hung up" their son, and his final retaliation was to hang himself. Another suicidal woman (referred to in Chapter 2) who was immobilized in her relations with her family recurrently dreamed of herself as a dead cat hanging on a clothesline.

The symbolic significance of other suicidal methods also varies with the individual. Even the use of multiple methods may be revealing. A 1972 report relates the account of a particularly enraged man who had lost his job, who owed money, and whose wife had been unfaithful before deserting him. "He expressed the deepest self-hatred when he committed suicide by sealing off the kitchen, turning on the gas, stabbing himself in the chest, and hanging himself."[9] The author does not say so, but one would assume that the multiplicity of methods helped this man express the intense feeling that he was being attacked on all sides.

In many cases the way in which another person is involved in the suicide is most revealing. When the suicide arranges to have a particular person find his body, he is usually blaming, reproaching, accusing, or revenging himself on that particular person. Sometimes the potential suicide may leave his life in someone else's hands. One woman took a large dose of pills, knowing her husband would come home to find her unconscious and forcing him to decide whether or not to save her. In fact he waited three to four hours before deciding to call an ambulance.

In some cases people important to the suicidal individual are directly injured in the suicide attempt. A 1964 study of a series of individuals who crashed their cars as a way of attempting suicide found that in several cases the passengers of the car included individuals whom the driver wished to hurt.[10] Although the driver denied any desire to injure anyone but himself, in several cases he later threatened to kill passengers who were in the car.

A suicide note is at times an integral part of the way in which an individual commits suicide. Such notes can be most revealing of the motive for suicide.

Edwin Shneidman and Norman Farberow reported that in Los Angeles each year, over a ten-year period, between 12 and 15 percent of the suicides left notes.[11] A study of suicide in Philadelphia over a four-year period revealed that of 742 suicides, 24 percent left notes.[12] Both the Los Angeles and the Philadelphia studies showed no significant demographic or socioeconomic differences between those who wrote notes and those who did not.

A study conducted in Pittsburgh found that 220 of 1035 cases of completed suicides in that metropolitan area involved written suicide notes.[13] Their findings are in general agreement with those of the Philadelphia study, except that they found that a significantly lower percentage of the nonwhites who committed suicide wrote notes. Both studies agreed that drugs were more commonly used by the note writers than by the general suicide population. Neither gives an explanation for this, but drugs do permit an individual to write a note while he is waiting for them to act.

Louis Gottschalk and Goldine Gleser point out that the socio-economic similarity of the writers and nonwriters does not mean they are psychologically similar. "The fact that some wrote notes and some did not, by itself, indicates that the motivation to communicate with others in some verbal form was quite different in the two groups."[14] The content analysis that Gottschalk and Gleser made of suicide notes leads them to conclude, "The very choice of words used in such notes reveals an unusual preoccupation with objects of the live world and, by inference, a wish to maintain some tie or produce some persistent effect on such objects, no matter how vague and tenuous. We strongly suspect the psychopathology of the note-writing suicidal person is different from the person who commits suicide without leaving a note."[15]

Gottschalk and Gleser probably overstate the point, since the communication with others and the desire to influence them are often expressed verbally by people who do not write notes. Since many suicides neither write nor communicate with others before their death, the researchers are certainly warranted in concluding that note writers are not a cross section of suicides.

The Pittsburgh study included a content analysis of suicide notes that indicated a high degree of similarity in the notes by men and women. There were three significant differences: the notes written by women expressed more grief and disappointment, contained more instructions and requests indicating a concern for others, and more frequently expressed wit, irony, and sarcasm. The authors attribute these differences to the fact that depression is a more common symptom among women than among men, to social norms that either encourage women to be more concerned with others or discourage men from expressing such feelings, and to the fact that humor, irony, and sarcasm may be means by which women learn to express indirectly what men express more directly.

The Philadelphia group did an analysis of the emotional context of the notes in its study. "Over half of the notes showed such positive affect as gratitude, affection, and concern for the welfare of others, while only 24% expressed hostile or negative feelings directed toward themselves or the outside world, and 25% were completely neutral in affect." They conclude that "the recognition that positive or neutral feelings are present in the majority of cases should lead to a more promising outlook in the care and treatment of attempted suicides if they can be identified."[16]

Since anyone killing himself is likely to have negative feelings toward himself and others, the absence of such feelings in notes would argue in favor of the presence of denial in the notes rather than for an favorable therapeutic prognosis. Most therapists would be more optimistic about a suicidal patient who was more in touch with his feelings. The Philadelphia study illustrates the danger of taking suicide notes too literally.

Most attempts to deal with suicide notes have classified them into types. Jerry Jacobs, who examined 112 notes, divided them into notes that ask forgiveness or indulgence, notes about illness, notes of direct accusation, notes of instruction or wills, and notes about an after life.[17]

Shneidman, who together with Farberow began the systematic study of suicide notes, has recently developed a classification of the notes based on how any explanation ("thesis") present in the note is elaborated.[18] Creating his own vocabulary, he described five categories of notes: thetical, antithetical, synthetical, athetical, and ambithetical. For example, a note by a man attributing his suicide to his wife's leaving him would be thetical; a note denying that her leaving is responsible for his suicide would be antithetical. A note that both blames the wife and denies she is at fault would be ambithetical. One that combines both ideas into a new insight—i.e., perhaps he provoked her into leaving— would be synthetical. An athetical note, one without a thesis, might simply give the wife instructions on how to dispose of his possessions.

Jacobs insists that suicide notes are rational, coherent documents written by individuals with a great deal of self-awareness. Shneidman points out, however, that the individual is likely to be in a detached, constricted, and confused state when he makes his attempt. Such a state, he believes, leads to psychologically barren, uninformative notes. This renders Shneidman somewhat pessimistic, in his recent writings, about the value of studying suicide notes.

Although I agree with Shneidman about the mental state of the suicidal individual, who often has little insight into his behavior, I believe that if the classifications developed by Jacobs, Shneidman, and others were to be supplemented by a more psychodynamic viewpoint, such notes could be more informative.

Shneidman, for instance, gives the following as an example of an athetical suicide note—i.e., one lacking a point of view and containing instructions or directions:

Dear Mary. I am writeing [sic] you, as our Divorce is not final, and will not be till next month, so the way things stand now you are still my wife, which makes you entitled to the things which belong to me, and I want you to have them. Don't let anyone take them from you as they are yours. Please see a lawyer and get them as soon as you can. I am listing some of the things, they are: A Blue Davenport and chair, a Magic Chef Stove, a large mattress, an Electrolux cleaner, a 9 × 12 Rug redish flower design and pad. All the things listed above are all most new. Then there is my 30-30 rifle, books, typewriter, tools and a hand contract for a house in Chicago, a Savings account in Boston, Mass. Your husband, William H. Smith.

Certainly the writer is revealing more than simply how he wants to dispose of his possessions. He is going to prevent the divorce and to see to it that his wife remains locked forever in her relationship to him as his widow, if not his wife. He presents himself as a generous and unreproachful husband.

Although he addressed his wife by her first name, he signs the letter "your husband, William H. Smith," which emphasizes the formal rather than the personal nature of the relationship. For many who are suicidal in response to loss, it is being married— or having a wife or husband rather than a relationship with a person—that is important.

Jacobs quotes the following as illustrative of a note asking forgiveness:

> It is hard to say why you don't want to live. I have only one real reason. The three people I have in the world which I love don't love me.
>
> Tom, I love you so dearly but you have told me you don't want me and don't love me. I never thought you would let me go this far, but I am now at the end which is the best thing for you. You have so many problems and I am sorry I added to them.
>
> Daddy, I hurt you so much and I guess I really hurt myself. You only wanted the very best for me and you must believe this is it.
>
> Mommy, you tried so hard to make me happy and to make things right for all of us. I love you too so very much. You did not fail, I did.
>
> I had no place to go so I am back where I always seem to find peace. I have failed in everything I have done and I hope I do not fail in this.
>
> I love you all dearly and am sorry this is the way I have to say goodbye.
>
> Please forgive me and be happy.
>
> (Your wife and your daughter.)

A psychodynamic reading of such a note suggests that much more than a desire for forgiveness is involved. Although the writer of the note says she is not wanted by three people she loves, she deals with her hurt by attempting to adopt a protective or solicitous attitude toward all of them. Even with her husband, with whom her tone is more accusatory than expiatory, she writes unconvincingly of the problems she caused him and of his being better off without her.

She tries to cover her hurt and anger by saying she is doing what is best for her husband. That she learned this device in her relation with her family may be inferred from her need to tell her father that he intended only what was best for her. The remark would seem to be more forgiving of him than asking his forgiveness. More important, it is an indirect way of calling attention to the pain he has caused her. "You wanted what is best for me and believe me this is it" suggests in an ironic way a relation between his attitude toward her and her self-destructiveness.

She tells her mother that her suicide is not her mother's failure, but the need to say so suggests it is probably a denial of what she wants to convey. She immediately goes on to write of her own failures, and the associative linkage suggests that she relates her failures in life to her mother's failure to give her what she needed.

The attempts to deny hurt and anger and to avoid direct accusation that are reflected in this woman's suicide note are characteristic of suicide notes in general. "You are not to blame" written to a husband, wife, or parent usually turns out to mean the opposite.

Writing a note, arranging to be found by a particular person, and informing someone ahead of time of one's suicidal intentions are all part of the method of suicide. Too often an exclusive concentration on the potential or actual instrument of death leads to the neglect of these factors.

The choice of method represents a convergence of cultural and personal significance. A particular method may serve as a form of communication of both personal and social needs. The method many people choose is not only their last message, but a climactic gesture that also expresses how they lived and how they hoped to resolve the conflicts that plagued them in life. One young man I saw who spent the night on the edge of the roof of his college dorm, thinking of jumping, spoke of it in terms of the continuing fame that suicide had given Marilyn Monroe. He told of never having gotten attention from his parents and of having felt very ignored at college. He had the fantasy that he would call to tell his parents he was going to jump, and while they got upset he would leave the receiver hanging and go up on the roof. They would call someone at school, but it would be too late. The fantasy reflected the blocked communication that had always existed in his family and his wish to make his parents experience the frustration he had endured in trying to reach them. He clenched and wrung his fists as he spoke of how much he wanted to strike back.

Perhaps most important was his preoccupation with Marilyn Monroe's suicide—the grotesque, grim wish to make a splash by jumping to a notorious death. The young woman, mentioned in Chapter 5, who survived a seven-story jump had wanted the attention that would come from it. But the need such young people had for a dramatic, newsworthy attempt derived from the intense experience of having been passed over by their parents. Several adolescents who had cut their wrists were disappointed that their parents never noticed the scars. "Do I have to die before you'll notice me?" was the complaint they seemed to be making. But such personal frustration is set in a cultural matrix of increasing numbers of young people who feel unrecognized and overlooked and are willing to pay any price to be noticed.

The individual suicide attempt often seems to be a psychological drama of suicidal motivation whose script is also written by the culture in which it occurs. In a modern version of a case comparable to Freud's, in which a suicide attempt by jumping had a motivation linking pregnancy and death, a woman in her late thirties jumped from a five-story window with a picture of her son in her brassiere and a message on the back of the picture saying, "Timmy knows I love him." Years before, at the time of her divorce, this woman had given her young son to his paternal grandparents, who actually raised him. She was tortured by her difficulties in love relationships and by her inability to love her son, although she still saw him. The picture and its message amounted to an attempt to deny the true state of affairs. Yet they furnished the first insight into the depth of her denial and her feeling that her life had ended when her son was born. Conflicts concerning the ability to love and care for children are more central to the suicide of women today (see Chapter 4) than is the sense of guilt over sexual wishes or behavior that was so prevalent in Freud's time.

The interplay among culture, character, and suicidal method and motive are illustrated in the following case. A 30-year-old man from a puritanical religious background in rural Norway described himself as the black sheep of his otherwise stable family. All of his siblings were married and leading responsible lives, while he had felt "superfluous" since childhood. Since the age of 18 he had been a moderately severe alcoholic. He had made an impossible marriage in which he had also felt "superfluous" and which quickly led to divorce. His employment had been mainly as a seaman, but his explosive temper and frequent fights aboard ship had made it impossible for him to continue in this capacity, and he was depressed over this.

He reported the following dream, which he had immediately before an impulsive suicide attempt in which he jumped in front of and was almost fatally injured by a rapidly moving car. "An atom bomb was falling. . . . I was in hell and about to be burned. My brother was above, saying that I should be burned."

The patient said he would end up in hell if he did not lead "a

more Christian life." Eight months earlier he had begun
attending church in an effort to force himself to live differently,
but without success. His mother was extremely religious and
opposed to drinking, smoking, or any amusement for its own
sake. Indeed this was the dominant emotional climate of their
community. He had never been close to her but had taken over
her religious beliefs, although he felt unable to live up to them.
The brother in the dream was the family member the patient had
felt closest to, although the relationship had been characterized
by fights and reconciliations until the time of his brother's death
three years earlier.

The patient had made several impulsive suicide attempts during the preceding eight years. Suicide for him was an act of
atonement, and death a punishment that he felt he deserved for
his explosiveness, for his anger toward his sibling and the world,
and for the asocial, immoral existence he was leading. His aspirations and his failures and his reaction to them occurred in the
context of the particular psychosocial expectations of his family
and his community. His rural, religious, puritanical subculture
did not produce a high suicide rate, but the suicide it produced
had a characteristic "moral" quality centering on self-punishment
for sin or evil.

Jumping suddenly in front of a car was consistent with the
impulsive quality of his behavior in his fights and his other suicide attempts. His dream image of deserving to burn in hell was
consistent with the psychology of his motivation for suicide.

Are any policy conclusions to be drawn from the relation of
method to motive in suicide? Since availability and familiarity
are significant in determining the choice of a particular method,
many people have wondered whether suicide could be prevented
by making a given method less available.

Past evidence had indicated otherwise. For example, twice as many suicides in the U.S. now use firearms as did so at the beginning of the century, but our suicide rate is no higher now than it was then. Most of the Western countries with higher suicide rates than ours have gun control: though these countries have few suicides due to firearms, drug overdose or hanging then become the methods most used. And in Denmark, where poison control measures helped reduce the number of suicides using toxic substances, the rate of suicide by hanging went up and the high suicide rate was unchanged.

However, in England, where one-third of the suicides resulted from domestic gas, the drop in the suicide rate over a seven-year period (1963–70) coincided with a change in the content of domestic gas: carbon monoxide was replaced with methane. The drop in the rate was equivalent to the proportion of suicides that had been caused by carbon monoxide poisoning.

In this country recent evidence indicating that gun control does reduce suicide, particularly among the young (discussed in Chapter 1) has changed our thinking. Young people are those most likely to make impulsive suicide attempts. When made with available household medications, these attempts are seldom fatal; when made with guns, they usually are.

The acceptance of guns in the U.S. is a reflection of the psychosocial forces that produce and accept violence in our culture. As with firearms, our use and abuse of drugs, although having a clear impact on suicide, is part of a wider psychosocial problem. Greater caution in prescribing drugs for depressed patients, however, is desirable and achievable, and would undoubtedly prevent some deaths by suicide.

Derek Humphry's book *Final Exit* recommends a relatively new method of committing suicide. While arguing for legalization of assisted suicide he describes a highly lethal method—the use of a plastic bag, over the head, along with ingestion of barbi-turates. Studies since publication of this book have shown a marked increase in the plastic-bag method of suicide; copies of *Final Exit* have been found next to the bodies of a number of people, some of them young people, who used this method.[19]

Social policy toward guns, drugs, and assisted suicide (as we shall see in Chapter 11) has other significance for suicide. This point can be made by referring to the on-going debate about the desirability of a guard fence at the Golden Gate Bridge to discour-age would-be suicides. A protective device was installed around the Empire State Building for similar reasons. Those opposed to a fence on the Golden Gate Bridge argue that the potential sui-cides would kill themselves in some other place. Although the fence opponents may be right, they draw the wrong conclusion. Leaving the bridge without a protective fence seems to imply a social sanction for those who would jump. Similarly, failure to restrict access to guns and drugs conveys the message that we are willing to accept the consequences of their uncontrolled use. Our policy choices should provide clear statements that we do not encourage destructive and self-destructive behavior, and equally clear notice that we value constructive ways of dealing with the pain and rage life contains.

8. Psychotherapy and Suicide

IN REVIEWING ARTICLES written in the past thirty years on the treatment of suicidal individuals, one is struck with how often the word *management* is used synonymously with *therapy*. Such articles are usually guides designed to help the therapist outmaneuver the potentially suicidal person. They contain a series of recommendations of a practical nature, such as "Make every effort to have firearms and potentially lethal medications removed from the home of the suicidal patient," "Control carefully the prescription of potentially lethal drugs," and "Advise the family to be watchful."[1]

Such precautions and warnings seem reasonable, but in practice they reflect a state of mind and a way of relating to suicidal patients that often make treatment unsuccessful. Since many suicidal patients are themselves preoccupied with management and control, therapy can become a contest in which the suicidal patient usually obtains his or her pills if he or she really wants them and in which the therapist is reassured that all possible precautions have been taken. All the precautions and all the management may result in encouraging one of the most lethal aspects of the suicidal individual, that is, his tendency to make someone else responsible for his staying alive.

In these articles the approach to therapy itself is usually based on similar attempts at manipulation. In a widely recommended article on the subject it is suggested that the therapist encourage the patient to believe that his current mood will pass; hold out hope by telling the patient about others who felt as he does and who got better; point out that actual suicidal behavior will interfere with treatment; indicate that the treatment cannot help the patient if he is dead; and remind the patient of his feelings for his spouse, children, or pets.[2]

Encouraging a suicidal patient to live for the sake of the therapy, the therapist, or his family reinforces what many such patients already feel: that they are living only for the sake of others. Such feelings are more apt to encourage suicide than prevent it.

Most articles on the treatment of suicide issue, in one form or another, the following warning: "No form of treatment is effective with a dead patient." A list of criteria for evaluating suicidal risk usually follows. In some cases the list is basically an evaluation of the degree of the patient's depression, based on his mood, energy, performance—socially and vocationally—and on the degree of his anxiety. A series of danger points may be enumerated: when the patient is on pass from the hospital, when he first goes home, and when stress in his life increases, to name a few. Such a list usually includes the clinically axiomatic warning that a lessening of depression often precedes a suicide attempt. In other words, if the patient remains depressed, be wary, and if he is getting less depressed, be even warier.

These articles reiterate in one way or another an injunction for "constant monitoring" in order to ascertain suicidal risk. A decision regarding increased risk is invariably accompanied by recommendations for more intensive management measures—hospitalization, medication, more medication or new medication, and electric shock. What such articles fail to include is any statement about how lacking in evidence we are that such measures are effective in preventing suicide.

In any case, it would be better for the therapist working in or out of a hospital to recognize that he is not likely to keep alive by surveillance, incarceration, or any form of precaution a patient who is determined to kill himself. The best chance for helping the patient lies in understanding and helping him with the problems that are making him suicidal, including most specifically the way in which he uses the threat of death. A therapist who feels threatened by the fact that a patient may kill himself while under his care is in no position to be a therapist to the patient. The rationalization that emergency measures are necessary to prevent suicide and to make therapy possible serves to conceal the reality that emergency measures, reflecting the therapist's anxiety, often render therapy impossible.

Only in psychotherapy does the nature of the suicidal individual's involvement with death and self-destructiveness become fully apparent. The therapist's own attitudes toward death, dying, and suicide, however, become almost as important as the patient's in determining the outcome. Fear of the responsibility for suicidal patients is a conscious motivation leading many therapists to avoid treating them. Among therapists who do treat suicidal patients, anxiety over the possibility of the patient's death often serves unwittingly to deaden their perceptions. Such anxiety is as apt to derive from guilt or a fear of being blamed for a patient's death as from any excess of compassion or empathy. Although suicide is a life-or-death matter for the patient, once the therapist begins to see the success of therapy as a life-or-death matter for his own self-esteem, his efforts are likely be futile.

Suicidal patients, though they may deaden themselves to much else in life, usually perceive such anxieties on the part of a therapist. Since so many of them (including those who eventually kill themselves) have learned to use the anxiety that they can arouse in others about their death in a coercive or manipulative way, they will usually test the therapist to see whether they can do the same thing with him. If the therapist meets unreasonable demands in response to death threats, the situation usually repeats itself, with escalation of the demands and increasing angry dissatisfaction if they are not met. Unless these character attitudes and expectations of the patient are explored and understood, the therapist is liable to go into bondage to the patient, with bad results.

One therapist was coerced into calling a patient every morning for a year because of the patient's implicit threat that if the therapist did not call, the patient might kill herself. This particular patient eventually did, despite the calls, leaving the therapist feeling both troubled and betrayed. Had more effort been spent in challenging and understanding the patient's attempt to structure how and in what manner the therapist was to show interest, rather than in gratifying the patient's demands, the therapy would have had more chance of success.

The suicidal person often makes conditions for life: if you don't save me, I'll die; if I can't make you happy, I'll end my life. Such attitudes are central to the patient's involvement with suicide; if their emergence does not arouse excessive anxiety on the part of the therapist, he is in a position to explore them to therapeutic advantage. The business executive (referred to on pages 156–60) whose wife had left him after years of an unhappy marriage came into treatment insisting that he would not rebuild his life until he knew his wife was happy. The dream in which he related my going away on vacation to funeral arrangements about which he was not being consulted helped make him aware of the similar way in which his response to his wife's leaving focused on the issue of control. His need to set the conditions under which he would be happy was an outgrowth of his inability to determine the conditions of her happiness. Therapy helped him to become aware of how much his response originated in fear of severing an unhappy relationship with his mother. He had felt frightened and despondent over his inability to influence her lack of interest in him, but he had also felt responsible for her unhappiness. As he perceived the interconnections and origins of his need to control his relationships with his wife, with his mother, and with me, and was able to use this insight constructively, his depression lifted, his drinking stopped, and he was no longer suicidal. He was once again able to be productive at work, although his difficulties in forming a close satisfying relationship with a woman were still present.

One young man had shot himself in the heart—the bullet grazed his heart, pierced his lung, and came to rest close to his spine. He came into treatment, telling me that he would give me six months to make him less lonely, isolated, and depressed before killing himself. This kind of ultimatum, whether given to a therapist, a lover, or to oneself, is designed not merely to bring about the end but to kill whatever relationship comes before it. This young man was treatable only when we focused on the way in which he tried to make our relationship one in which he would be dead and challenge or resist any efforts to bring him back to life. Life is not, as it seems, or as the individual often says, unbearable with depression, but it may sometimes be inconceivable without it.

Occasionally, the conditions the patient wishes to set on therapy include involving the therapist actively during a suicide attempt. A therapist's own inclination to see himself as the savior or rescuer of the suicidal patient can be responsible for perpetuating suicidal behavior, particularly in young people. One young woman had made five suicide attempts in her past therapy. She called her therapist during her attempts and managed to have him come to one hotel or motel after another in order to save her. He dealt with his irritation at her behavior by a fierce determination to save her and a pride in being her rescuer. His willingness to do so seemed to intensify the severity of her attempts. After her last attempt, which she was lucky to survive, her parents, her therapist, and the patient agreed on the need for some change in therapy.

This young woman came from a family in which little interest, affection, or attention was paid to her. She had learned to use illness or suicide attempts coercively in order to gain attention. She felt secure only when she was able to use crises to control the interest and attention given to her, and she had to learn to value affection of any other kind.

Despite progress in her therapy, it seemed likely that she would eventually test me, as she had tested her parents and her prior therapist, with her coercive use of the suicide threat. She did. She called one evening from a motel in the suburbs just after swallowing some sleeping pills. I told her to go to a nearby hospital and to have them call me. My knowledge of her, and her progress, made me feel that this decision was reasonably safe and necessary. Yet I was considerably relieved when the hospital called after having pumped out her stomach. She came in for her next appointment initially angry with me for not coming to her rescue, but this was the end of her suicide attempts and the beginning of a dramatic overall therapeutic improvement.

There is a risk of being misunderstood in relating such an incident. A therapist must know a patient well, and have extensive experience, in order to make such a decision. But there is a greater risk in allowing to go uncorrected the widespread misconception that a therapist does such a suicidal patient a service by allowing himself to become her constant savior. A therapist in such a coercive bondage, no matter how well intentioned, is of little use to a patient.

If suicidal young people arouse rescue fantasies in therapists, older people who are suicidal are more apt to arouse irritation and to be dealt with by medication or hospitalization without psychotherapy. The false assumption that little can be done with psychotherapy for older people in general is even more wrong in regard to older people who are suicidal.

Yet many older people who are suicidal have, despite their problems, demonstrated varying degrees of adaptive capacity throughout a lifetime. Adaptive capacity in the past is probably a better indicator than age in determining the prognosis in psychotherapy.

The sociology professor (discussed on pages 98–102) who became suicidal after a stroke left him partly paralyzed is a good case in point. He was someone who had dealt with his anxieties since childhood by attempting to tightly control the circumstances of his life and the people who were important to him. When the stroke made his past adaptation no longer possible, he became demanding and critical of his wife and stepchildren. Although his behavior was an exaggeration of previous tendencies, it now became unbearable for his family.

During a session in which he related to me several instances in which he had helped to resolve some friction between two attendants in the hospital, I responded positively to what he had done. He immediately replied that he used to be much more capable. His comparison of any current satisfaction or achievement in a derogatory way with his past abilities became a central issue in his therapy. As he ceased doing this his mood improved.

Even more critical was a passive, resigned attitude he had toward his progress in rehabilitation therapy in particular and toward his life in general. He wanted greater mobility within the hospital grounds, yet he did not request such privileges. He was passive about caring for himself, waiting for his wife to visit to help him button his shirt. His passivity was in marked contrast to his behavior before the stroke. When this behavior was pointed out, he became quite angry. The word *passivity* irritated him, but also challenged him, and he began doing everything for himself, becoming remarkably agile with his walker. He began many subsequent sessions by letting me know how much he had accomplished and how wrong I had been to see him as passive.

The man (discussed on pages 154–56) who had lost his wife and son in a boating accident ten years earlier, reacted with an almost fatal suicide attempt, and then spent the next decade destroying his life with alcohol, made excellent progress in psychotherapy. When he was helped to explore his tragedy, to understand his anger toward his wife and son, and to deal with his own feelings of responsibility and guilt, he ceased blaming his in-laws and successfully began to pick up the pieces of his life. Although he did not go back to accounting, he was able to function well as a bookkeeper, he stopped drinking, and he developed meaningful social relationships for the first time in ten years. When he was freer of the emotions that bound him to the death of his family, when he was able to feel entitled to live, his former ability to enjoy work and to care for other people was a strength that was soon in evidence.

Before the past few years when the loneliness and depression caused by her unhappy marriage had made her suicidal, the woman from Austria (discussed on pages 92–95) had had a successful career at work and a good relationship with her son (who lived in another state), whom she had raised virtually without help from her husband. Although the situation was complicated by her view of her unhappy marriage as her just due for having left her mother and sister, who later died in concentration camps, she responded well to psychotherapy.

At first this patient needed the therapist to give her the permission to live that she had vainly and recurrently sought in her dreams of her dead sister. Even before the loss of her mother and sister, and despite her intelligence and ability, she had never felt entitled to shape the circumstances of her life. Since childhood, after her father's death, she and her family had been dependent on her uncle's permission for every choice they wished to make. The major decision she had made independently—to leave Austria—saved her life but left her feeling guilty for having survived.

As she came to understand the relation of her past life to her present situation, she was able to make a satisfying life for herself apart from her husband. She moved to where her son lived, became more involved with him, his wife, and her grandchildren, and was able for the first time in years to take a trip by herself to visit old friends in Vienna.

Even in older patients whose past adaptive capacity was poor, psychotherapy can make suicide much less likely. The man (discussed on pages 96–98) who suffered from chronic schizophrenia and nearly killed himself while hospitalized is a case in point. Dependent on, but abused by, first his mother and then his two wives, he was unable to function on his own.

In the hospital, he was treated primarily with medication for his anxiety, the dosage being increased whenever he seemed more upset. His periods of disturbance were considered to be due to the vicissitudes of his schizophrenia, and the hospital usually restricted his freedom to leave the ward for fear that he might kill himself. His response was to become more agitated.

When this man was seen in psychotherapy, it soon became evident that all his disturbed periods were triggered by episodes in which he felt rejected or abandoned by the hospital staff or by his brothers and sisters, who refused to visit him in the hospital. His sensitivity to such rejection was great, but his agitated response and attempts at suicide occurred only when the staff responded to his difficulties with restriction, seclusion, or more medication rather than with empathy for what he was feeling. When such empathy was provided in psychotherapy, he changed from a nonfunctioning, angry, depressed, suicidal individual to an active and productive member of the hospital community.

Since many suicidal patients were in psychotherapy at the time of their suicide, researchers have sought to examine such cases systematically in order to see what might have gone wrong. William Wheat did a retrospective study of therapeutic interaction in the case of thirty patients who committed suicide during or after hospitalization.[3] He emphasized three factors in attempting to explain these suicides: the refusal of the therapist to tolerate infantile dependency, so that the therapist conveyed to the patient an expectation of mature behavior exceeding the patient's capacity; the discouragement on the part of the therapist about the progress of treatment; and an event or environment crisis of overwhelming importance to the patient that was unrecognized by the therapist or beyond the control of the therapeutic situation. The family's refusal to visit the patient last mentioned, despite his requests, is an example of such a precipitating event.

"All of these processes," Wheat writes, "can lead to a breakdown in the therapeutic communication resulting in the patient's feeling abandoned or helpless, thus setting the stage for the disastrous result of suicide." Victor Bloom, in a similar review of known suicides in treatment at a psychiatric training center, identifies the following as significant precipitants: rejecting behavior on the part of the therapist, including verbal and facial expressions of anger; premature discharge of the patient; reduction of the frequency of psychotherapeutic sessions; and unavailability of the therapist.[4]

Uri Lowental complains of a lack of empathy on the part of therapists treating suicidal patients.[5] He lists a number of causes: the greater potential for guilt if the therapist is close to a patient;

the shame over a potential suicide as reflection on the therapist's capacity or competence; and, most important, the therapist's inability to come to terms with suicidal impulses in himself or in his patients as a possibly reasonable alternative to life's dilemmas. He implies that only a therapist who has seriously contemplated suicide can properly empathize with a suicidal patient. He provides no evidence for this conclusion; he is content to state his admiration for the empathy with the suicidal individual that the author A. Alvarez expresses in his book on suicide, *The Savage God*—an empathy that Lowental believes stems from the fact that Alvarez himself had made a serious suicide attempt.[6]

Although personal involvement with a problem—if a therapist has satisfactorily resolved it—may be of aid in the treatment of others, it does not guarantee greater insight or empathy. I have seen many suicidal individuals, including therapists, who attempted suicide but gained neither insight into themselves nor greater understanding of their own or others' desire for suicide. In any case, studies by suicide prevention centers suggest that counselors who are not depressed or suicidal, who indeed are reasonably happy with their own lives, do best with suicidal patients.

On the other hand, I have long been impressed by the fact that most articles on suicide, including Lowental's, seem more comfortable with abstractions than with people; they usually do not present a single suicidal individual with a view toward conveying a sense of the quality of the person's life or wish to die. Such articles stand in startling contrast to publications on virtually any other clinical problem. The absence of such case descriptions bespeaks the distance and lack of empathy about which Lowental complains.

John Maltsberger and Dan Buie, in one of the few fine articles on the subject of therapy with suicidal patients, deal with many of the harmful countertransference reactions aroused in therapists by suicidal patients, particularly by those who are borderline or psychotic. By their primitive attacks on the therapist, ranging from attempts to frustrate his therapeutic efforts to expressions of contempt for him as a person, such patients are often able to arouse "countertransference hatred." "The three most common narcissistic snares," they write, "are the aspirations to heal all, know all, and love all. . . . such gifts are no more available to the contemporary psychotherapist than they were to Faust."[7] The attack by the suicidal patient, who may sense the therapist's vulnerability, can lead to destructive reactions in the therapist that vary from malice to aversion.

Maltsberger and Buie go on to point out that the therapist's repression of these reactions may lead him to lose interest in the patient or to reject the patient as hopeless. The projection of countertransference hatred, on the other hand, taking the form of "I do not wish to kill you, you wish to kill yourself," leads to a paralyzing preoccupation on the therapist's part with the danger of suicide by the patient. Reaction formation to such countertransference feelings can contribute to oversolicitousness, exaggerated fear of suicide, fantasies of rescue, and overprotection of the patient.

In the past fifteen years, I have been consulted on numerous occasions by therapists who wished help in understanding a patient's suicide attempts or suicide and their reactions to this behavior. In most cases, the problem was the therapist's failure to understand what was going on in the interaction between the patient and therapist, rather than any basic lack of concern for the patient. In fact, a major therapeutic difficulty often stems from the therapist's assumption that by simply supplying a care and concern that had been missing in the patient's life—that is, by not being rejecting—he will somehow give the patient the desire to live. Often, however, the patient's hidden agenda is an attempt to prove that nothing the therapist can do will be enough. The therapist's wish to see himself as the suicidal patient's savior may blind the therapist to the fact that the patient has cast him in the role of executioner.

For example, one young woman jumped in front of a train when her therapist was about to leave for a vacation. On the day she jumped, she called a local TV station to tell them that at 8 P.M. a man—she gave her therapist's last name without indicating that he was treating her—would push a girl in a pink dress in front of a train at a particular station. Her warning was not heeded, and at eight o'clock, dressed in a pink dress, she jumped. Although she survived, she lost both legs.

She considered she had "died" when her father left the family when she was eight or nine. Throughout her adolescence she was preoccupied with death. She could remember the death scenes in many novels, vividly recalling Anna Karenina's suicide in front of a train. Her relationships with men had been painful recapitulations of the earlier rejection by her father, and one unhappy love affair had been followed by a suicide attempt.

The following dream concerning her present suicide attempt made her wish to die more understandable. She was in a long, narrow tunnel and could see a light at the end of it. She walked toward the light, and there she saw a man and a woman standing over a manger. In her associations to the dream, the tunnel suggested to her the subway, where she had jumped as the train was coming out of the tunnel and into the lighted platform area. Moving from the darkness of the tunnel and into the light seemed to her like being born. The child in the manger was both the Christ child and herself. She particularly identified with the sense that the crucifixion reunited Christ with his Father. She saw her life as having been set on a course in which gratification of her fantasies was possible only through her death. One can see how much she accomplished in her death fantasy. She is reborn, is a boy, is reunited with her father, and, finally, is ominpotent. For a patient with such fantasies, the thought of dying has a very strong appeal.

The grandiosity expressed in the dream of a rebirth as Christ is a common feature in the psychodynamics of suicide. It reflects the illusion of total mastery that suicide may provide, as well as suggesting the profound narcissistic injury that underlies the need for such grandiosity.

This young woman's therapist had tried to be available in a way that her father was not. He was made uncomfortable by the manner in which the patient had actually incorporated him into her suicidal fantasies, but he did not recognize until later that she was determined to perceive him—like her father—as responsible for her death, while binding him to her through death. She structured the relationship this way and used his leaving on vacation as an excuse for her suicide attempt. Even in the method by which she tried to kill herself, she appeared to be asking him to rescue her, but in fact she was trying to make sure that he could not and that he would be blamed for her death.

When seen in consultation after her suicide attempt, she was still interested in punishing her therapist. She suggested that I should write up her case, being sure to include her therapist's name. At the same time she behaved as if she had accomplished a rebirth. And paradoxically in her new life as a cripple, with vastly reduced expectations, she made a much better adjustment than she had previously. One suspects that her need for self-punishment may in some fashion have been permanently satisfied by the self-inflicted injury.*

---

* Her response to the incapacity that followed her suicide attempt was paralleled by the suicide attempt of a man who had shot himself in the head as a college student, blinding himself, but surviving. When I met him thirty years later, he insisted his life had been changed for the better by the experience and he had published a book detailing the transformation.

Successful therapy cannot be conducted with the suicidal patient unless the therapist understands the ways in which the patient uses his potential death as part of his adaptation. Such knowledge may minimize the risk of suicide, but therapy requires that the therapist be able to accept and live with some risk. In the words of the authors of a 1974 article on the subject, "the only method of reducing the long-term risk of suicide may be one that risks its short-term commission."[8]

As we have seen, suicidal patients often use the threat of suicide as a means of controlling the behavior of others. This is true of those who eventually kill themselves and of those who do not. Thomas Szasz points out correctly that many therapists respond to the patient's need to control with their own need to control.[9] In order to avoid the risk of suicide, they coercively hospitalize the patient. Although hospitalization and involuntary commitment of the suicidal patient may at times be necessary, and will be the subject of a later chapter in this book, it should be noted here that ultimately, in or out of a hospital, successful psychotherapy cannot be conducted by a "policeman."

Psychotherapy, supplemented by psychotropic drugs when necessary to relieve severe depression or paralyzing anxiety, is the treatment of choice for seriously suicidal patients. Seriously suicidal patients are either too depressed, too withdrawn, or too fragile to tolerate the anxiety that is generated in the psychoanalytic process. Yet many suicidal patients, like most of the individuals discussed in this chapter, can work psychodynamically in psychotherapy and should be given the opportunity to do so.

Suicide and Social Policy

9. Suicide Prevention

THE NATIONAL SAVE-A-LIFE League, started in New York in 1906, was the first of the suicide prevention organizations in this country. The league is said to have originated in an incident involving a young woman and a clergyman. Staying at a New York hotel, the woman called the desk clerk and said she wished to speak to a minister. The Reverend Harry M. Warren, who held regular nonsectarian services in various hotels in addition to performing his pastoral duties at the Central Park Baptist Church, was called but could not be reached that evening. He subsequently came to her bedside at Bellevue Hospital, where she had been taken after she had made a suicide attempt, from which she eventually died. She told him, "I think maybe if I had talked to someone like you, I wouldn't have done it."

Whether the young woman was expressing gratitude or regret or whether she wanted to make the Reverend Warren feel guilty, the Reverend Warren is said to have become determined to see to it that someone was always available for such people in times of stress. He made suicide the subject of his next sermon, put an announcement in the newspaper, and urged anyone considering such a step to call upon him. The story of the minister and the young woman became the story of Genesis for the Save-a-Life League and for other organizations modeled on it.[1]

A sense of responsibility for potential suicides who had no one to look after them grew in the last half of the nineteenth century, as increasing numbers of unfortunate people seemed to be casualties of modern industrial life. The clerical expression of such concern was perhaps epitomized by the Salvation Army, which began operating an antisuicide bureau in London in the same year that the Save-a-Life League started in New York.

Three quarters of a century later, the league still functions in the Episcopal Church Center building in lower Manhattan. It serves primarily as a twenty-four-hour-a-day referral service for people who telephone in distress. Those who answer the phones are mainly volunteers who have received some training from professional people affiliated with the league.

Clergymen were among the first to organize and direct suicide prevention facilities. Some influenced their churches to sponsor or provide a home for these programs. The Samaritans, organized in England in 1955 by the Reverend Chad Varah, became the model for a worldwide organization. Although the inspiration for such programs is often spiritual—the Samaritan gain their name from the parable of the Good Samaritan—their approach is usually secular, pragmatic, and nonsectarian. [2]

Many suicide prevention services have a more directly religious orientation. Contact USA is an organization of over one hundred telephone counseling ministries throughout the United States that attempt to listen to, help, or befriend the suicidal as well as others in distress. [3] The organization sees itself as a Christian ministry that aims at "sharing the goodness of God's compassionate love with each and every person" and requests its telephone workers to "undertake to counsel in accordance with Christian insights." Contact is an American affiliate of Life Line International, a worldwide organization with the same mission. [4]

The suicide prevention movement was small in scope and received little public attention until the 1960s, when suicide was attacked as a social problem with the same enthusiasm that accompanied the war on poverty. A proliferating network of suicide prevention programs grew up with the public expectation that they would reduce the number of suicides—an expectation to some degree fed by the programs themselves in their effort to attract community support.

Enthusiasm for suicide prevention led the National Institute for Mental Health in 1966 to establish the Center for the Studies of Suicide Prevention. Under the direction first of Edwin Shneidman and then of Harvey Resnik, the center stimulated and coordinated research into suicide. But, as the director of NIMH, Dr. Stanley Yolles, wrote, the primary role of the center was "to effect a reduction in the present rate of suicidal deaths and to do it in such a way as to demonstrate unequivocally that lives have been saved."[5] The major step in the suicide prevention program outlined by Dr. Yolles was the encouragement of the formation and development of more suicide prevention centers.

Most of the two hundred secular suicide prevention programs currently operating in this country have developed in the past twenty years. The major stimulus has come from the mental health associations of local communities. In some cases the local association simply helps the programs get started or provides ongoing financial support; in others it remains closely involved with the administration of the suicide prevention program.

Professional health groups and hospitals have been responsible for a smaller number of programs. Some of these are directly connected with county departments of health or welfare, some are located in or affiliated with hospitals, while others are situated in mental health clinics or community mental health centers.

The programs are almost entirely the result of local initiative and involve both nonprofessional and professional people; most of the programs depend solely upon community support. A few that are integrated with community mental health centers receive federal matching grants. None receives any special federal grant support for their general service community operations.

The Suicide Prevention Center of Los Angeles, the only such program that received major federal support in its development, became a catalyst and model for many other suicide-prevention programs. As Edwin Shneidman and Norman Farberow, who founded the Los Angeles Suicide Prevention Center, relate the story, the center originated thirty years after their discovery of several hundred suicide notes in the Los Angeles County coroner's office.[6] The two decided to collaborate in a study of those notes, and obtained a National Institute for Mental Health grant to support their research. They also began to study case histories of individuals who survived suicide attempts, and were inevitably drawn to clinical activity with suicidal patients, including consultations, assessments, and therapeutic endeavors. In 1958, with further grant support from NIMH, they formed an independent, nonprofit foundation and expanded into educational and training activities as well as clinical and research efforts.

The major service of all suicide prevention programs is the availability twenty-four hours a day of a knowledgeable person who can make a referral for someone in crisis. All of the programs rely heavily on volunteers to answer the phones. Much research has been done on the effectiveness of these volunteers, but the consensus is that if properly selected, properly trained, and properly supervised, they function effectively.

The great majority of the programs do not provide treatment as such, but typically refer people to an affiliated hospital, clinic, or community mental health center. Some of them are able to ask callers to come in for evaluation or treatment, but this occurs infrequently.

The English based Samaritans utilize volunteers to "befriend" a selected number of the clients who might profit from it.[7] A depressed, isolated, bereaved person is considered an ideal condidate for such befriending. The volunteer tries to provide a mixture of companionship and guidance. Some of the American programs, including several associated with the Samaritans, are also based on befriending. Most, however, do not provide any comparable sustained service, although a few can send someone to help an individual in an immediate crisis.

The variation in the services provided and the staff personnel of the programs is considerable. About a third of the programs have no paid staff, and another third have only one or two paid staff members. The larger programs usually have professional administrators, professional therapists (primarily psychologists and social workers), full-time lay counselors who have been given special training and take daytime calls, and volunteers ranging from medical students to housewives who work part-time and take night calls.

The need for standards for these suicide prevention programs has become more and more apparent. Contact USA now certifies the programs that wish to be affiliated with the parent organization only if they meet certain standards for the services provided and the quality of training for volunteers.

The American Association of Suicidology, an organization formed in 1968 to bring together individuals and organizations interested in suicide prevention, developed criteria for evaluating and certifying suicide prevention programs; they included such factors as their administration, training procedures, general service delivery, suicide services, and community integration. Since 1976, when certification was begun, about a fifth of the association's approximately seventy-five member organizations have been certified.[8]

Concern about regulatory standards was partly a response to

the increasing disappointment many felt with suicide prevention programs. That disappointment had deeper roots than the great variation in the quality of services that exists among such programs; it reflected a more basic questioning of the effectiveness of all of them. The exaggerated hopes generated by suicide prevention programs and the exaggerated claims made by some of them began to be evaluated more objectively.

For example, the literature distributed by the National Save-a-Life League, which is basically a New York organization, claims without any evidence that in its seventy-five-year history the organization has saved over 75,000 lives, giving a prevention rate of 1,000 suicides per year. Professionals in the field of suicide accepted prematurely the tentative conclusions of a 1968 English study attributing a decline in suicide in England to the presence of the Samaritans.[9] On the other hand, a study by I. William Weiner of four California cities, two with suicide prevention centers and two without them, which showed that the centers had no effect on the suicide rates of those communities,[10] was criticized for coming to a conclusion too soon.

More systematic analysis appeared in U.S. government studies in the early 1970s.[11] Suicide rates in twenty-five cities that had no suicide prevention centers were compared with seventeen cities that did. Over an eight-year period, from 1960 to 1968, there were no significant differences in the changes in the suicide rates of the two groups of cities. David Lester, who pointed out that the cities with centers were larger than those without, did a similar study examining cities of comparable size.[12] He found that even when population size was controlled for, there were no significant suicide rate changes based on whether cities had or did not have a suicide prevention center.

Lester was at a loss to explain the English results that seemed so contradictory to his own. A few years later such explanations proved unnecessary. A carefully controlled study in England has now demonstrated that there is no difference in the suicide rates of comparable communities that have and those that do not have active Samaritan organizations. [13]

The evidence by 1980 is fairly conclusive that suicide prevention programs have had no demonstrable effect on the suicide rate of their communities. Few responsible suicide prevention centers in this country now make claims about the number of lives they have saved.

Basic conceptual, structural, and logistical problems made this situation inevitable and predictable. The overwhelming number of calls and contacts do not come from the seriously suicidal segment of the population but from troubled individuals who need to talk to someone. In one study sampling ten suicide prevention centers, the proportion of calls received in which the caller had at least been considering suicide was 33 percent. [14] The number of calls in which the individual was seriously suicidal had been estimated to be a much smaller percentage of the total number of calls. Nor do such studies count incomplete calls. Lester reported that of several thousand calls received monthly at the Suicide Prevention Crisis Service in Buffalo, more than half are from people who hang up immediately or after making humorous or obscene remarks. [15]

Ronald Maris compared clients of the Chicago suicide prevention center with those who actually killed themselves. [16] The typical caller was young, black, and female. The typical suicide, on the other hand, was elderly, white, and male. Lester found a similar phenomenon in Buffalo, where the typical center caller was female, middle-aged, white, single or married, and not living alone. Again, however, the typical suicide was a white solitary elderly male. [17]

Maris suggested that prevention center programs must be reoriented to accommodate the life-style of the completed suicide group. Since they rarely come to the centers and since little information appears on death certificates, most prevention agencies simply do not know much about the behavior and attitudes of the group they seek to service. He pointed out that the very notion of a *center* for suicide prevention may be at odds with the reality that the population it seeks to reach is socially isolated, marginal, and at the periphery of the community, not in the center or mainstream.

Another way of looking at the utilization of suicide prevention centers is to try to determine how many completed suicides actually contacted the local centers. Lester reported three estimates.[18] In Los Angeles and St. Louis fewer than 2 percent of completed suicides had called the center. In the Buffalo center, with which Lester is affiliated, there was no record of a completed suicide's having called the center. Robert Litman reported, however, that in 1972, 8 percent of those whose deaths were certified as suicide in Los Angeles had been in touch with the Los Angeles Suicide Prevention Center.[19] A Cleveland study found fifty-three suicides who had contacted the Cleveland suicide prevention center over a period of four years.[20] The researchers calculated that the Cleveland center had been in contact with almost 6 percent of the officially recognized suicides in the county.

A study by the Los Angeles Suicide Prevention Center that sought to find out whether extended care affected suicidal outcome had the serendipitous result of demonstrating that some high risk suicidal individuals do call the center.[21] Four hundred cases classified as high risks on the basis of telephone calls were followed. With half of these an attempt was made to maintain a continuing relationship by phone and in person on a weekly basis over a two-year period.

It turned out that there were seven suicides in the extended-care group, compared with two in the control group. While the difference was not statistically significant, the results were disappointing. The center found that its volunteers, who had been carefully screened, felt overwhelmed by the sustained contact with the seriously suicidal and often wanted to transfer the cases to the professional staff. Litman, in reporting results of the study, considered the possibility that the discouragement of the workers contributed to the outcome.[22] He also believed that for some in the extended care group the program aroused hopes and expectations that were not fulfilled. Thus, suicidal tendencies may have been aggravated. Litman concluded that the continuing relationship offered by the volunteers was "too little, too late."

The study would seem to indicate that it is possible to use a telephone crisis service to identify a more seriously suicidal group but that it is an extremely inefficient way of doing so. Moreover, the problem remains of how to provide adequate help for the relatively large high risk group.

When experience with the centers demonstrated that they had no effect on the suicide rate and could not prove unequivocally that they saved lives, NIMH reacted by eliminating the National Center for the Studies of Suicide Prevention. With it unfortunately went a major impetus for research into the problem of suicide.

Yet neither the NIMH decision nor the inability of the local centers to prevent suicide should lead us to abandon them with the same alacrity with which we embraced them. The suicide prevention centers have given aid and comfort to a great number of people in distress. They have helped to make us aware of the need for walk-in and call-in facilities for people in all sorts of emotional crises. This is worth doing for its own sake, without the illusion that we are reducing the suicide rate. Judged moreover as a research endeavor, from an educational and training standpoint, or as catalysts in stimulating interest in suicide prevention, institutions like the Los Angeles Suicide Prevention Center have been an outstanding success.

Suicide is a problem of considerable magnitude. It is estimated that there are several hundred thousand suicide attempts in this country each year and that five to six million individuals in all have made suicide attempts. Follow-up studies have shown that about 10 percent of an attempted-suicide population go on to kill themselves within a ten-year period.[23] Other retrospective studies in the United States have shown that between 20 percent and 65 percent of those who kill themselves have a history of prior attempts.[24] These findings indicate that the attempted suicide population contains much of the eventual suicide population, plus an even larger number of people who will not go on to kill themselves.

Clearly, it is impossible to try to find and refer all potential suicides for treatment. But it is possible, on the basis of current clinical knowledge, to identify the high risk cases among attempted suicides. A study of 193 persons admitted after a suicide attempt to San Francisco General Hospital attempted such an identification.[25] Retrospectively applying a checklist evaluation instrument of demographic and diagnostic data that could often be ascertained at admission or soon after, and without any clinical evaluation, they were able to identify a high-risk subgroup consisting of 17 percent of the original population, 49 percent of which subsequently attempted to commit suicide.

The identification and treatment of the high risk population might involve as many as ten thousand new cases a year throughout the country, but such a program would still be far more manageable—and probably more fruitful—than one attempting to identify and somehow treat the literally millions who call in to suicide prevention centers. Such treatment would have to include individual psychotherapy, the use of psychotropic medications when indicated, and in many cases the use of volunteers to work as befrienders in combination with a therapist. The efficacy of such an approach could first be tried and tested in a limited way in order to avoid the sequence of enthusiasm and disillusion that characterizes the history of the suicide prevention centers.

Disillusionment with the centers led to a decline in interest in suicide. The awareness of the rise in suicide among the young and our belated interest in the problems of older people, including that of suicide, have begun to change this situation. Whether we are pessimistic or sanguine about resolving the problem, the question remains of what to do with the seriously suicidal.

10. *Involuntary Commitment*

with Lois Waldman, LL.D.

WHEREAS SUICIDE PREVENTION centers are vulnerable to the criticism that they do too little and do not reach the right people, the practice of involuntary commitment has been faulted for doing too much in the wrong way for psychiatric patients in general and for suicidal patients in particular. In recent years efforts have been made to abolish involuntary commitment or at least to reduce it substantially. These efforts, intended to protect the rights of the mentally ill, are similar to those on behalf of other previously neglected segments of society, such as women, blacks, juveniles, and prisoners.

Critics of involuntary commitment urge that all the due process protections that are provided to criminal defendants be granted to people faced with involuntary hospitalization. They further urge that the standards for commitment of the mentally ill be limited to persons who can be shown to be dangerous to themselves or others or unable to care for themselves, and that the state should be required to prove that claim to be a certainty.[1]

Implicit in most of the criticisms of forced commitment are the following beliefs:

1. The psychiatric diagnoses used to justify hospitalization are invalid and unreliable.

2. The psychiatric predictions of dangerous behavior, both to others and to self, that are used to justify hospitalizations are unreliable.

3. There is no evidence that individuals do better in hospitals than in the community or that drug and electric shock treatments—staple treatments for hospitalized suicidal patients—are particularly effective in preventing suicide.[2]

DIAGNOSIS AND DANGER

Although objective clinical determinations of both the diagnosis and the dangerousness of psychiatric patients are supposed to be the bases for involuntary commitment, research indicates that social factors such as age, sex, and marital and social status all influence the outcome.[3] Whether or not a patient has an attorney at the hearing is equally important in determining the disposition of the case.[4]

Most commitment statutes specify that the potentially suicidal individual must be considered dangerous to himself and also be mentally ill. Civil libertarians fear that the diagnosis of mental illness may be used to confine someone to prevent suicide or that the danger of suicide may be exaggerated to achieve what is felt to be the desired end of commitment.

Whether or not such reasoning is correct, studies make clear that in making commitment determinations, psychiatrists consistently tend to overestimate the dangerousness of the patients they evaluate.[5] In the case of potentially suicidal patients, the difficulty in predicting an actual suicide, combined with a fear of being held responsible for mistakes, probably contributes to such an overestimation.

There is also evidence to suggest that knowledge that someone has attempted or committed suicide influences both the determination that someone is mentally ill and the diagnosis given to that person. A group at Harvard that reviewed the subject found that the highest estimate of mental illness when the diagnosis had been made before the suicide was 22 percent. When the estimates were made afterward, the highest estimate was 90 percent.[6] In a study done in St. Louis of 134 consecutive cases of suicide, 94 percent were given a retrospective diagnosis of psychiatric illness, 45 percent were considered to have had psychotic depressive disorders, and none were given a diagnosis of psychoneurotic depression.[7] In a Los Angeles study of hospital patients seen before their suicide, the diagnosis of psychoneurotic depression was frequently made.[8] In studies of attempted suicide there is an even wider range in the distribution of diagnoses. Critics of commitment procedures with regard to suicide have understandably come to believe that the diagnosis of mental illness is too uncertain and too subject to fluctuation to provide a reliable basis for depriving individuals of their liberty.

Many of the diagnostic inconsistencies in psychiatry are being resolved through the introduction of better defined criteria, as reflected in the recently published Diagnostic and Statistical Manual of the American Psychiatric Association (DSM III). More reliability in diagnoses will not fully resolve the problem, however, since it is the patient's ability to function outside of a hospital rather than a diagnosis that should ultimately be involved in decisions concerning commitment.

HOSPITALIZATION

It is remarkable how uncritically hospitalization has been accepted as a means of helping the seriously suicidal. A 1956 study showed that a number of hospitalized suicidal patients killed themselves while home on pass.[9] The assumption was made that it was a return to the problems at home that precipitated the suicide. The possibility that the dread of returning to the hospital could be a factor was not even considered. In the last century Kraepelin had already been aware that many patients leave a hospital on pass or for good only "in order to be able to accomplish their suicidal intentions outside."[10] Being home may permit them greater freedom in choosing how to commit suicide, rather than cause them to attempt it.

Another study, arguing for hospitalization of the suicidal patient, points out that an analysis of suicide in Los Angeles showed that 15 percent of the suicides had received but not followed a recommendation for psychiatric hospitalization in the weeks before their deaths.[11] We are not told under what circumstances the recommendation was made or whether the patient was offered any alternative, or what percentage of the overall sample killed themselves during hospitalization. We are told, however, that 7 percent of the sample committed suicide immediately after discharge from a psychiatric hospital. There is as much justification for concluding that the recommendation for hospitalization or the experience of hospitalization contributed to the suicide as there is for maintaining that hospitalization would have prevented it.

Hospitalization *per se* does not prevent suicide, since few populations have suicide rates as high as those found in mental hospitals. Studies of suicide rates in hospitals have indicated rates varying from 20 to 2,000 patients per 100,000.[12] After corrections for age and sex, suicide is estimated to be at least five times more common among the mental hospital population than among the general population.

Hospitalization certainly serves to calm some individuals and to give them a measure of relief from the pressures of their lives. For some acutely suicidal patients it may be life saving. Some suicidal patients even use their attempts as a way of dramatizing their need for hospitalization. Other suicidal patients, however, are made more upset by their confinement. The decision for hospitalization is too often made, not on the basis of a realistic evaluation of whether it will help a particular patient, but because therapists want to shift the responsibility for a possible suicide onto an institution.

The evidence to date indicates that shock treatment and psychotropic drugs, the staples of hospital treatment, although effective in alleviating depressive symptoms, have not been effective in preventing suicide. Experienced psychotherapists who are comfortable in dealing with suicidal patients are few and far between, and such patients, even at expensive private hospitals, are often in the hands of inexperienced residents who do not have adequate supervision.

If individual therapists react out of fear and anxiety rather than considered judgment in deciding to hospitalize patients, similar fears on the part of the hospital staff often govern the treatment of the patient in the hospital. Many precautions now prevalent in hospitals reflect the staff's fear of responsibility for failure rather than any evidence of their positive effect on patient behavior. For example, seclusion or round-the-clock observation are commonly used to prevent suicide. Seclusion can be a terrifying experience for a patient; round-the-clock observation is usually demoralizing and dehumanizing. Patients often commit suicide while under the aegis of these precautionary measures. We do not know whether such measures contribute to suicides in these cases.

When a patient in a hospital kills himself, steps are often taken to prevent future suicides, based on a hastily formed perception of what might have been a factor in the case at hand. If the patient had extensive freedom within the hospital, then the restriction of all patients in whom suicide is suspected may become the policy, without proper concern for the negative effects of such a policy on individual patients. The focus on suicide prevention within hospitals can become, as a study at the University of California at Los Angeles indicates, an obstruction in the treatment of suicidal patients. [13] The authors of that study point out that measures instituted after a suicide to prevent future suicides are counterproductive largely because each case is different. Their analysis also indicates that the measures taken would not have prevented the suicide that occurred, let alone the ones that are feared.

Lawrence Woolley and Arnold Eichert examined changing rates of both suicide and escape in the Sheppard and Enoch Pratt Hospital in Baltimore during the 1930s. [14] They attributed a declining incidence of both of these actions to a decrease in special precautionary measures over that period. They concluded that such special measures act to increase suicide or escape by focusing attention on those actions rather than on the patients as people.

Studies of suicide among hospitalized patients have examined such things as their diagnosis, social background, and past history of suicide attempts. We know of no study that has examined whether the patient was admitted to the hospital voluntarily or whether he remained in it willingly. Yet given the psychology of suicide and the need of so many suicidal patients to control the most minor circumstances of their lives, it is not surprising that many of them react poorly to even the minimal regimentation of the best psychiatric hospitals.

Unless and until comparable groups of suicidal patients are studied who are not hospitalized, there is no sure way of knowing whether hospitalization prevents suicide, contributes to it, or, as clinical experience makes one suspect, can do either depending upon the patient. The absence of such knowledge has led many civil libertarians to advocate revisions in commitment laws that in the view of some psychiatrists would have the effect of doing away with involuntary commitment for suicidal individuals altogether.

REVISIONS

Some of these revisions have already been enacted into law in a number of states, and they also find expression in the suggested statute on civil commitment drafted by the Mental Health Law Project (MHLP) for publication by a journal of the American Bar Association.[15] These revisions have focused on the standards for commitment and the burden of proof required to show that these standards have been met.

A number of states have recently enacted statutes requiring that there be a showing that "dangerousness" to oneself or to others has been manifested in recent overt dangerous behavior.[16] Under some statutes and legal decisions, such behavior may include verbal threats; in others, like the model statute of the Mental Health Law Project, it would appear that the only types of suicidal behavior that can be considered are actual destructive acts.

MHLPS's apparent insistence that only actual acts be considered as evidence and that statements of the intention to kill oneself not be so considered disregards all psychiatric knowledge about suicide. Apart from cases involving adolescents, in which statements of suicidal intention and actual suicide attempts have a relatively low correlation with eventual suicide, statements of suicidal intention have been shown to be one of the best indicators we have of eventual suicide. If the purpose of any code is to be of some help to the patient, the exclusion of such statements makes no sense.

Parallel with the effort to tighten the standards of commitment has been the drive to adopt the "beyond a reasonable doubt" standard of proof used in criminal cases, as opposed to the looser civil standard of proof by a "preponderance of the evidence." The Supreme Court, in *Addington* v. *Texas* (1979), has held that the due process clause of the Fourteenth Amendment to the Constitution requires neither the application of the strict criminal standard nor the looser "preponderance of the evidence" rule but rather an in between rule—that of "clear and convincing" evidence.[17] Some states, however, impose the criminal standard in civil commitment proceedings despite the Supreme Court view that there is a serious question as to whether a state could ever prove beyond a reasonable doubt that an individual is both mentally ill and dangerous.[18]

A few states have evolved even more stringent safeguards against unwarranted commitment. They may require evidence that treatment is available for the person's mental illness or that confinement is actually necessary to prevent harm to the patient; other states require a finding that hospitalization is the best available treatment and that no less restrictive treatment is available.[19]

The MHLP's model statute goes further still in limiting the circumstances under which a suicidal individual may be involuntarily committed. It not only incorporates a requirement of evidence of actual recent self-destructive acts going beyond mere threats before commitment is undertaken; it also requires that it be shown that the individual lacks the capacity to make informed judgments about his treatment. In addition, under the proposed model statute there must be a showing that the treatment has a good chance of helping the individual.

James Bray, president of the National Association of State Mental Health Program Directors, has made an incisive critique of these provisions of the model statute. He points out, "Even though the court finds that the respondent presents a likelihood of serious harm to himself or others, it may not commit him unless it also finds that there is a reasonable possibility the treatment will improve the respondent's mental condition. In the absence of such a finding, it must release the patient even though he is dangerously mentally ill according to all competent clinical testimony. . . . [Assume that a patient] is found to be dangerous to himself or others, but that he does not lack capacity to make informed decisions about treatment. It would be a travesty of justice and common sense if capacity is deemed to mandate a court order granting his release."[20]

In addition to urging reform of the standards for forcible commitment and a higher standard of proof in those proceedings, civil libertarian critics of forcible institutionalization have also sought to give mental patients almost all the rights of criminal defendants. The due process safeguards that are available to a criminal defendant include notice in sufficient detail and in sufficient time to permit preparation of defense; prompt judicial hearings; presence and opportunity to be heard at the hearings; the right to counsel, including the right to appointed counsel; the right to trial by jury; insistence on the rules of evidence; and the privilege against self-incrimination.

Despite the fact that effective notice of the date, time, and nature of the hearing is necessary to the exercise of a patient's other due process rights, some state commitment statutes do not make notice mandatory; some require that the patient be given only the minimal amount of information.[21] This policy is justified on the ground that the service of technical and confusing legal papers might traumatize a mentally disordered person. It has been rightly pointed out, however, that forced confinement in an institution is itself a traumatizing experience unlikely to be aggravated by the service of papers. In fact, information that he has the opportunity for a hearing to tell his side of the story may actually reduce a patient's anxiety. For these reasons a federal district court has held unconstitutional a Wisconsin statute providing only for discretionary notice. The court held that due process required—in addition to notice of the time and location of the hearing—notice to the individual of the reasons for his detention, the standards for commitment, the identities of the persons who will testify at his hearing, and the probable content of their testimony.[22]

In a nonemergency situation, detention prior to a hearing would appear to violate due process standards. At the very least, hearings that take place after detention prejudice the detainee, since he is viewed differently when he appears in hospital garb, often heavily medicated and perhaps confused by being thrust into strange and impersonal surroundings. All these factors may make it more difficult for him to convince the judge that he does not require hospitalization. In addition, once he is hospitalized, the stigma of hospitalization, even if later shown to be unnecessary, may lead to loss of friends, a job, and even custody of children. However, in the case of patients whose detention is sought to prevent imminent harm to themselves, detention prior to a hearing is the most likely situation. Even in an emergency situation, due process considerations dictate that a hearing may not be too long delayed. Due process requires prompt, even if temporary, disposition of the case in order to preserve the rights of the detainee.

Civil libertarians and most courts also reject the view that possible trauma to the alleged patient excuses his presence at the hearing. They argue that the presence of the subject at the hearing assures that he can assist in his defense and protect his interests. His presence also gives the fact finder the chance to speak to the patient, observe his demeanor, cut through the medical terminology in written reports, and test his own observations of the patient against those of the psychiatrist.

For these reasons, too, civil libertarians urge that there be no forced medicating before the appropriateness of commitment is determined. Federal courts in several states have discussed the issue. All of these decisions prohibited prescribing drugs that inhibit meaningful participation in the hearing; Nebraska banned all prehearing treatment, including the use of drugs that might interfere with the subject's ability to assist in the presentation of his defense.[23]

Some civil libertarians call for jury trials in commitment proceedings, believing that juries will be less likely than a single jurist to be guided by medical testimony advocating commitment. There is no convincing evidence to support this assertion. Although some judges who refuse to commit a nonsuicidal individual solely on the grounds that such a person needs treatment may nevertheless forcibly hospitalize a suicidal individual to save him from himself, the likelihood that a jury will be less protective of suicidal patients is slight. While jury trials serve to introduce community values and judgments into the commitment process, they seriously delay proceedings, introduce additional formality into them, and make them much more expensive for the state.

The issue of whether a jury trial is an element of due process in civil commitment has not yet been dealt with by the courts. It is unlikely that the due process clause of the Constitution requires a jury trial for forced hospitalization. Many states, nevertheless, provide a statutory right to jury trial.[24]

Some civil libertarians and the Mental Health Law Project maintain that an individual should be permitted to remain silent in a psychiatric interview when his statements can be used as a basis for civil commitment. MHLP argues that if danger to self is the standard for commitment, then the patient's serious disorder, his inability to make informed decisions, and the fact that he is actively violent or self-destructive should be obvious to jurors and judges from the testimony of lay witnesses and the individual's own behavior. They believe, therefore, that the psychiatrist's testimony is not essential and that the patient's liberty and privacy rights outweigh all other concerns.

At least one court has held that a person has the right to refuse to answer questions in a psychiatric interview if the evidence obtained in it is to be used for the purpose of commitment.[25] The Supreme Court, however, has recently declined to review a decision of an Oregon court which held that due process did not require that a person be afforded the right to remain silent in involuntary commitment proceedings.[26]

Since what a patient says and how he says it is the most important tool a psychiatrist has in evaluating dangerousness or the inability to care for oneself as well as in making a clinical diagnosis, any legal encouragement of the individual to remain silent becomes a way of making the psychiatrist's role meaningless. Knowledge of the psychological dynamics of any overt behavior as well as information about how the individual reacts in the interview are essential if the psychiatrist is to evaluate the possibilities of treatment, one of the factors that the MHLP wishes to be a decisive determinant of commitment. MHLP tries to distinguish between the patient's silence when treatability is being determined and his silence concerning evaluations of his mental state—a distinction that may be possible on paper but not in life. In any case, criticizing the accuracy of psychiatric evaluations while trying to deprive the psychiatrist of the major tool to make such evaluations, his interview with the patient, indicates a stubborn determination to impose procedure over common sense. Most courts have rejected this approach.

Specific rules of evidence that govern the admissibility of certain types of testimony and the admission of certain documents are generally applied to judicial hearings. In the past, commitment hearings were not conducted under these rules. The main evidence rule that has been ignored is the one governing the use of "hearsay" evidence. If a psychiatrist testifies as to what other persons—such as nurses, orderlies, or family members—told him a patient said, or if he refers to a psychiatric report by another doctor of an interview with the patient, or if he discusses a ward chart in which another doctor noted that the individual threatened self-destructive acts, such evidence is considered hearsay since the facts are not subject to verification through cross-examination of the individual making the statement.

A number of courts have recently held that the rules of evidence are applicable to commitment hearings, and Washington's statute governing involuntary hospitalization guarantees the application of these rules to commitment proceedings.[27] The enforcement of the rules of evidence along with jury trials has the effect of introducing more formality into these proceedings. Since witnesses would be required to appear for cross-examination, court appearances by nurses, ward attendants, social workers, neighbors, and relatives would be more common and trials would be lengthened, thus making it far more expensive and difficult to hospitalize individuals without their cooperation.

Most state commitment statutes provide that persons facing involuntary hospitalization have a right to be represented by an attorney during the commitment hearing. A number of courts have held also that there is a constitutional requirement that counsel be provided for indigent patients who wish to challenge their hospitalization.[28] Provision for the appointment of counsel in civil commitment cases if the patient has none is by no means universal, however. There is some question as to how early in the proceedings such counsel should be made available—whether, for example, as the California statute requires, he may be present at the initial psychiatric examination—and as to precisely what role the attorney should play.[29] Most writers on the subject assert that the attorney should assume a fully adversary role on the client's behalf, vigorously asserting his client's right to freedom in almost every situation. [30] Others see the attorney acting in a more paternalistic fashion, even recommending commitment when it appears appropriate. [31]

At hearings for retention in a state hospital in New York, for example, an assistant attorney general usually represents the hospital. But when other hospitals make applications for confinement, they are usually represented by psychiatrists. [32] This type of situation gives rise to the criticism that doctors in the civil commitment process serve as adversaries to their patients, a role inimical to their therapeutic capacity. If hospitals were in all cases to be represented by counsel and the appearance of conflict at the hearing was thus limited to the legal profession, this adversary role of the psychiatrist might be less conspicuous. At best, however, the adversarial nature of the psychiatrist's position would not be eliminated but only concealed. The documented unwillingness of judges to release against the wishes of psychiatrists and the inevitable tension between the patient's desire for release and the hospital's desire to retain—the tension that brought the parties into court in the first instance—would remain.

LANTERMAN-PETRIS-SHORT ACT (LPS)

The Lanterman-Petris-Short Act (LPS), adopted in California in 1967, was considered a landmark in the reform of involuntary commitment for the suicidal in particular and for psychiatric patients in general. [33] In California, prior to LPS, a person could be indefinitely committed if the court found that the person was "of such mental condition that he is in need of supervision, treatment, care or restraint" or "dangerous to h—self, or to the person or property of others . . ." Under this system California courts were committing over one thousand persons per month to state institutions, usually after only the most cursory psychiatric examination and court hearing.[34] For this procedure, LPS substitutes one that prohibits involuntary detention for longer than seventy-two hours unless the person is certified as dangerous to himself or others or so "gravely disabled" as to be "unable to provide for his basic personal needs for food, clothing, or shelter." If either of these conditions is met, he can be certified for fourteen days of "intensive treatment." After the expiration of the fourteen-day certification period, suicidal persons can be confined for up to fourteen additional days, but only if the person threatened or attempted to take his own life during the period of observation or intensive treatment.

ENKI Research Institute undertook to study whether the release of suicidal patients under LPS had resulted in an increased suicide rate.[35] They did follow-up studies of patient cohorts admitted to primary psychiatric service units in California before and after the implementation of LPS. ENKI found in its original study, and confirmed in a recent and as yet unpublished report, that (1) there was no increase in the suicide rate because of the early and mandatory release provisions of LPS and that (2) the statute's recertification provisions for suicidal patients were rarely used.[36]

The original ENKI report states, "The paradox exists in that professionals voiced great concern for extending the duration of involuntary treatment, yet when they had the option of continuing treatment, it was used in less than 1% of eligible cases.

"Our findings indicate that mental health services seemed to have little, if any, impact on the suicide rates in the community (for example in 1963 82% of the suicides in Los Angeles County had never been seen at the county hospital). Based on the findings of our cohort study, one conclusion is that it may be more effective and humanitarian to limit, rather than extend involuntary hospitalization for suicidal persons."

However, considering the difficulties placed in the way of recertification, the fact that California hospital psychiatrists do not avail themselves of the second fourteen day option is of little significance. If anything, it argues against the value of two fourteen-day time periods. And if, as ENKI says, the vast majority of the suicides in Los Angeles have never been to the county hospital, using the county suicide rate to evaluate LPS is equally questionable.

California psychiatrists working in psychiatric hospitals with whom we have discussed LPS believe that while it has partially resolved old problems, it has created a new one. The short-term hospitalization span mandated by LPS does not permit psychiatric staff to involve the suicidal patient constructively in any effective treatment plans, whether as in-patients or out-patients. Many patients discharged from state hospitals have been found to quickly turn up in municipal hospitals. Of course, the trend in the past decade to "de-institutionalize" psychiatric patients has created the same problem in states that do not have laws comparable to LPS.

LPS would have been a big step forward if it had been accompanied by adequate provision for help to the suicidal individuals as well as to others who were not committed or were quickly released. It has helped to free us from a system that was not very effective, but since no suitable alternative was provided, it is not clear that we are better off. In place of the tragedy of patients who were unfairly and unnecessarily kept in psychiatric hospitals, deinstitutionalization has created a small army of disabled patients, including those who are suicidal, floundering on their own in towns and cities throughout the county.

Another source of legal protection for the suicidal patient and for hospitalized psychiatric patients in general is the patient advocacy services, of which New York State's Mental Health Information Service (MHIS) was a forerunner.[37] The New York law was enacted to ensure that no New York State patient became a "forgotten man."[38]

MHIS, staffed primarily by lawyers, functions as an arm of the court, informing patients and families of their rights and providing information to the courts. Its purpose is to review the status of both involuntary and voluntary patients and to inform them of their rights under the law. Most cases of conflict between the patients and the hospital are resolved by negotiation. Often the mere request for the hearing and the consequent discussion with the patient's doctors, social worker, and his MHIS counsel result in release or a satisfactory alternative solution. In the event of a hearing, MHIS is charged with providing a report to the court regarding all the relevant facts surrounding the hospitalization: the social background and medical history of the patient, including suicidal attempts, available alternatives to hospitalization, and summaries of interviews with the hospital staff, family, and friends.[39] MHIS also represents patients who seek to challenge their confinement and assert other legal rights. The MHIS advocacy approach has been adopted in a number of other states. The recently enacted federal Mental Health Systems Act provides federal grants to states to fund the delivery of independent external advocacy services.[40]

CONCLUSION

The introduction of due process protections and of advocacy services, although setting up significant barriers to inappropriate confinements, has also raised complex legal, social, and economic problems. De-institutionalization has created the problem of caring for patients outside of hospitals. Halfway houses offer a potentially promising solution, but the trend to decrease government welfare spending makes it unlikely that such care will soon be provided. Decreased government spending would also affect the movement to inject greater legal protections into the commitment process. There is no doubt that the effectiveness of any kind of advocacy program in preventing inappropriate confinement depends on the state's willingness to fund these programs adequately and to attract able and dedicated personnel.

The United States Supreme Court, at least, has not fully accepted the civil libertarian's equation of the commitment process with criminal proceedings or their rejection of the possibility that confinement is therapeutic. Nor does the Court appear to believe, as it does in criminal cases, that it is better for a mentally ill person to go free than for a normal individual to be committed.

In a larger sense the furor over commitment has been a struggle between a traditional medical-psychiatric approach to suicide and a legal model based on the rights of defendants in criminal proceedings. Both models have had serious weaknesses.

The traditional approach has been neglectful of patient's rights; it is also not based on sound psychiatry. It assumes without evidence that enforced hospitalization benefits seriously suicidal patients. As a result there has been little effort to find out for which patients it may be beneficial and for which detrimental. Some of the medical arguments defending the status quo are obvious rationalizations, such as the contention that patients will be upset by having to deal with legal procedures when it is their doctors who often see these procedures as an interference or imposition.

The commitment of suicidal individuals was never conceived of as a social preventative likely to affect the rate of suicides in society. It was meant to be used more as an emergency measure in dealing with a crisis in which family, friends, or physicians did not know what else to do. Unfortunately, the fear and anxiety of individuals close to the suicide attempter often persist long beyond the few weeks following the attempt. Partly out of a sense of inadequacy to deal with the situation and partly out of a desire to shift the responsibility for the patient's life to an institution, they often seek to keep the individual hospitalized. As the chapter dealing with the treatment of the suicidal patient explained, these reactions are often witnessed in the psychiatrist treating the patient as well as in the family and friends. In such cases, there is no one available to challenge the family's, friend's, or physician's desire for continued hospitalization. In addition, once the individual has been committed to a mental hospital for treatment, the justification for continued hospitalization—based on the diagnosis of mental illness—has already been established and assumes a force all its own.

To a larger extent than is recognized, commitment has been motivated by the therapist's fear of being responsible and of actually being held responsible for the suicide of a patient. Such fears, as we saw in Chapter 7, often make it difficult to render decisions that are in the patient's best interests. Therapists pass the responsibility on to hospitals, whose staffs are often guided by comparable fears that prevent them from exercising sound judgment.

It complicates the issue of commitment that many patients cannot directly admit they wish or need to be in a hospital but behave in a manner that makes their hospitalization likely. Failure to heed such unspoken communication can be disastrous.

Writing under a pseudonym, an English author documented the story of his wife's mental disintegration and suicide, in which his and her therapist's refusal to hospitalize her played a major role.[41] She became increasingly regressed, rolling in the dirt, screeching hysterically, contorting her body, and breaking windows and cups, with "self-destruction in her eyes." Her husband persuaded himself that he was following the wish that his wife had once expressed not to be rehospitalized if a psychiatric breakdown reoccurred. His position did not change when she attempted to kill their youngest child.

Everything she did conveyed a wish to be taken out of her home. She even ran away to a local mental hospital, where she did somewhat better, but was brought home because her husband and her therapist were philosophically opposed to hospitalization. Finally she poured gasoline on herself, set herself afire, and died a slow and painful death.

If a patient is hospitalized, some fixed time limit to see whether hospitalization can help makes sense; but two arbitrary fourteen-day periods as exacted in LPS and incorporated in the Mental Health Law Project's model statute do not. Involuntary suicidal patients can at times be helped, but if they are, they have essentially become voluntary patients. A period of four to six weeks is enough to give the hospital a chance to help. If the patient shows no improvement by then, it is not likely that hospitalization is going to help. If the hospital cannot help, then the possibility of suicide alone should not be a sufficient reason for keeping a patient.

Even if a fixed period of time is established, some sort of ombudsman like that established in the New York MHIS is necessary. It is not usually the initial commitment that constitutes the major source of abuse. It is, rather, the continued confinement of individuals who are not being helped but are kept primarily because they are potentially suicidal. Some of these individuals will remain suicide risks for a lifetime. If they are able to care for themselves, keeping them indefinitely confined, often under the strict restrictions of hospital suicide prevention procedures, is usually poor psychiatric practice as well as an abuse of patients' rights.

One recently seen 55-year-old woman had become depressed and overtly suicidal following the breakup of her marriage. She was treated for months in a hospital without improvement. Her own hatred of being hospitalized made it probable that nothing the hospital could do would be beneficial. She seemed likely to remain suicidal throughout her lifetime, but when the hospital was persuaded to make arrangements for her to live with some friends and to be treated as an out-patient, her overall condition improved.

Another recently seen suicidal patient was kept on round-the-clock observation for nine months because he had nearly died in a serious suicide attempt while in the hospital. The constant presence of an attendant created enormous difficulties for the patient and caused his overall condition to deteriorate; however, supervisory personnel were unwilling to take the responsibility for changing the situation. When they were finally persuaded to take the patient off round-the-clock observation, he became more responsive to treatment and his condition improved dramatically.

These two patients, having recently made serious suicide attempts, would have been certifiable even under the LPS law in California. And although they were New York patients, the insufficient personnel available under MHIS did not take up their cases. They were helped by the accident of having been seen by one of the authors in connection with his research. His willingness to take responsibility for a change in the treatment plan was necessary because of the staff's concern about being blamed if anything went wrong. Such situations suggest it would be of value to have psychiatrists knowledgeable about suicide working with attorneys as ombudsmen. * A psychiatrist freed of the need to support a hospital position with regard to commitment and without direct responsibility for the care of the patient would be in a position to make an informed recommendation in the patient's best interests, and one that would probably be heeded. Such cooperation between lawyer and psychiatrist would be more effective than current practice, which places the two professions in an intrinsically adversary position. †

---

*The New Jersey statute that provides that a nonlawyer or a mental health professional be part of a team to help and protect patients is a small step in this direction. [42]

† Statutes authorizing the state to pay for a psychiatrist for the patient give the poor some protection, but they maintain the adversary nature of the proceeding. [43]

11. Assisted Suicide and Euthanasia

INCREASINGLY, SUICIDE IS advocated as a fundamental human right. In this view attempts to prevent suicide are an interference with that right. Nietzsche succinctly expressed this position when he wrote, "There is a certain right by which we may deprive a man of life, but none by which we may deprive him of death."[1] Removed from its social and psychological context, suicide then becomes an issue of personal freedom.

The psychiatrist Thomas Szasz has been an articulate contemporary spokesman for this point of view.[2] Szasz believes that we rationalize an oppressive policy toward behaviors like suicide and drug abuse by labeling them illnesses and calling on psychiatrists and psychologists to enforce that policy. Of suicide prevention, Szasz writes, "He who does not accept and respect those who want to reject life does not truly accept and respect life itself." Causing one's own death, Szasz goes on, "should be called 'suicide' only by those who disapprove of it; and should be called 'death control' by those who approve of it."[3]

Szasz does not acknowledge the often transient and ambivalent quality of the impulse to commit suicide; he simply believes that successful suicides intend to die and unsuccessful ones do not. The clinical evidence contradicts him. Three-fourths of all suicides indicate ambivalence by communicating their intentions, often with the hope of intervention. In numerous cases, the pleas for help are varied, repeated, and expressed to more than one person. Studies of those who have survived serious suicide attempts have revealed that a fantasy of being rescued is often present.

What has misled clinicians who make a rigid separation between those who survive suicide attempts and those who do not is the evidence that many so-called "attempted suicides" clearly want to live. This in no way contradicts the clinical evidence that a large number of those who kill themselves are ambivalent in the sense that they do something irrevocable in a state of uncertainty.

Many people have speculated that if you could talk to someone who was in midair after jumping from a tall tower, you might find out that he no longer was so sure he wanted to die. Over the past forty years I have seen four people who survived six-story suicide jumps. Two wished to survive as soon as they had jumped, two said they did not, but one of the latter two who professed to be furious at having survived made no subsequent suicide attempts.

Moreover, in a majority of cases, we do not know at once how serious the individual is about suicide. It is estimated that only one out of ten suicide attempts results in death, a figure that tends to confirm the view that suicidal individuals are conflicted about dying. Similarly, studies of the subsequent mortality rates of survivors show that only about 1 percent of all survivors kill themselves within one year. Thus intervention—even if it is short-term and circumscribed—seems warranted and desirable.

Is every suicidal person mentally ill and in need of hospitalization, as Eli Robins, an authority on psychiatric diagnoses and the epidemiology of suicide, believes?[4] Or is the suicidal person simply called mentally ill for the purpose of controlling his or her behavior, as Szasz believes? Or does he have the right to kill himself whether or not he is mentally ill, as Eliot Slater, an English psychiatrist and advocate of euthanasia, believes?[5] My own view is that each of these positions contains some truth, but no one of them should be the guide for social policy. Most suicides can be diagnosed as mentally ill; diagnoses of mental illness are influenced by the threat of suicide and the desire to prevent it through hospitalization. But the diagnosis of mental illness is insufficient to explain suicide and does not justify taking away an individual's rights indefinitely.

The right to kill oneself can be exercised without involving society by most of those who are sufficiently determined to do so. Someone on the window ledge of a tall building who is threatening to jump or someone who is found unconscious after swallowing sleeping pills has forced society to pay attention, whether or not that person is hoping to be saved or helped. Surely, confinement for a limited period with the hope of providing help is indicated. When pathology is psychosocial—when the community has a stake in it—personal rights are not unlimited.

Coercive treatment, however, is less effective. It is usually possible to persuade someone who is depressed and acutely suicidal to accept hospitalization even if he or she is otherwise functional. Some who say they do not want hospitalization behave in ways that suggest they do. Such individuals' subsequent acceptance of hospitalization suggests a need for someone else to take the responsibility for the decision.

Whether an individual is hospitalized voluntarily or not, great care has to be exercised to assess benefit from treatment or continuation of a hospital stay. Hospitalization of the suicidal can be lifesaving as an emergency measure; it becomes a danger when it is extended out of inertia or for fear of further suicide attempts.

Our efforts to prevent suicide should not devalue life more than suicide does.

Szasz and other civil libertarians who agree with him make no claim that society should help, support, or encourage the suicide in his efforts to kill himself. They believe that it would be sufficient if society recognized that it had no right to interfere. But supporters of euthanasia go further with "the right to suicide." They believe in the utility of suicidal death and want support, encouragement, and even help in carrying out suicide.

Until the last decade, arguments for legalizing assisted suicide or euthanasia focused on the social problems presented by the elderly and the chronically ill. The increasing number of old people, the inadequate care provided by nursing homes, and the economic cost to both families and society were used to support the view that euthanasia must be accepted, encouraged, and protected. Mary Rose Barrington, an English jurist and a past chairperson of the British Voluntary Euthanasia Society, tells us that "the problem of three or four contemporary generations peopling a world that heretofore has had to support only two or three is with us here and now."[6]

Barrington and Slater feel that chronic illness—without regard for age—is a justification for suicide. Slater tells us, "If a chronically sick man dies, he ceases to be a burden on himself, on his family, on the health services and on the community. If we can do nothing to get a patient better, but do our best to retard the process of dying—extend it perhaps over months and years—we are adding to the totality of ill health and incapacity. To take an obvious example, transplant surgery, in providing a spare set for people who have run through one pair of kidneys, one liver or heart, increases the number of people in the community who at one time are suffering from diseases of the kidneys, liver or heart. There is, of course, absolutely no limit to the burdens we can go on piling up, by trying to keep badly damaged individuals alive."[7] Such social Darwinism, if carried to a logical conclusion, would force us to cease our efforts on behalf of the disabled, chronically ill, or handicapped.

Barrington informs us that, unlike people, sick animals have the good sense to stop eating and die. Actually, some human beings do so too; they are usually people whose spirit has been so crushed by life that they offer little resistance to illness. We need not believe that suffering is good for the character in order to understand that the capacity to deal with adversity, including illness, is one of the features of psychosocial stability.

Recently the argument for euthanasia in this country has centered on more humane considerations, that is, the personal suffering of the terminally ill. The desire to have medical help in ending one's life is seen as an extension of the right to refuse to be sustained on life support systems or to request not to be resuscitated. Advocates of euthanasia see no difference between a doctor's withdrawing futile treatment and his becoming a more direct participant in inducing death.

Although both assisted suicide and euthanasia have been put forward as an expression of the individual's "right to die," some advocates have drawn a distinction between assisted suicide, where the doctor prescribes medication and informs the patient how much is needed to end life, and euthanasia in which the doctor induces death, usually by the injection of drugs. Assisted suicide has been seen as protecting against medical abuse by giving the patient more control over his death. Advocates see it as a first step that is more likely to be accepted than euthanasia.

Opponents regard euthanasia as a form of medical killing in violation of social, ethical, and medical traditions. There is concern that it will be applied in an involuntary way to the terminally ill who are elderly, particularly those who are poor.

Proponents of this view see little protection in assisted suicide since influence or coercion do not require a physician or relatives to take direct action.

They fear that social acceptance itself may become a form of coercion. University of Michigan professor of law Yale Kamisar asks, "in a suicide-permissive society, in a climate in which suicide is the 'rational' thing *to* do, or at least a 'reasonable' option will it become the unreasonable thing *not* to do? The noble thing *to* do? In a society unsympathetic to justifying an impaired or dependent existence, a psychological burden may be placed on those who do not think their illness or infirmity is reason for dying. The presence of a socially approved option becomes a subtle pressure to request it."[8]

Opponents see death as a biological fact, not a right. And, as Daniel Callahan points out, while we may debate about how far we should go to prevent an individual from killing himself, we do not permit an individual—nor does he have a right—to authorize someone else to kill him.[9] Decriminalization of both suicide and attempted suicide and the abolition of such punishment as confinement in prison and ignominious burial did not come about because society approved of suicide or considered it a human right. The changes reflected the view that punishment was unfair to the relatives of the suicide and, more importantly, because it was acknowledged that those who attempted or committed suicide were usually suffering from mental illness.

For two decades the discussion over assisted suicide and euthanasia has been dominated by philosophers, theologians, and physicians who are often uninformed about the psychiatric and psychosocial dimensions of the problem. They deferentially quote Camus's view that the question of suicide—that is, "judging whether life is or is not worth living"—is the fundamental question in life and for philosophy.[10] It is not the central question for most people nor has it been for most philosophers, but it is the central question for suicidally depressed patients and for a few twentieth-century existential philosophers. For those who are suicidal, control over whether they live or die provides the illusion of control over many of life's existential anxieties, including those of dying.[11]

Many people have experienced situations where hastening the death of a terminally ill relative or friend who has not been suicidal may be humane and where a physician may be justified in providing such help. For reasons that I will try to make clear, legalizing physician-assisted suicide and euthanasia would be one of the worst possible answers to a problem that needs to be addressed. Since the movement toward legalization represents such a drastic departure from established social policy and medical tradition, it is helpful to look first at current psychiatric knowledge about suicide and terminal illness.

Suicide, Depression, and Euthanasia

We know that 95 percent of those who kill themselves have been shown to have a diagnosable psychiatric illness in the months preceding suicide.[12] The majority suffer from depression, which can be treated. This is particularly true of the elderly, who are more prone than younger people to take their lives during the type of acute depressive episode that responds most effectively to treatment.[13] Other diagnoses among the suicides include alcoholism, substance abuse, schizophrenia, and panic disorder; treatments are available for all of these illnesses.

Advocates of physician-assisted suicide and euthanasia maintain that in terminally ill patients the wish to die is completely different from that of other suicidal patients. Although the terminally ill constitute only 3 percent of the total number of suicides,[14] like other suicidal individuals, patients who desire an early death during a terminal illness are usually suffering from a treatable mental illness, most commonly a depressive condition.[15] Strikingly, the overwhelming majority of the terminally ill fight for life to the end. Some may voice suicidal thoughts in response to transient depression or severe pain, but these patients usually respond well to treatment for depressive illness and pain medication and are grateful to be alive.

Studies of those who have died by suicide underscore the non-rational elements of the wish to die in reaction to serious illness. More individuals, particularly elderly individuals, killed themselves because they feared or *mistakenly* believed they had cancer than those who killed themselves who knew they actually had cancer.[16] Similarly, preoccupation with suicide is higher for those awaiting the results of tests for HIV antibodies than in those who know they are HIV positive.[17]

Given the advances in our medical knowledge and treatment ability, a thorough psychiatric evaluation for the presence of a treatable disorder may literally make a life or death difference for patients who say they wish to die or to have a physician help them to do so. This is not an evaluation that can be made by the average physician who does not have extensive experience with depression and suicide.[18]

In studies of assisted suicide and euthanasia, most of which have been done in the Netherlands, physicians reported that loss of dignity, pain, not wishing to die in an "unworthy way," being dependent on others, and being tired of living were the reasons patients have for requesting euthanasia.[19] The fear of death itself is not mentioned.

My own experience has been that many patients and physicians displace anxieties about death onto the circumstances of dying: pain, dependence, loss of dignity, and the unpleasant side effects resulting from medical treatment, or, for the physician, frustration at not being able to offer a sure cure. Focusing on or becoming enraged at the process of dying distracts from the fear of death itself.

Giving death its due may focus a patient on what he can achieve in whatever life can still offer. A few years ago an attorney I will call Tim was referred to me for psychiatric consultation. In his early thirties, he was diagnosed as having acute myelocytic leukemia; with treatment he was given a 25 percent chance of survival. His immediate reaction was a desperate preoccupation with suicide and a wish for support in carrying it out. At first he could not consider how he felt about death and its meaning, but he remained preoccupied with concerns about being dependent and with his unwillingness to tolerate the symptoms of his disease or the side effects of proposed treatment. Once we could talk about the possibility or likelihood of his dying—what it meant to him in terms of separation and bodily disintegration—his desperate avoidance subsided. He decided to undergo medical treatment, complained relatively little about the unpleasant side effects, and used the remaining months of his life to connect with his wife and parents in ways that were moving and meaningful for him. Two days before he died, Tim talked of what he would have missed without the opportunity for a loving parting.

Tim's expectations of painful circumstances surrounding his dying were not irrational, but all his anxieties about death and dying were displaced onto amplifying them. If the ravages of illness and the painful side effects of treatment were not accompanied by the fear of imminent death, they would be more bearable, and many who choose suicide might not do so. Conversely, if life were so structured that we all knew we would die on the day of our eighty-fifth birthday, but live in good health up to that time, it is likely that many people would kill themselves in the months or years prior to their eighty-fifth birthday so as to avoid anxiety over the inevitability of their fate and their lack of control over it.

Potential for Abuse

If euthanasia were to be legalized, certain groups would be at a higher risk for abuse than others: the elderly, those particularly frightened by illness, and the depressed of all ages. The elderly often feel that their families would prefer that they were gone. Societal sanction for physician-assisted suicide for the terminally ill is likely to encourage family members so inclined to pressure the infirm and the elderly, and to collude with uninformed or unscrupulous physicians to provide such deaths. According to philosophers Karen Lebacqz and N. Tristan Englehardt, that an individual might choose to die rather than burden the family is socially affirming.[20] Just as love-pact suicides rarely turn out to be affirmations of love, so the self-sacrificial suicide may lend itself to becoming the instrument of tyranny of the healthy over the aged and infirm.

Margaret Battin, an advocate of euthanasia, admits that social acceptance of euthanasia would undoubtedly lead to situations in which families that wish to be free of the burden of caring for the elderly pressure them to end their lives. She recognizes that this pressure could be expressed through an appeal to the older person that suicide would be for the good of all concerned; but such an appeal would be effective only in a climate that sanctioned suicide for infirm older people. She warns of the dangers of institutional abuse of euthanasizing the elderly in a health care system in which coverage is inequitable, costs are out of control, a high proportion of these costs are associated with terminal illness, and patients who choose death would provide the cheapest alternative. Although Battin is conscious of the "moral quicksand" into which the right to suicide "threatens to lead us," she believes it must be accepted on moral grounds.[21]

Most of the older suicidal patients discussed in this book who responded to treatment or recovered on their own would have been candidates for assisted suicide or euthanasia during the prolonged period when they were depressed or suicidal. Recall the sociology professor (Chapter 3) who, after his stroke, tormented his wife and children before a suicide attempt with an overdose of pills. His wife told me he wanted her to bring him bullets for his gun, which she might have done, but she feared he might hurt her and their children as well. Both she and her husband are now happy with the life they have made together, despite his partial paralysis.

If assisted suicide and euthanasia were to be extended to depressed psychiatric patients who are suicidal regardless of their physical health, as has taken place in the Netherlands, depressed patients with or without medical conditions who did not respond quickly to treatment could be vulnerable. Recall the woman (see Chapter 3) who had had a major depressive episode after her husband died of a heart attack while greeting her upon her return from work. She had made several serious suicide attempts and when I first saw her she had just come out of a barbiturate-induced coma. Following her husband's death she was hospitalized several times, received virtually every antidepressant medication then available, and was given two courses of electric shock treatment, all to no avail.

Her condition was incurable, she insisted, and suicide was the only solution. She would not consider treatment, but came for a few therapy sessions, and I remained in touch with her and her family to see how she was doing. Her children had reached a point where they half hoped she would die, since they spent so much time thwarting her suicide attempts. Two more distressing years were followed by a nearly fatal suicide attempt in which she awoke after several days of coma to tell her daughter that she was finished with suicide. She agreed to see me, but could only tell me that she had had a dream in which her husband came to her and said, "That's enough—you've put yourself and everyone else through enough suffering." She claimed she awoke the following morning free of her depression. When I spoke to her a year later and to her daughter a few years after that, they told me she was living by herself, had made a new social life, and was no longer depressed or suicidal. In her case, under a system that permitted legalized assisted suicide, she would have ended her life with the concurrence of her family and the assistance of her doctor long before showing signs of a recovery.

The general public has encountered the question of assisted suicide and euthanasia mainly through the publicity afforded Dr. Jack Kevorkian and Derek Humphry. Many of the patients who have been drawn to Kevorkian have been people whose terror of illness persuades them that quick death is the best solution. Janet Adkins, a woman in the early stages of Alzheimer's who was fearful of the progress of the disease, was seen by Kevorkian, a retired pathologist in Michigan with a passionate commitment to promoting assisted suicide and the use of his "suicide machine." After a brief conversation he decided she was a suitable candidate. He used the machine to help her kill herself. Clearly, his lack of knowledge of her and his investment in promoting assisted suicide disqualified him from making such a determination. No Michigan law then prohibited assisted suicide (most states have such laws) but he was admonished by the court not to engage in the practice. Disregarding the admonition, Kevorkian subsequently helped to end the lives of many others, some of whom were seriously ill but not near death.[22] Dr. Kevorkian's license to practice medicine has since been summarily suspended, but a Michigan judge ruled that he could not be prosecuted for murder in the absence of a state law prohibiting assisting a suicide. In 1993, Michigan passed such a law, which Kevorkian violated with the avowed intention of testing its constitutionality.

Kevorkian advocates creation of a board-certified medical specialty, "obitiatry," based on a four-year medical residency that would train physicians in the practice of "medicide." A grandfather clause would permit pioneers like Dr. Kevorkian to be certified to develop the program. Kevorkian presents a detailed model plan for the state of Michigan, dividing it into eleven geographically mapped zones, each with its own headquarters and death clinic. He talks the reader through the process by which Wanda Endittal, a hypothetical patient with multiple sclerosis, seeks help to end her life. Her physician, Dr. Frieda Blame, refers her to an obitiatrist, Dr. Will B. Reddy. After an elaborate consultation process with other obitiatrists including Dr. Lotte Goode, a psychiatrist, Wanda's case is referred to the "action obitiatrists." One of them, Dr. Dewey Ledder, makes a last review of her file, and the other, Dr. Shelby Donne, performs the medicide. Kevorkian's account reads much like a Swiftian satire on the world we would create if Kevorkian's vision were followed. Kevorkian recognizes that his plan "may sound overblown, overly grandiose or impractical."[23]

Derek Humphry, like Kevorkian, was tapping into deeply felt anxieties concerning dying in intolerable circumstances that led some to support his efforts without regard for their consequences. Initially, Humphry and the Hemlock Society would not send instructions on how to commit suicide to the public at large, presumably because the information might get into the wrong hands.[24] At some point Humphry changed his mind and published a how-to-kill-yourself book and promoted its sale to the general public.[25] Since the publication of his book, however, there has been a significant increase in the number of people— some of them young people found dead with the book nearby— who have asphyxiated themselves with plastic bags, one of the methods recommended by Humphry.[26]

Humphry's participation in the suicide pact of his former wife's parents also raised questions. Ann Wickett, the former wife of Derek Humphry, and a co-founder of the Hemlock Society, made clear in her book, letters, conversations with friends, and her own taped suicide note that she was tormented by having actively participated with Humphry in the suicide pact of her parents.[27] Although her 92-year-old father may have been ready to die, she was aware that her 78-year-old mother was not. Such pacts have been romanticized and considered rational suicides, but published case reports confirm my own clinical experience that in most such pacts a man who wishes to end his life coerces a woman into joining him to prove her love.[28]

Today, proponents of what is called "rational suicide" draw on the concept of *bilanz selbstmord* or "balance-sheet suicide," developed by German philosophers in the early part of this century.[29] Individuals assumed to be mentally unimpaired dispassionately took stock of their life situation and, having found it unacceptable or untenable and foreseeing no significant change for the better, decided to end their lives. Contemporary advocates see a close analogy between a rational decision for suicide and the decision of the directors of a firm to declare bankruptcy and go out of business.[30]

The idea that life can be measured by balancing assets and liabilities is itself a characteristic of suicidal people. Some of the most depressed suicidal patients spend years making elaborate lists of reasons why they should go on living to counter the many reasons they can think of for dying. They are prone to make conditions on life: "I won't live if I can't be in control," "without my husband," "if I lose my looks, power, prestige, or health," or "if I am going to die soon." Depression, often precipitated by discovering a serious illness, exaggerates the tendency toward seeing problems in black or white terms. If society sanctions the view that life is only worth living if certain conditions are met, the patient's rigidity is reinforced.[31]

THE DUTCH EXPERIENCE

Anyone interested in the consequences of social sanction of euthanasia is inevitably led to the Netherlands, a western democracy with a distinguished medical tradition, where doctors, provided they follow certain guidelines, can practice euthanasia and assisted suicide with impunity and public acceptance. That acceptance has now been extended to suicidal patients who are not physically ill.

In the spring of 1993 in the city of Assen, a court of three judges acquitted a psychiatrist who had assisted in the suicide of his patient, a 50-year-old woman who had lost her two sons and who was recently divorced from her husband. The Assen case is joining the handful of internationally known Dutch cases of assisted suicide and euthanasia, each referred to by the name of the city where it was tried.[32] Before I left for the Netherlands on a trip to study euthanasia and assisted suicide in medical and psychiatric cases and the subject of involuntary euthanasia, Dr. Boudewijn Chabot, the psychiatrist in the Assen case, responded positively to my letter asking to discuss the case with him.

Is the Netherlands the place where Jack Kevorkian's vision has come to pass? How much can the Dutch experience with euthanasia help to guide or caution us?

De facto legalization of euthanasia and assisted suicide exists in the Netherlands. Although the criminal law provides punishment for euthanasia and a lesser punishment for assisted suicide, the same code stipulates that there can be exceptions to the law in special circumstances. The Dutch courts, in a series of cases tried during the past twenty years, have ruled that euthanasia is such a special circumstance. It is permitted by a doctor driven by force majeure, an overpowering conflict between the law—which makes euthanasia illegal—and his responsibility to help a patient which makes euthanasia necessary and overrides a conflict with the law.

The Dutch courts and the Royal Dutch Medical Association (KNMG) separately established the same guidelines for physicians to follow whether practicing assisted suicide or euthanasia: 1) voluntariness—the patient's request must be made freely, persistently, and consciously; 2) there must exist unbearable suffering that cannot be relieved by other means; and 3) consultation—the attending physician should consult with a colleague. Doctors are expected to report cases of euthanasia as deaths due to "unnatural causes" with the understanding that they will not be prosecuted if the guidelines were followed.

Few cases have been brought to trial. The recommended guidelines are not fixed conditions, so even when they were not followed, judges have consistently exonerated physicians on the grounds of force majeure. Only one doctor, the physician in the infamous De Terp nursing home case, who pled guilty to putting to death without their consent patients under his care, has been sent to prison.

Despite accepting euthanasia, prior to 1991 the Dutch did not have hard facts about the practice. Estimates of the number of euthanasia cases had ranged from 5,000 to 20,000 of the 130,000 deaths in the Netherlands each year. Charges by doctors and others that involuntary euthanasia was widespread were made.

To ascertain actual Dutch medical practice regarding euthanasia, a government commission, headed by Professor Jan Remmelink, arranged a study by investigators at Erasmus University in which physicians were granted anonymity and immunity from prosecution for information revealed in the study. The investigators found that 49,000 deaths in the Netherlands each year involve a medical decision at the end of life (MDEL). Ninety-five percent of these MDEL cases involve, in equal numbers, either withholding or discontinuing life support, or the alleviation of pain and symptoms through potentially lethal narcotic injections. Outright euthanasia was the cause of death in 2,300 (2 percent) of all Dutch deaths. Assisted suicide was relatively uncommon, occurring some four hundred times per year. Over 50 percent of Dutch physicians admitted to practicing euthanasia, with cancer patients being the majority of their cases. Only 60 percent of doctors kept a written record of their cases, and only 29 percent of doctors filled out the death certificates honestly in euthanasia cases.[33]

The Dutch were hoping the Remmelink Report would put to rest concerns about euthanasia. Indeed, many have tried to put such a spin on it. Instead, and largely because of the integrity of the study, the report opened up a Pandora's box of questions that need to be addressed. Moreover, the more serious side of the problem turned out to be so-called involuntary euthanasia, a term that is disturbing to the Dutch.

Of obvious concern to Dutch and foreign observers of euthanasia in the Netherlands was the revelation that in over one thousand cases physicians admitted they had actively caused or hastened death without the request of the patient. The impossibility of treating pain effectively was given as the reason for killing the patient in about 30 percent of these cases. The remaining 70 percent were killed with a variety of justifications ranging from "low quality of life" to "all treatment was withdrawn but the patient did not die." The Remmelink Commission considered that these cases were not morally troublesome, because the suffering of those patients had become unbearable and they would usually have died soon anyhow. Twenty-seven percent of physicians indicated that they had terminated the lives of patients without a request from the patient to do so; another 32 percent could conceive of doing so.

According to the report, other forms of hastening death without the patient's consent are common practice in the Netherlands. In over four thousand cases the doctor's explicit intention in administering pain medication or withdrawing or withholding treatment was to shorten life; in over eleven thousand cases this was a "secondary goal." In half of the forty-nine thousand MDEL cases, apart from the euthanasia cases, decisions that might or were intended to end the life of the patient were made without consulting the patient. In about 80 percent of these cases physicians gave the patient's impaired ability to communicate as their justification. This left about five thousand cases in which physicians made decisions that might, or were intended to, take the lives of competent patients without consulting them.

Involuntary euthanasia raised such large questions that only the report's principal investigator seemed able to address them. Dr. Paul van der Maas, chair of the Department of Public Health and Social Medicine of Erasmus University in Rotterdam, had led the investigative effort.

I asked van der Maas about the decision to include all medical decisions at the end of life and not just euthanasia in his study. He said people claim that termination of life without request does not occur, but every doctor knows it does and it should be looked at as well.

Van der Maas followed the Dutch practice of never using the

term "involuntary euthanasia." The Dutch define euthanasia as the ending of the life of one person by another at the first person's request. If a life is terminated without explicit request, it is not considered to be euthanasia. For me, "involuntary euthanasia" has a far less Orwellian and sinister connotation than "termination of the patient without explicit request."

Van der Maas and I talked about a boundary area where it is not clear if the death is the result of medicine given to alleviate pain and symptoms, or the result of either euthanasia or the termination of life without explicit request. It seemed that a case could be classified as euthanasia when the doctor is giving medication with the explicit intention of shortening life, and the patient knows and consents. The only real difference, van der Maas pointed out, is that in ordinary euthanasia cases death is immediate whereas in the borderline cases death may take a day or two. If the patient is given medication to end his life and does not know it, the case would seem to fall into the "termination of life without request" category. Because of these and other problems defining the exact category of a death, van der Maas would not be surprised if the actual number of euthanasia cases was higher than the official figure.

More alarming were the statistics in the report indicating that there were thousands of cases in which decisions that might or were intended to end a fully competent patient's life were made without consulting the patient. It was therefore surprising that the report did not include a recommendation for doctors to discuss their plans with competent patients. Van der Maas said he would make such a point in other contexts but, in order to secure the cooperation of the KNMG and the participating doctors, it was understood the report would make as few recommendations as possible.

In the interests of maintaining harmony, virtually all of the explanations of the physicians in the study appear to have been accepted at face value, even when follow-up questions seemed necessary. For example, in 13 percent of the cases, physicians who did not communicate with competent patients concerning MDELs that might or were intended to end their lives gave as a reason for not doing so some previous discussion of the subject with the patient. Yet it seemed incomprehensible that the physician would terminate the life of a competent patient on the basis of prior discussion without checking to see if the patient still felt the same way. One could only conjecture that the physician, actually knowing that the patient would not agree or had changed his mind, did not want to hear the answer because he felt it appropriate to end the patient's life, and to do so after a negative reply would amount to murder. Another possibility was that the physician was justifying the death by stretching the patient's words, which may, according to the study, have been no more than an urgent request for the relief of pain. Challenging such explanations could have clarified the doctors' rationale for ending a patient's life without ascertaining his or her wishes.

Other areas warranted further inquiry. Failure to obtain consultation, not providing alternative treatment plans, the claim that in almost all cases life was shortened only a few hours or days—all these were accepted without challenge. Van der Maas seemed concerned that to do otherwise would compromise the investigation's neutrality. I had the impression that the study's interviewers—who were primarily physicians—were questioning their colleagues in a somewhat collegial manner.

The Remmelink Commission accepted the report with one major addition. They felt that even if it was appropriate to terminate cases without explicit request, such cases should also be reported to the authorities. In November 1993 legislation was subsequently passed putting into law what had previously been case law: if force majeure applied, the physician would not be prosecuted for assisted suicide and euthanasia (although both still remained illegal), but physicians would be required to report all cases in which life was terminated without explicit request. The KNMG is opposed to this broadening of the notification procedure, particularly since the new legislative protection does not include cases terminated without request, which would have to be decided on a case-by-case basis. The new law, however, also includes the physician's "mental duress" as an exceptional circumstance that could exempt a doctor from prosecution, and, conceivably, it could be used in a defense of involuntary euthanasia since the consent of the patient killed is irrelevant in such a defense.

If in his private comments van der Maas seemed concerned about terminations of life without request, in his public utterances he was more restrained in his criticism. Following publication of the report, he wrote an article demonstrating that in many of the cases in which patients' lives were ended without their consent, doctors had been required to make emergency decisions about patients who were not competent or fully competent.[34] However, when I asked how he felt about broadening the notification procedure to include such cases, he said it was right to do so. That seemed to say more than anything else that he regards the problem as serious.

In an earlier study of euthanasia in Dutch hospitals, doctors explained to H. W. Hilhorst that they resorted to active euthanasia of sick people without their patients' knowledge when they did not have either the courage or the cruelty to talk openly to the patient and offer the option of death.[35] From a psychological point of view, cowardice, cruelty, and guilt are probably involved in equal measure. The frequency of this practice in the Netherlands suggests that Dutch doctors are no more comfortable than their American counterparts in dealing with the terminally ill as people.

Doctors and nurses told Hilhorst that more requests for euthanasia came from the patient's family than the patient; he concluded that the family, the doctors, and the nurses often pressured the patient to request euthanasia. Others have reported such pressure outside of the hospital environment. A Dutch medical journal noted an example of a wife who no longer wished to care for her sick husband; she gave him a choice between euthanasia and admission to a home for the chronically ill. The man, afraid of being with strangers in an unfamiliar place, chose to be killed. His doctor, although aware of the coercion, ended the man's life.[36] The Remmelink Report provided little information about such pressure apart from the finding that more than half of Dutch physicians considered it appropriate to introduce the subject of euthanasia with their patients. Virtually all the euthanasia advocates I spoke to in the Netherlands saw this as enabling the patient to consider an option that he or she may have felt inhibited about bringing up and not as a form of coercion.

The attitudes, needs, and limitations of the physicians are as critical as those of the patient in determining the outcome in euthanasia cases. While I was at the Dutch Voluntary Euthanasia Society (NVVE) the staff wanted me to see *An Appointment with Death*, a film (in English) about euthanasia. One of the cases presented involved a man of about 60 who was diagnosed with cancer and told he had a year to live. He arranged for his doctor to help end his life when the symptoms became intolerable, and discussed his decision with his wife and grown children. He felt the peace of mind his decision had given him left him free to fight the disease. Several years later he was still active, pleased that he had lived longer than predicted, and satisfied with how he had handled matters. His case was surely as reasonable an argument for euthanasia as one could make. The man had no suicidal intention to begin with, was not trying to end his life prematurely, and used the knowledge that he could die comfortably to live as long as he could without anxiety.

Another case involved a young man, seemingly in his mid-30s, who was diagnosed as HIV-positive. He had no physical symptoms, but he had seen other AIDS patients suffer and he wanted his physician's assistance in dying. The doctor compassionately explained to him that he might live for some years symptom-free. Over time the young man repeated his request and eventually his doctor acceded to it. The young man was clearly depressed and overwhelmed by the news of his situation. The doctor kept establishing that the young man was persistent in his request, but did not address the terror that underlay it. I was convinced that with the care of a psychologically sensitive physician, this young man would not have needed to be put to death.

Most recently the Dutch have begun to accept psychological distress as justification for assisted suicide or euthanasia whether or not physical illness is present. Although assisted suicide for a small number of psychiatric patients who are suicidal has been practiced for some time, the trial in 1993 of Dr. Boudewijn Chabot established a legal basis for assisting in such suicides and brought the issue to international attention.[37]

Chabot told me that he first became interested in euthanasia through a personal experience in 1989. A young woman he knew who was not ill medically or psychiatrically wanted to die. He referred her for therapy so she could consider it in a "balanced way." Her therapist agreed to assist in the suicide if she was unable to transform the young woman's wish to die into a wish to change her life. Although the young woman made one suicide attempt during psychotherapy, she did not kill herself. If the patient is told in advance, Chabot added, that the doctor will never assist in suicide, there is no reason for the patient to talk. He was impressed by the therapist's approach to and management of the case and wished to treat patients in a similar way, including entering into an agreement that the therapist will provide death if treatment fails.

Chabot contacted the NVVE for referrals. In July 1991 he was called about "Netty Boomsma"—the fictional name he has given to his Assen patient—who had lost her 20-year-old second son to cancer in May 1991. Her first son had died by suicide some years earlier, also at the age of 20. Netty was now interested only in suicide. Chabot told the NVVE caller that Netty was in a state of bereavement and needed time to complete the process. Try to convince her, his caller urged.

Since she had to travel a long distance, Netty was seen for two ninety-minute sessions on her first visit. On that day, she told Chabot that the suicide of her first son had been completely unexpected. He was on military duty in Germany and was involved in his first serious love affair when the young woman he was seeing left him for another young man. While home on a visit Netty's son was sad but never spoke of suicide and he returned to Germany for the last weeks of his tour. While on guard duty, he carried a loaded gun and shot himself in the heart. He left a note for his mother, brother, and father saying they were the best, but that he could not live without his girl friend. On the day her second son died of cancer, Netty bought a burial spot between her two sons. That evening, after her friends left and she was alone, Netty took pills in a suicide attempt. She wanted a funeral together with her second son.

Netty, Chabot told me, was a social worker, trained to be introspective. She knew the sort of information he wanted to hear. They could go into issues quickly. At the end of the first day she asked for Vesparox, a mixture of short- and long-acting barbiturates used by some in assisted suicide. "You are not the first person I have been to," she said. She had asked her general practitioner, a psychologist, and a psychiatric social worker to assist in her suicide. All had refused her. She showed him letters she had written requesting help. All the replies advised her to see a psychiatrist. One wrote, "If there is really no possibility for you, the psychiatrist will soon know."

Chabot told her he needed time. "There may be alternatives," he said, "I don't know." He assured her that he would not drag on the interviews. She told him that every day was awful for her. She was not a "believer," but felt she was "pulled to her boys." Chabot made a commitment to help her with her suicide if she would really go into her life in her sessions with him.

From August 3, 1991, when he saw her for the first time, to September 7, when the decision to go ahead was made, he saw her a total of thirty hours. Some sessions included her sister, some her sister and brother-in-law since, Chabot said, they were all close. Netty's sister and her husband loved Netty, he said, but supported her decision. Her sister said Netty had wanted to die since the death of her first son, who was her favorite, but felt she could not do it because of her second boy, a dyslexic who had difficulties in school and who ought not to be left with his alcoholic father.

Chabot told me that Netty's marriage was a disaster from the beginning. She was 23 and her husband was 28. She was not really in love but married to get away from an unpleasant relationship with a domineering mother and a father who went along with whatever her mother wanted. Her husband believed a woman should stay at home, which she did for a while, although she felt caged. She decided to work and earn her own money. Netty told Chabot she started to live the day her first child was born. The child made it possible for her to be something apart from her disapproving mother. Six years later she had her second son. When her children were small she went to social work school at night, while she held a job she enjoyed during the day. Netty continued to work until January 1990, when her son's chemotherapy started.

Netty's husband blamed her for their eldest son's death, saying that she was responsible for their son's education and so was responsible for his suicide. He would beat up Netty when he was drunk. She would leave him, but then she would go back because of her second son. She planned at one point to kill herself and her second son by driving into a canal, but felt she could not take his life.

At the end of 1988, a few weeks after her father died, she left her husband and her son went with her. By then her son had become a comfort to her. He understood her grief and tried to console her. Over the years he became even more important to her.

Netty felt guilty that she had not divorced her husband earlier. She had thought things would improve when they had children, but then felt she could not separate her children from their father, which she later realized was an excuse not to divorce. Remaining in the marriage was the main failure of her life, she said. If she had left perhaps things would have been different and her son would not have killed himself.

By the summer of 1989 both her sister and her brother-in-law felt she was almost her old self, but her former energy never returned. Before her son's suicide, Netty was involved in many activities, particularly painting. Those interests ceased with his death.

In November 1990 her second son went to the hospital for injuries sustained in an auto accident. While there it was discovered that he had a malignant, inoperable teratoma of the lung.

The only possible treatment was chemotherapy. Her son died as a consequence of the chemotherapy, which destroyed his white blood cells. At the end he was being maintained on a respirator that Netty agreed to have disconnected.

On August 25, 1991, Netty told Chabot they had gone into all the details of her life, and that she had not come for bereavement therapy, although she had gone through that briefly after her first son's death. She needed an answer to her question: Was he going to help her with her suicide? Although the process might be going too quickly for him, she was not coming back unless he agreed to help her. If he did not help her, she might do it herself.

Chabot told her that he needed to have the opinion of consultants regarding the decision. He made a complete written summary of her case as he knew it. He asked a number of experts for their opinion, two of whom, including Joost Schudel, professor of psychiatry at Erasmus University, did not recommend that Chabot go forward. Schudel felt it was not appropriate because the patient needed bereavement therapy and not assisted suicide, and he felt her condition was not irremediable, so if she refused treatment, suicide should not be permitted. Chabot contended that Netty was comparable to the patient who can refuse chemotherapy for cancer and request euthanasia if there is only a small chance for treatment to succeed. The other experts agreed with him, seemingly because Netty's suffering was unbearable and there was little chance that therapy would help. They said it was appropriate for Chabot to assist in the suicide. Among these was Carlo Mittendorf, a clinical psychologist specializing in bereavement.

Chabot asked only Dr. Frank van Ree, one of the few Dutch psychiatrists publishing on assisted suicide, to see the patient, but van Ree felt it was not necessary. Since the majority of the consultants agreed with Chabot, and particularly since the expert in bereavement therapy thought the chances for improvement were slight, Chabot went ahead.

Chabot had one more session with Netty, her sister, and brother-in-law where he still tried to persuade her to postpone the decision. She persisted in saying she did not want bereavement therapy. Her sister was emotional in saying good-bye. She said she and Netty had cared for their father when he was dying and now she and her husband would be with Netty till the end. Chabot said he needed them to come back one more time since he had not received all the replies to his letters requesting consultation.

Her last visit to his office was on September 20. She brought a friend, a married woman, along with her sister. He said he would get her the pills by the first of October. (It would not be a mixture of barbiturates, which might not be lethal for twenty-four hours.) The Royal Dutch Association for the Advancement of Pharmacy, in a manual available only to doctors, recommended a mixture that would act more quickly and that Chabot eventually had a pharmacist prepare for him.

Chabot said the most difficult time he had was the week prior to Netty's death. She had been so grateful and so considerate of his feelings, and had said to him, "I feel so good, but I know you are having a hard time."

Prior to September 27, Netty's final day, Chabot said he had much to do. He typed up a report of all his interviews so they would be available for the public prosecutor after her death. He met with Netty and her friend once more to discuss the details. Netty's ex-husband did not accept her decision. He said he would call the police and that she would be put in a hospital, and he told Netty he would report Chabot to the police if he assisted her. Since her ex-husband could drop in at her house at any time and could be violent, her car was moved so her husband would not know she was home. Chabot said he felt like he was in a detective film.

Netty's sister and brother-in-law changed their minds about being with Netty until the end. Her sister said they did not want to be there because their children would then ask for details. Netty's friend would be there, however. At the last minute Chabot invited a colleague and friend who was a general practitioner to witness the death so he could testify in court as to how Chabot behaved. Chabot complained that his friend is now in trouble and may have to appear before a medical tribunal to explain his participation in the case.

Chabot, his friend, Netty, and her friend sat around a table at Netty's home. Chabot told Netty, "I hope you don't feel pressed to go on just because we are here." She said she wanted to go ahead. She asked to be in the room of her younger son, on his bed. They all went upstairs and Chabot gave her the liquid as well as some capsules. She opened the capsules as she had been advised and put them in some yogurt. Jokingly she asked him if he could not have given her some capsules before to practice with. She sat down on the bed and asked them to play the recording of a Bach flute sonata that had been played at her son's funeral. She drank the liquid, saying it was not too bad. The music was playing and there was a photograph of her two sons next to the bed. Netty kissed the picture. She asked her friend to sit next to her. Her friend was stroking her hair. Netty said she had made a great effort to fix her hair and her friend was messing it up. The friend replied she would make it beautiful later. Netty asked Chabot, "Why do young kids want suicide?" Chabot recalls saying to her after five minutes, "Think of your boys." Within seven minutes, she lost consciousness while being held by her friend. Then she slept. Her heart stopped in a half-hour.

Although Chabot followed the approved procedure for officially reporting an unnatural death, nearly one year after Netty's death, in the summer of 1992, there was a police investigation. He said, "They spoke to her friend, her sister, her former husband, her former psychiatrist, me, everybody." Chabot waited through a long difficult period until December 1992, when he was told that he would have to go to court.

The court case was heard in Assen in April 1993. The trial took an entire day. In Dutch courts there is no jury; decisions are made by three judges. The defendant speaks first and last, if he so chooses. The judges had all the written reports solicited by Chabot, including the two that were negative. An ethicist whom Chabot had later asked for an opinion had sided with Chabot. Three consultants who agreed with Chabot, including Dries Van Dantzig, a professor of psychotherapy, were asked to appear in person. The prosecutor's expert witness, Robert Giel, a professor of social psychology at the University of Groningen, also wrote an opinion that the assisted suicide was justified. The prosecutor asked for a one-year conditional sentence, which meant that if he were found guilty, Chabot would go to prison for a year only if he repeated the offense.

After the prosecutor and Chabot's defense attorney delivered their summations, Chabot was asked if he wished to make concluding remarks. He did and asked them to judge him, not Netty. He read from portions of letters she wrote to him. She spoke of their closeness through the shared experience of her impending death; she expressed her gratitude to Chabot for facilitating the anticipated peaceful reunion with her boys. Chabot said she was not a patient, but a woman who did not want to live. Later that month, Chabot learned that he was acquitted. The court said he was guilty of assisting in her suicide, but with good reason—that he had had an overpowering conflict of duties, he had followed the guidelines, and that there was only a small chance of success with bereavement therapy. The court felt Netty had irremediable suffering and the fact that the source of her suffering was mental rather than physical was not relevant.

The ministry of justice took the case to an appeals court in Leeuwaarden. There van Ree was asked to testify as to why he did not see the patient himself. Van Ree explained that he felt he understood the case and that it would only cause the patient pain to be seen again. Was it less harmful to her to help her commit suicide?

At the end of September 1993 Chabot learned that he had been exonerated by the appeals court. The Leeuwaarden court, as is common in the Netherlands, slightly modified the Assen court's opinion in the matter. The Leeuwaarden court ruled that since the source of the suffering was not somatic, it was relevant to look into psychiatric pathology since the competence of the person was at stake. Since all the experts agreed the patient was competent, the court upheld the decision, adding to the case law that now constitutes the de facto legalization of assisted suicide and euthanasia the idea that a patient a physician claims is not suffering from either psychiatric or physical illness can receive assisted suicide simply because he or she is unhappy.

The Dutch Supreme Court, which ruled on the Assen Case in June 1994, agreed with the lower courts in affirming that mental suffering can be grounds for euthanasia, but found Chabot guilty of not having had a psychiatric consultant see the patient. Although the court expressed the belief that such consultation was necessary in the absence of physical illness, it imposed no punishment since it felt that in all other regards Chabot had behaved responsibly. The case was seen as a triumph by euthanasia advocates since it legally established mental suffering as a basis for euthanasia.[38] It was clear that Chabot could have persuaded a consultant who agreed with him to see the patient had he known that would be necessary.

Netty Boomsma's relationship with Chabot seems to illustrate what one would suspect: that some suicidal patients would use an agreement to assist in their suicide to mark time until the therapist feels obliged to fulfill the promise. This type of contract seems to me psychologically unsound, similar to one often made in America requiring suicidal patients to not kill themselves before calling the therapist.

Suicidal patients often have fantasies, sometimes conscious but more often unconscious, that cast the therapist in the role of executioner. A commitment on the therapist's part to become that if treatment fails plays into and reenforces these fantasies. It may also play into the therapist's illusion that if he cannot cure the patient, no one else can either. Since no therapy could be said to have been undertaken with Netty, it is not surprising that Chabot insists she was not a patient, but simply a woman who wanted to die. Therapy would have required challenging the premise under which she contacted and visited him.

Chabot stated that if he did not agree to her terms Netty would have never come back. I asked why, if she did not follow *his* prescription for treatment, he would feel obliged to follow *hers*. Certainly at the end he appeared to be succumbing to emotional blackmail.

Chabot may be right that if he refused her demand she would have sought another physician: in the Netherlands assisted suicide is an available option Netty could have obtained from another doctor. Clearly, she was a patient who needed someone to play the role of her executioner. Both she and Chabot experienced a closeness in her death. There seemed to be some feeling on Chabot's part of needing to be included in the patient's death if he were unable to help the patient live.

Chabot seems to have entered into Netty's fantasy of death as a reunion. His comment to Netty right before her death that she should think about her boys suggests that he, too, saw her death

metaphorically, as a return to her lost children. By metaphoriz-
ing death as something other than death, it is made to appear
an attractive, fairytale-like option. But beneath the surface, such
metaphors, like fairytales, contain some of the most tormented
and savage emotions there are. Not treating Netty as a depressed
patient but as a devoted mother whose desire to join her sons in
death was not a sign of her disturbance but a legitimate and real-
izable goal, makes it impossible to explore her guilt toward her
children and her need for punishment.

From what Chabot was able to elicit from Netty in the sessions
where her relatives were not present, it was clear that bereavement counseling was likely to fail, but that less narrowly focused
psychotherapy might have succeeded. Netty's personality problems far anteceded her bereavement. She had told Chabot she
became a person only when her first son was born and that she
stayed alive only for the sake of her second son. Chabot was playing into her way of relating by asking her to give him more time,
that is, to stay alive for his sake.

Netty needed someone who could tell her in a firm but kind
way that she had never really lived for herself and that it was not
too late to try. She could always kill herself but she ought to give
life a chance first. Netty's guilt over her first son's suicide had
sources deeper than her failure to get a divorce. Caring for her
second son seems to have had something of the quality of an
atonement. One suspects that therapy might have engaged her
had it provided her with the opportunity to understand her relationship to her sons *before* she decided to join them in death.

No one should underestimate the grief of a mother who has
lost a beloved child, but neither should one ignore the many
ways life offers us to deal with the feelings of loss, guilt, and pain
a child's death is likely to arouse. The Dutch like to present
patients with concrete alternatives. For Netty, my suggestion

would have been to utilize her skills as a social worker and involve her in a facility or project devoted to youth suicide prevention. Her last words to Chabot, "Why do young kids want suicide?" suggest that work that permitted her to deal with that question might have engaged her in a way that would have been more positive for her as well as for those she might have helped.

Opposition to assisted suicide and euthanasia is limited in the Netherlands and estimated in polls at 20 to 25 percent of the population. Most of the opposition, both medical and in the community at large, is dismissed by advocates as coming from religious conservatives and those people, mainly Jewish, who lost families in Nazi concentration camps and are said by some advocates to be unable to be objective about euthanasia.

Karl Gunning is a now-retired physician who helped found the Dutch Physicians' Association, a small group of doctors that split off from the KNMG because of disagreements on abortion and euthanasia. He told me the association's membership has dwindled from 1,200 to 600 members, approximately 2 percent of the KNMG's total of 30,000. Gunning believes that if more people were aware of the extent of involuntary euthanasia, the situation might change.

Some people, concerned that their lives might be ended without their consent, have joined the Dutch Patients Association (60,000 members), a group organized by Protestants opposed to both euthanasia and abortion. The association receives inquiries from people wanting to know if a particular hospital is "safe," and, together with the Stichting Schuilplaats (Sanctuary Foundation), a religious group also opposed to euthanasia, they distribute a "passport for life" indicating that, in medical emergencies, a patient does not want his or her life terminated without their consent.

Dutch euthanasia advocates are dismissive of or defensive

about any criticism of assisted suicide or euthanasia in the Netherlands. I was not entirely reassured to find that the most knowledgeable supporters of euthanasia are privately willing to discuss the abuses in their system even if they publicly deny that there are problems. The Dutch overreactions to criticism of their euthanasia policies, and their many published articles that deny their problems, lead one to fear that they might never address the need for reform.

Most opponents of euthanasia are willing to concede that no one is going to undo de facto legalization of euthanasia in the Netherlands. The Dutch have accomplished something they wanted: giving their citizens the reassurance that they will not have to endure an unnecessarily prolonged, painful ending to their lives. Even if the Dutch public were fully aware of the contents of the difficult-to-read Remmelink Report or its implications, they would probably not want to undo what they consider their right to euthanasia, although they might insist on some better control.

The issue for the Netherlands is whether or not the Dutch can gain better control of euthanasia and also the process by which patients' lives are ended without their consent. There is no consensus on removing the criminal penalties against euthanasia and assisted suicide, penalties that the public has the impression serve as a form of control over the doctor's behavior. With prosecutors, consultants, experts, attorneys, and probably judges concerned that any legal decision must protect euthanasia, and hence the doctor, from its opponents, with public sympathies on the side of the doctor, who in most instances would not be on trial if he had not reported the case, and with what is known about the case being primarily what the doctor chooses to reveal, in euthanasia cases the Dutch judicial system presents a ritualized drama that allows for some subtle, minor improvisation before admonishment or acquittal. If our adversarial judicial system could be said at times to sacrifice justice on the altar of victory, in the Netherlands the sacrifice seems to have been for the sake of what the Dutch would regard as the higher goal of social harmony.

American, British, and some Dutch jurists do not like the way in which force majeure, a concept ordinarily invoked to justify extreme actions taken when necessary to defend, not to take, life, has been used as the legal underpinning for the support and medicalization of euthanasia and assisted suicide. Originally the Dutch courts interpreted force majeure as applying if virtually anyone in the doctor's situation would have acted as he did. Subsequently, the courts have interpreted it as applying if any other member of the medical profession would have acted as the doctor did. Joseph Welie, an ethicist at the University of Nijmegen, points out that this ruling elevates physicians to a superior moral status whose judgments on life and death are always just. When combined with Dutch acceptance of the use of a sympathetic colleague as a consultant, there is an increasing tendency to free the physician from legal control.[39] Moreover, considering the unexpected frequency with which physicians end the lives of patients without their consent, several Dutch euthanasia advocates have conceded privately that the general acceptance of euthanasia has probably encouraged doctors to feel they can decide for patients what is an acceptable quality of life.

Euthanasia, fought for on the basis of the principle of autonomy and self-determination of patients, has actually increased the paternalistic power of the medical profession in the Netherlands. Doctors' organizations behave like groups or unions everywhere—they protect the interests of their members. Doctors are especially unaccustomed to explaining their decisions to nonphysicians. American medicine has reluctantly accepted that in matters of what we call "quality assurance," the different perspectives of nurses, social workers, psychologists, and even lay administrators can be invaluable even if the initial impulse is to resent it.

The acceptance of euthanasia for psychiatric patients who are suicidal is simply bad psychiatry. It seems the inevitable consequence of allowing such criteria as "competence" and "intolerable suffering" to determine the outcome rather than sound clinical judgment. The idea that a depressed patient can make a decision for suicide uninfluenced by his pathology only demonstrates how limited "competence" is as a criterion for evaluating those who are suicidal. In these cases, the psychiatrist is in the position of working to prevent suicide until the patient asks for his assistance in committing suicide; then, the rules of the game change and the psychiatrist negotiates with the patient as to whose approach is best.

Seriously suicidal patients want suicide. In a society that makes euthanasia accessible for them they will be harder to treat, not easier. Many of them fantasize closeness in death with a person who kills them, and given that some psychiatrists and general practitioners have complementary fantasies, euthanasia fulfills their needs as much as the patient's.

The Assen case has given psychiatrists and psychologists in the Netherlands reason to question where they are going. Unless one is prepared to declare that in euthanasia the Dutch have found a cure for suicide, one can only hope the Dutch will take a second look at their current policies. Even patients who desire an early death during a terminal illness are usually suffering from a depression that is treatable; they are likely to be different from those who seek to avoid pain in the last days of terminal illness. Strikingly, the vast majority of the terminally ill fight for life to the end. Some may voice suicidal thoughts in response to transient depression or severe pain, but those patients usually respond well to treatment for depressive illness and pain medication, and are usually grateful to be alive. Those who need to bring suicide and death into the relationship with their physician and use it coercively may be expressing a more severe depression than their doctors may recognize.

Evaluation of the prospective euthanasia patient by psychiatrists knowledgeable about suicide, depression, and terminal illness cannot provide us with a simple solution to a complex social problem. Nor should psychiatrists be sanguine at being reduced to the role, suggested by some, of simply determining if a patient is competent to make a decision regarding euthanasia. It was the fact that I was not the arbiter of his case that permitted the patient I described with acute myelocytic leukemia to talk freely about his fears of death and eventually to change his mind about wanting an immediate end to his life.

Psychological issues play an equally important role in cases that are medical in origin. Doctors both in the Netherlands and the United States are insufficiently sensitive to the influence a doctor has on a patient's decision in these matters. Those doctors who are most emotionally involved in euthanasia and most interested in actually performing it may be those whose own needs in the matter should disqualify them.

Virtually all Dutch advocates of euthanasia familiar with the United States see our legalizing assisted suicide and/or euthanasia as unwise for a variety of reasons. From their perspective, the United States is not characterized by either a legal or medical system that fosters social harmony, but that instead pits one profession against the other. They believe the tendency of American patients in general to litigation would make euthanasia a nightmare for physicians. They cite social and economic disparities in health care as another source of contention and recognize that without comprehensive care for the sickly poor and the elderly, assisted suicide and euthanasia will tend to become their only options. The Dutch believe their hospitals are not subject to the economic pressure to get rid of the terminally ill that would be present in this country. The relative absence of the family doctor, the core of medical practice in the Netherlands, eliminates what the Dutch perceive as a major source of patient protection. Further contaminating the process in the United States would be the difficulty of preventing the profit motive from making euthanasia and assisted suicide a lucrative business.

If assisted suicide and euthanasia were legalized in this country, it is likely to encourage involuntary euthanasia, as has happened in the Netherlands. If involuntary euthanasia with competent patients alone were to take place in the United States at the same frequency as it does in the Netherlands, at the most conservative estimate it would lead to 75,000 such deaths a year—more than the current number of suicides and homicides combined.

The Dutch have had twenty years of experience, court cases, and KNMG deliberation to help them reach a social consensus on euthanasia. In contrast, in our country, proposals for legalizing assisted suicide and euthanasia have been hastily introduced without a sufficient body of case law or procedures to define acceptable perameters for all.

Nor would a social consensus be simply the answer to the question "Are you in favor of euthanasia?" A majority of people are, by which they mean little more than that they would rather die painlessly than painfully. If the question were asked "If terminally ill, would you rather be given treatment to make you comfortable or have your life ended by a physician?" responses might be different. The question "If terminally ill, should you (or someone you delegate) or your doctor decide when you should die," is also likely to evoke a different set of responses.

Kevorkian and other doctors are testing the American judicial system in the same way that some Dutch doctors tested the Dutch system. It has been suggested that prosecutors would feel freer to exercise their own discretion as to where to prosecute if they could consult with an arbitration panel representing diverse perspectives. This would permit us to deal with euthanasia and assisted suicide on a case-by-case basis without giving it legal sanction.[40]

Kevorkian's acquittal in the case in which he assisted in the suicide of a patient dying painfully of amyotrophic lateral sclerosis, does not open the floodgates for such cases as feared by opponents of assisted suicide, nor does it suggest the need for legalization of assisted suicide, as hoped for by its advocates.[41] There have been many comparable cases where a suffering, dying patient's life has been ended by a doctor, and in no case so far has an American jury convicted a physician. Some of Kevorkian's cases, who were not terminally ill but were fearful of becoming so, might arouse a less sympathetic response from a jury.

More is needed than case-by-case testing in the courts. We need a national commission to explore and develop a consensus on the care and treatment of the terminally ill in the United States—a scientific commission similar to the President's commission that in 1983 gave us guidelines about foregoing life-sustaining treatment with dying patients.[42] Work of a wider scope needs to be done now. There is a great deal of evidence that in the United States, as in the Netherlands, doctors are not sufficiently trained in the relief of pain and other symptoms in the terminally ill. Hospice care is in its infancy in both countries. We have not yet educated the public as to the choices they have in refusing or terminating treatment that prolongs a painful process of dying. Nor have we devoted enough time in our medical schools to educating future physicians about coming to terms with the painful truth that there will be patients they will not be able to save but whose needs they must address.

The relationship between doctor and patient and the attitude of each in facing serious or terminal illness is at the heart of the matter. Dr. C. Everett Koop captured this in discussing "the intent of the heart" in treating a hypothetical older woman with a powerful painkiller. "The intent behind the gradual administration of drugs is to be her ally in her remaining hours or days of her life and to keep her comfortable as she slips away. The intent behind . . . the drug overdose, is to get her 'out of her misery' and 'off our hands' as quickly as possible."[43]

It will not always be possible to know the "intent of the heart" or to uncover the intense ambivalence that illness, treatment, and imminent death inflame in both doctors and patients. There are now, and will continue to be, abuses. But as long as producing death with the intent of doing so is illegal, as long as physicians know that in case of a complaint they will have to be able to justify their actions to their peers and to the legal system, the amount of such abuse will be limited. If a doctor chooses to break the law he should do so with full knowledge of the seriousness of his action. The protection of the honorable physician does not now warrant legalizing physician-assisted suicide or euthanasia in a society where the public is relatively uninformed of present abuses and where there exists the potential for much greater abuses if legalization occurs.

How we deal with illness, age, and decline says a great deal about who and what we are, both as individuals and as a society. The growing number of people living to old age and the increasing incidence of depression in people of all ages presents us with a medical challenge. Our efforts should concentrate on providing treatment, relieving pain for the intractably ill, and, in the case of terminal illness, helping the individual come to terms with death.

If those advocating legalization of assisted suicide prevail, it will be a reflection that as a culture we are turning away from efforts to improve our care of the mentally ill, the infirm, and the elderly. Instead, we would be licensing the right to abuse and exploit the fears of the ill and depressed. We would be accepting the view of those who are engulfed in suicidal despair that death is the preferred solution to the problems of illness, age, and depression.

My primary aim in going to the Netherlands was to learn what I could that might be applicable to this country. The people I met on both sides of the question in the Netherlands were intelligent and caring. If they had not been, their experience would have less relevance for us. Yet, in the name of humanitarian goals, bright and compassionate people can inappropriately end other people's lives. There seems to be much we can learn from the Dutch experience.

References

Introduction

1. H. Hendin, *Suicide and Scandinavia* (New York: W. W. Norton, 1965).
2. H. Hendin, *Black Suicide* (New York: Basic Books, 1969); H. Hendin, *The Age of Sensation* (New York: W. W. Norton, 1975); H. Hendin and A. P. Haas, *The Wounds of War: The Psychological Aftermath of Combat in Vietnam* (New York: Basic Books, 1984).
3. K. Minkoff, E. Bergman, A. T. Beck, et al., "Hopelessness, Depression, and Attempted Suicide," *American Journal of Psychiatry* 130 (1973): 455–59.
4. A. T. Beck, R. A. Steer, M. Kovacs, and G. Garrison, "Hopelessness and Eventual Suicide: A Ten-Year Prospective Study of Patients Hospitalized with Suicidal Ideation," *Am J Psychiatry* 142 (1985): 559–63.
5. R. E. Drake, C. Gates, P. G. Cotton, and A. Whitaker, "Suicide among Schizophrenics: Who Is at Risk?" *Journal of Nervous and Mental Disorders* 172 (1984): 613–17; R. E. Drake, C. Gates, A. Whitaker, and P. G. Cotton, "Suicide among Schizophrenics: A Review," *Comprehensive Psychiatry* 26 (1985): 90–100.
6. B. Winchel, B. Stanley, and M. Stanley, "Behavioral Aspects of Suicide," in *Suicide and the Life Cycle,* ed. S. J. Blumenthal and D. J. Kupfer (Washington, D.C.: American Psychiatric Press, 1990).
7. M. Åsberg, P. Thuren, L. Traskman, et al., "Serotonin Depression: A Biochemical Subgroup within the Affective Disorders?" *Science* 191 (1976): 478–80.
8. G. L. Brown, M. H. Ebert, P. F. Goyer, et al., "Aggression, Suicide, and Serotonin: Relationship to CSF Amine Metabolites," *Am J Psychiatry* 139 (1982): 741–46; H. M. Van Praag, "CSF 5-HIAA and Suicide in Nondepressed Schizophrenics," *The Lancet*, 2 (1983): 977–78; M. Linnoila, M. Virkunnen, M. Scheinin, et al., "Low Cerebrospinal Fluid 5-Hydroxyindoleacetic Acid Concentration Differentiates Impulsive from Non-Impulsive Violent Behavior," *Life Sciences* 33 (1983): 2609–14; M. Virkunnen, A. Nuutila, F. M. Goodwin, et al., "Cerebrospinal Fluid Monoamine Metabolite Levels in Male Arsonists," *Archives of General Psychiatry* 44 (1987): 241–47; S. S. Kety, "Genetic Features in Suicide: Family, Twins, and Adoption Studies," in *Sui-*

cide Over the Life Cycle, ed. S. J. Blumenthal and D. Kupfer (Washington, D.C.: American Psychiatric Press, 1990).

9. L. Traskman-Bendz, M. Åsberg, L. Bertilsson, et al., "CSF Mondamine Metabolites of Depressed Patients during Illness and after Recovery," *Acta Psychiatr Scand* 69 (1984): 333–42.

10. M. Åsberg, P. Nordstrom, and L. Traskman-Bendz, "Biological Factors in Suicide," in *Suicide*, ed. A. Roy (Baltimore: Williams and Wilkins, 1986).

11. J. J. Mann and M. Stanley, eds., *Psychobiology of Suicidal Behavior* (New York: New York Academy of Science, 1986).

12. F. J. Kallman and M. M. Anastasio, "Twin Studies on the Psychopathology of Suicide," *J Nerv Ment Dis* 105 (1947): 40–55; F. M. Kallman, J. DePorte, E. DePorte, et al., "Suicide in Twins and Only Children," *American Journal of Human Genetics* 1 (1949): 113–26.

13. N. Juel-Nielsen and T. Videbech, "A Twin Study of Suicide," *Acta Geneticae Medicae et Gemellologiae* 19 (1970): 307–10; A. Bertelsen, B. Harvald, and M. Hauge, "A Danish Twin Study of Manic-Depressive Disorders," *British Journal of Psychiatry* 130 (1977): 330.

14. A. Roy, "Family History of Suicide," *Arch Gen Psychiatry* 40 (1983): 971–74; D. Brent, J. A. Perper, C. E. Goldstein, et al., "Risk Factors for Adolescent Suicide: A Comparison of Adolescent Suicide Victims with Suicidal Inpatients," *Arch Gen Psychiatry* 45 (1988): 581–88.

15. F. Schulsinger, S. S. Kety, D. Rosenthal, et al., "A Family History of Suicide," in *Origin, Prevention, and Treatment of Affective Disorders*, ed. M. Schou and E. Stromgren (New York: Academic Press, 1979).

16. J. D. Egeland and J. N. Sussex, "Suicide and Family Loading for Affective Disorders," *Journal of the American Medical Association* 254 (1985): 915–18.

17. B. Mitterauer. "A Contribution to the Discussion of the Role of the Genetic Factor in Suicide Based on Five Studies of an Epidemiologically Defined Area (Province of Salzburg, Austria)," *Comp Psychi* 31 (1990): 557–65.

18. S. S. Kety, "Factors in Suicide: Family, Twins, and Adoption Studies in Suicide Over the Life Cycle," ed. by S. J. Blumenthal and D. Kupfer (Washington, D.C.: American Psychiatric Press, 1990, pp. 127–33).

19. H. Hendin, "Psychodynamics of Suicide, with Particular Reference to the Young," *Am J Psychiatry* 148 (1991): 1150–58.

20. R. Plutchik and H. M. van Praag, "Psychosocial Correlates of Suicide and Violence Risk," in *Violence and Suicidality: Perspectives in Clinical and Psychological Research*, ed. H. M. van Praag, R. Plutchik, and A. Apter (New York: Brunner / Mazel, 1990).

21. M. Gould, D. Shaffer, and M. Davies, "Truncated Pathways from Childhood to Adulthood: Attrition in Follow-up Studies Due to Death," in *Straight and Devious Pathways to Adulthood*, ed. L. M. Robins and M. R. Rutter (Cambridge: Cambridge University Press, 1990).

22. J. T. Maltsberger, *Suicide Risk: The Formulation of Clinical Judgment* (New York: New York University Press, 1981).

23. R. Lifton, "Suicide: The Quest for a Future," in *Suicide: Understanding and Responding*, ed. D. Jacobs and H. Brown (Madison, Conn.: International Universities Press, 1989).

24. J. Fawcett, W. A. Scheftner, L. Fogg, D. C. Clark, M. A. Young, D. Hedeker, and R. Gibbons, "Time-Related Predictors of Suicide in Major Affective Disorder," *Am J Psychiatry* 147 (1990): 1189–94.

25. H. Hendin and A. P. Haas, "Suicide and Guilt as Manifestations of PTSD in Vietnam Combat Veterans," *Am J Psychiatry* 148 (1991): 586–91.

26. O. Kernberg, "Diagnosis and Clinical Management of Suicidal Potential in Borderline Patients," in *The Borderline Patient*, vol. 2 (Hillsdale, N.J.: Analytic Press, 1987).

27. H. Hendin, "Psychodynamics of Suicide," *Am J Psychiatry* 148 (1991): 1150–58.

28. S. Freud, "Mourning and Melancholia" (1917 [1915]), in *The Standard Edition of the Complete Psychological Works*, trans. and ed. J. Strachey, vol. 14 (London: Hogarth Press, 1957; New York: Norton, 1976), pp. 243–58.

29. H. Hendin, "Psychodynamics of Suicide," *Am J Psychiatry* 148 (1991): 1150–58.

30. E. Kilpatrick, "A Psychoanalytic Understanding of Suicide," *American Journal of Psychoanalysis* 8 (1948): 13–23.

31. O. Kernberg, "A Psychoanalytic Classification of Character Pathology," *Journal of the American Psychoanalytic Association* 18 (1970): 800–822.

32. H. Hendin, *Suicide and Scandinavia*.

33. H. Hendin, "Psychodynamics of Suicide," *Am J Psychiatry* 148 (1991): 1150–58.

34. H. Hendin, "Suicide: A Review of New Directions in Research," *Hospital Community Psychiatry* 37 (1986): 148–54; H. Hendin, "Growing Up Dead: Student Suicide," *American Journal of Psychotherapy* 29 (1975): 327–38; H. Hendin, "Youth Suicide: A Psychosocial Perspective," *Suicide and Life-Threatening Behavior* 17 (1987): 151–65.

35. H. Hendin, "Psychodynamics of Suicide," *Am J Psychiatry* 148 (1991): 1150–58.

36. G. L. Klerman, "Clinical Epidemiology of Suicide," *Journal of Clinical Psychiatry* 48 (1987: December supplement): 33–38; R. Mintz, "Basic Considerations in the Psychotherapy of the Depressed Suicidal Patient," *Am J Psychother* 25 (1971): 56–73; C. Pfeffer, *The Suicidal Child* (New York: Guilford Press, 1985).

37. H. Kohut, *The Analysis of the Self* (New York: International Universities Press, 1971); H. Kohut, *The Restoration of the Self* (New York: International Universities Press, 1971); O. Kernberg, *Borderline Conditions and Pathological Narcissism* (New York: Jason Aronson, 1985).

38. Hendin, "Psychodynamics of Suicide," *Am J Psychiatry* 148 (1991): 1150–58.

39. C. E. Koop and G. D. Lundberg, "Violence in America: A Public Health Emergency / Time to Bite the Bullet Back," *JAMA* 267 (1992): 3075–76.

40. R. E. Markush and A. A. Bartolucci, "Firearms and Suicide in the United States," *American Journal of Public Health* 74 (1984): 123–27; D. Lester and M. E. Murrell, "The Influence of Gun Control Laws on Personal Violence," *Journal of Community Psychology* 14 (1986): 315–18; D. Lester and M. E. Murrell, "The Preventive Effect of Strict Gun Control Laws on Suicide and Homicide," *Suicide Life-Threatening Behav* 12 (1982): 131–41; D. Lester and M. E. Murrell, "The Influence of Gun Control Laws on Suicidal Behavior," and *Am J Psychiatry* 137 (1980): 121–22; C. Loftin, D. McDowall, B. Wiersema, and T. J. Cottey, "Effects of Restrictive Licensing of Handguns on Homicide and Suicide in the District of Columbia," *New England Journal of Medicine* 325 (1991): 1615–20.

41. A. L. Kellermann and D. T. Reay, "Protection or Peril? An Analysis of Firearm-Related Deaths in the Home," *NEJM* 314 (1986): 1557–60.

42. A. L. Kellermann, F. P. Rivara, G. Somes, D. T. Reay, J. Francisco, J. G. Banton, J. Prodzinski, C. Fligner, and B. B. Hackman, "Suicide in the Home in Relation to Gun Ownership," *NEJM* 327 (1992): 467–72; D. A. Brent, J. A. Perper, G. Moritz, M. Baugher, and C. Allman, "Suicide in Adolescents with No Apparent Psychopathology," *Journal of the American Academy of Child and Adolescent Psychiatry* 32 (1993): 494–500.

43. C. H. Browning, "Suicide, Firearms, and Public Health," *American Journal of Public Health* 64 (1974): 313–17; R. Frierson, "Women Who Shoot Themselves," *Hospital and Community Psychiatry* 40 (1989): 841–43; A. L. Kellermann, F. P. Rivara, G. Somes, D. T. Reay, J. G. Banton, J. Prodzinski, C. Fligner, and B. B. Hackman, "Suicide in the Home in Relation to Gun Ownership," *NEJM* 327 (1992): 467–472; L. G. Peterson, M. C. Peterson, G. J. O'Shanick, and A. Swann, "Self-Inflicted Gunshot Wounds: Lethality of Method versus Intent," *Am J Psychiatry* 142 (1985): 228–31.

44. D. A. Brent, J. A. Perper, G. Moritz, M. Baugher, J. Schweers, and C. Roth, "Firearms and Adolescent Suicide: A Community Case-Control Study," *American Journal of Diseases of Children* (in press); W. G. Hlady and J. P. Middaugh, "Suicides in Alaska: Firearms and Alcohol," *Am J Public Health* 78 (1988): 179–80; J. H. Sloan, F. P. Rivara, D. T. Reay, J. A. J. Ferris, and A. L. Kellermann, "Firearm Regulations and Rates of Suicide—A Comparison of Two Metropolitan Areas," *NEJM* 322 (1990): 369–73; D. A. Brent, J. A. Perper, C. E. Goldstein, D. J. Kolko, M. J. Allan, C. J. Allman, and J. P. Zelenak, "Risk Factors for Adolescent Suicide: A Comparison of Adolescent Suicide Victims with Suicidal Inpatients," *Arch Gen Psychiatry* 45 (1988): 581–88; D. A. Brent, J. A. Perper, C. J. Allman, G. M. Moritz, M. Wartella, and J. P. Zelenak, "The Presence and Accessibility of Firearms in the Homes of Adolescent Suicides: A Case-Control Study," *JAMA* 266 (1991): 2989–95.

45. B. Barraclough, D. Shepherd, and C. Jennings, "Do Newspaper Reports of Coroners' Inquests Incite People to Commit Suicide?" *Bri J Psychi* 131 (1977): 528–32; D. P. Phillips and L. L. Cartensen, "Clustering of Teenage Suicide after Television News Stories about Suicide," *NEJM* 315 (1986): 685–89; I. M. Wasserman, "Imitation and Suicide: A Reexamination of the Werther

Effect," *American Sociological Review* 49 (1984): 427–36; S. Blumenthal and L. Berger, "Suicide and Newspapers: A Replicated State," *Am J Psychiatry* 130 (1973): 468–71; J. Motto, "Newspaper Influence on Suicide," *Arch Gen Psychiatry* 23 (1970): 143–48.

46. M. S. Gould, "Suicide Clusters and Media Exposure," in *Suicide Over the Life Cycle*, ed. S. Blumenthal and D. Kupfer (New York: American Psychiatric Press, 1990).

47. N. C. Andreasen, "Creativity and Mental Illness," *Am J Psychiatry* 144 (1987): 1288–92.

48. Ibid.

49. H. S. Akiskal and K. Akiskal, "Reassessing the Prevalence of Bipolar Disorders: Clinical Significance and Artistic Creativity," *Psychiatry and Psychobiology* 3 (1988): 29s–36s.

50. H. Akiskal, letter, Sept. 20, 1988, cited in K. R. Jamison, *Touched with Fire: Manic-Depressive Illness and the Artistic Temperament* (New York: Macmillan, 1993).

51. K. R. Jamison, "Mood Disorders and Patterns of Creativity in British Writers and Artists," *Psychiatry* 52 (1989): 125–34.

52. Jamison, *Touched with Fire.*

53. P. J. van der Maas, J. J. M. van Delden, and L. Pijnenborg, *Euthanasia and other Medical Decisions Concerning the End of Life*, Health Policy Monographs (New York: Elsevier, 1992).

1.   A Psychosocial Perspective

1. Freud, "Mourning and Melancholia," in *The Standard Edition of the Complete Psychological Works*, trans. and ed. J. Strachey, vol. 14 (London: Hogarth Press, 1957; New York: Norton, 1978), pp. 243–58.

2. Freud, "The Psychogenesis of a Case of Homosexuality in a Woman," in *The Standard Edition*, vol. 18 (London: Hogarth Press, 1955; New York: Norton, 1976), pp. 147–72.

3. Freud, *Civilization and Its Discontents* (1930), trans. J. Riviere (London: Hogarth Press, 1949), p. 99.

4. Freud, *Beyond the Pleasure Principle* (New York: Norton, 1975).

5. Dewey, *Human Nature and Conduct* (New York: Modern Library, 1930).

6. Zilboorg, "Considerations on Suicide: With Particular Reference to That of the Young," *American Journal of Orthopsychiatry* 7 (1937): 17.

7. Freud, *Totem and Taboo* (1913), trans. and ed. J. Strachey (New York: Norton, 1952), p. 1.

8. Menninger, *Man against Himself* (New York: Harcourt, Brace, 1938).

9. Durkheim, *Suicide: A Study in Sociology*, trans. J. Spaulding and G. Simpson (New York: Free Press, 1951).

10. *Burnett v. People*, 68 N.E. 505 (Sup. Ct. Ill. 1905).

11. *Sanders v. State*, 112 S.W. 68 (Ct. Crim. App. Tex. 1908).

12. D. Rothman, *The Discovery of the Asylum: Social Order and Disorder in the New Republic* (Boston: Little, Brown, 1971).

13. D. Rothman, *Conscience and Convenience: The Asylum and Its Alternatives in Progressive America* (Boston: Little, Brown, 1980).

14. Lewis, *La Vida: A Puerto Rican Family in the Culture of Poverty—San Juan and New York* (New York: Random House, 1966).

2. Suicide among the Young

1. A. J. Schwartz and L. C. Whitaker, "Suicide among College Students: Assessment, Treatment, and Intervention," in *Suicide Over the Life Cycle*, ed. S. J. Blumenthal and D. J. Kupfer (Washington, D.C.: American Psychiatric Press, 1990), 303–40.

2. M. L. Peck and A. Schrut, "Suicidal Behavior among College Students," *HSMHA Health Report* 86 (1971): 149–56.

3. W. Temby, "Suicide," in *Emotional Problems of the Student*, ed. G. Blaine and C. McArthur (New York: Appleton-Century-Crofts, 1961), pp. 109–28; H. Parish, "Epidemiology of Suicide among College Students," *Yale Journal of Biology and Medicine* 29 (1957): 585–95; R. Seiden, "Campus Tragedy: A Study of Student Suicide," *Journal of Abnormal Psychology* 71 (1966): 389–99.

4. Seiden, "Campus Tragedy: A Study of Student Suicide," *J Ab Psych* 71 (1966): 399.

5. T. Raphael, S. Power, and W. Berridge, "The Question of Suicide as a Problem in College Mental Hygiene," *American Journal of Orthopsychiatry* 7 (1937): 1–14.

6. Ross, "Suicide among College Students," *American Journal of Psychiatry* 126 (1969): 221–22.

7. H. Hendin, "Student Suicide: Death as a Life Style," *Journal of Nervous and Mental Disease* 160 (1975): 204–19; H. Hendin, "Growing Up Dead: Student Suicide," *American Journal of Psychotherapy* 29 (1975) 327–38; H. Hendin, *The Age of Sensation* (New York: Norton, 1975).

8. Zilboorg, "Differential Diagnostic Types of Suicide," *Archives of Neurology and Psychiatry* 35 (1936): 270–91.

9. T. Dorpat, J. Jackson, and H. Ripley, "Broken Homes and Attempted and Completed Suicide," *Arch Gen Psychiatry* 12 (1965): 213–16.

10. S. Greer, "The Relationship between Parental Loss and Attempted Suicide: A Control Study," *British Journal of Psychiatry* 110 (1964): 698–705; J. Bruhn, "Broken Homes among Attempted Suicides and Psychiatric Out-Patients: A Comparative Study," *Journal of Mental Science* 108 (1962): 772–79.

11. J. Jacobs and J. Teicher, "Broken Homes and Social Isolation in Attempted Suicides of Adolescents," *International Journal of Social Psychiatry* 13 (1967): 139–49.

12. Ibid.

13. A. Schrut, "Some Typical Patterns in the Behavior and Background of Adolescent Girls Who Attempt Suicide," *Am J Psychiatry* 125 (1968): 69–

74; R. Gould, "Suicide Problems in Children and Adolescents," *Am J Psychother* 19 (1965): 228–46.

14. Sabbath, "The Suicidal Adolescent—The Expendable Child," *Journal of the American Academy of Child Psychiatry* 8 (1969): 272–89.

15. J. Teicher and J. Jacobs, "Adolescents Who Attempt Suicide: Preliminary Findings," *Am J Psychiatry* 122 (1966): 1248–57.

16. R. Easterlin, "Relative Economic Status and the American Fertility Swing," in *Family Economic Behavior: Problems and Prospects*, ed. E. Sheldon (Philadelphia: Lippincott, 1973), pp. 170–223; R. Easterlin, "The Conflict between Aspirations and Resources," *Population and Development Review* 2 (1976): 417–25; V. Oppenheimer, "The Easterlin Hypothesis: Another Aspect of the Echo to Consider," *Pop Dev Rev* 2 (1976): 433–57; R. Lee, "Demographic Forecasting and the Easterlin Hypothesis," *Pop Dev Rev* 2 (1976): 459–68.

17. R. Easterlin, *Birth and Fortune: The Impact of Numbers on Personal Welfare* (New York: Basic Books, 1980).

18. D. Gurak, Personal communication, 10 Oct. 1980.

3. Suicide among Older People

1. E. Busse and E. Pfeiffer, *Mental Illness in Later Life* (Washington: American Psychiatric Association, 1973), pp. 123–26.

2. J. Sendbuehler and S. Goldstein, "Attempted Suicide among the Aged," *Journal of the American Geriatric Society* 25 (1977): 245–48.

3. Sainsbury, *Suicide in London: An Ecological Study* (New York: Basic Books, 1956), p. 30.

4. P. Sainsbury, "Suicide in Old Age," *Proceedings of the Royal Society of Medicine* 54 (1961): 267.

5. E. Shanas et al., *Old People in Three Industrial Societies* (New York: Atherton, 1968).

6. E. Busse and E. Pfeiffer, "Functional Psychiatric Disorders in Old Age," in *Behavior and Adaptation in Late Life*, ed. E. Busse and E. Pfeiffer, 2d ed. (Boston: Little, Brown, 1977), pp. 158–211.

7. P. O'Neal, E. Robins, and E. Schmidt, "A Psychiatric Study of Attempted Suicide in Persons over Sixty Years of Age," *Archives of Neurology and Psychiatry* 75 (1956): 275–84.

8. I. Batchelor and M. Napier, "Attempted Suicide in Old Age," *British Medical Journal* (Oct.–Dec. 1953): 1188.

9. M. Weissman, K. Fox, and G. Klerman, "Hostility and Depression Associated with Suicide Attempts," *American Journal of Psychiatry* 130 (1973): 450–55.

10. K. Minkoff et al., "Hopelessness, Depression, and Attempted Suicide," *Am J Psychiatry* 130 (1973): 455–59.

11. Weiss, "Suicide in the Aged," in *Suicidal Behaviors: Diagnosis and Management*, ed. H. Resnik (Boston: Little, Brown, 1968), pp. 255–67.

4.   Suicide and Violence

1. Henry and Short, Suicide and Homicide: Some Economic, Sociological, and Psychological Aspects of Aggression (Glencoe, Ill.: Free Press, 1954).

2. H. Hendin, "Black Suicide," Archives of General Psychiatry 21 (1969): 407–22; H. Hendin, Black Suicide (New York: Basic Books, 1969).

3. Wolfgang, Patterns in Criminal Homicide (Philadelphia: University of Pennsylvania, 1958); Wolfgang, "Suicide by Means of Victim-Precipitated Homicide," Journal of Clinical and Experimental Psychopathology and Quarterly Review of Psychiatry and Neurology 20 (1959): 335–49.

4. Wolfgang, The Subculture of Violence: Towards an Integrated Theory in Criminology (London: Tavistock Publications, 1967).

5. Wolfgang, "An Analysis of Homicide-Suicide," Journal of Clinical and Experimental Psychopathology 19 (1958): 208–18.

6. West, Murder Followed by Suicide (Cambridge, Mass.: Harvard University Press, 1966).

7. Camus, The Fall, trans. J. O'Brien (New York: Modern Library, 1964).

8. F. Nietzsche, On the Genealogy of Morals, trans. W. Kaufmann (New York: Vintage Books, 1967).

9. F. Alexander and H. Staub, The Criminal, the Judge, and the Public, rev. ed., trans. G. Zilboorg (Glencoe, Ill.: Free Press, 1956), pp. 151–63.

10. Dorpat, "Suicide in Murderers," Psychiatry Digest 27 (June 1966): 54.

11. P. Resnick, "Child Murder by Parents: A Psychiatric Review of Filicide," American Journal of Psychiatry 126 (1969): 325–34.

12. K. Cole, G. Fisher, and S. Cole, "Women Who Kill: A Sociopsychological Study," Archives of General Psychiatry 19 (1968): 1–8.

13. Resnick, "Child Murder by Parents," Am J Psychiatry 126 (1969): 325–34.

14. S. Myers, "The Child Slayer: A Twenty-five Year Survey of Homicides Involving Preadolescent Victims," Arch Gen Psychiatry 17 (1967): 211–13.

15. Siciliano, "Risultati preliminari di un'indagine sull'omicidio in Danimarca," La scuola positiva, 4th ser. 3 (1961): 718–29.

16. H. Hendin, "Suicide in Denmark," Psychiatric Quarterly 34 (1960): 443–60.

5.   Suicide and Homosexuality

1. D. Shaffer, "Political Science," The New Yorker, May 3, 1993, p. 116.

2. E. Robins, The Final Months: A Study of the Lives of 134 Persons Who Committed Suicide (New York: Oxford, 1981).

3. C. L. Rich, R. C. Fowler, D. Young, and M. Blankush, "San Diego Suicide Study: Comparison of Gay to Straight Males," Suicide and Life-Threatening Behavior 16 (1986): 448–57.

4. Shaffer, "Political Science," The New Yorker, May 3, 1993, p. 116.

5. A. Kinsey, W. B. Pomeroy, and C. E. Martins, Sexual Behavior in the

Human Male (Philadelphia: W. B. Saunders, 1948); A. Kinsey, W. B. Pomeroy, C. E. Martins, and P. H. Gebhard, *Sexual Behavior in the Human Female* (Philadelphia: W. B. Saunders, 1953).

6. J. O. G. Billy, R. Tanfer, W. R. Grady, and D. N. Klepinger, "The Sexual Behavior of Men in the United States," *Family Planning Perspectives* 25 (1993): 52–60.

7. P. M. Marzuk, H. Tierny, K. Tardiff, E. M. Gross, M. A. Hsu, and J. J. Mann, "Increased Risk of Suicide in Persons with AIDS," *Journal of the American Medical Association* 259 (1988): 1333–37; T. R. Cole et al., "Risk of Suicide among Persons with AIDS: A National Assessment," *JAMA* 268 (1992): 2066–68.

8. M. Saghir, E. Robins, B. Walbran, and K. Gentry, "Homosexuality: IV. Psychiatric Disorders and Disability in the Female Homosexual," *American Journal of Psychiatry* 127 (1970): 147–54; idem, "Homosexuality: III. Psychiatric Disorders and Disability in the Male Homosexual," ibid. 126 (1970): 1079–86.

9. S. G. Schneider, N. L. Farberow, G. N. Kruks, "Suicidal Behavior in Adolescent and Adult Gay Men," *Suicide and Life-Threatening Behavior* 4 (1989): 381–94; G. Ramafedi, "Male Homosexuality: The Adolescent Perspective," *Pediatrics* 79 (1987): 326–30. G. Ramafedi, "Adolescent Homosexuality: Psychosocial and Medical Implications," *Pediatrics* 79 (1987): 331–37; T. Roesler and R. W. Deischer, "Youthful Male Homosexuality," *JAMA* 219 (1972): 1018–23.

10. J. Carmen and A. Blaine, "A Study of Suicide Attempts by Male and Female University Students," *International Psychiatric Clinics* (1970): 181–99.

11. H. Hendin, *The Age of Sensation* (New York: Norton, 1975).

12. H. Hendin, *Black Suicide* (New York: Harper & Row, 1971).

13. Baldwin, *Another Country* (New York: Dial Press, 1962).

14. Baldwin, *The Fire Next Time* (New York: Dial Press, 1963).

6. Suicide and Alcoholism

1. C. Schmid, "Suicide in Minneapolis, Minnesota: 1928–32," *American Journal of Sociology* 39 (1933): 30–48; J. Tuckman and M. Lavell, "Study of Suicide in Philadelphia," *Public Health Reports* 73 (1958): 547–53.

2. E. Robins et al., "Some Clinical Considerations in the Prevention of Suicide Based on a Study of 134 Successful Suicides," *American Journal of Public Health* 49 (1959): 888–99; E. Palola, T. Dorpat, and W. Larson, "Alcoholism and Suicidal Behavior," in *Society, Culture, and Drinking Patterns*, ed. D. Pittman and C. Snyder (New York: Wiley, 1962), pp. 511–34.

3. D. Goodwin, "Alcohol in Suicide and Homicide," *Quarterly Journal of Studies on Alcohol* 34 (1973): 144–56.

4. Lemere, "What Happens to Alcoholics," *American Journal of Psychiatry* 109 (1953): 674–76.

5. Rushing, "Suicide as a Possible Consequence of Alcoholism," in *Devi-*

ant Behavior and Social Process, ed. W. Rushing (Chicago: Rand McNally, 1969), pp. 323–27; Rushing, "Alcoholism and Suicide Rates by Status Set and Occupation," *Quarterly Journal of Studies on Alcohol* 29 (1968): 399–412.

6. Tamerin and Mendelson, "The Psychodynamics of Chronic Inebriation: Observation of Alcoholics during the Process of Drinking in an Experimental Group Setting," *Am J Psychiatry* 125 (1969): 886–99.

7. D. Mayfield and D. Montgomery, "Alcoholism, Alcohol Intoxication, and Suicide Attempts," *Archives of General Psychiatry* 27 (1972): 349–53.

8. Whitehead, "Notes on the Association between Alcoholism and Suicide," *International Journal of Addictions* 7 (1972): 525–32.

9. Frederick, "Drug Abuse: A Self-Destructive Enigma," *Maryland State Medical Journal* 22 (1973): 19–21; Frederick, "Drug Abuse as Self-Destructive Behavior," *Drug Therapy* 2 (1972): 49–68.

10. Menninger, *Man against Himself* (New York: Harcourt, Brace, 1938), p. 184.

11. Palola, Dorpat, and Larson, "Alcoholism and Suicidal Behavior," in *Society, Culture, and Drinking Patterns*, 511–34.

12. Murphy and Robins, "Social Factors in Suicide," *Journal of the American Medical Association* 199 (1967): 303–8.

13. G. Murphy, J. Armstrong, S. Hemele, J. Fisher, and W. Clendenin, "Suicide and Alcoholism," *Arch Gen Psychiatry* 36 (1979): 65–69.

14. A. Beck, M. Weissman, and M. Kovacs, "Alcoholism, Hopelessness, and Suicidal Behavior," *Journal of Studies on Alcohol* 37 (1976): 66–77.

7. *Method and Motive*

1. H. Hendin, *Suicide and Scandinavia* (New York: Grune & Stratton, 1964).

2. H. Hendin, *Black Suicide* (New York: Harper & Row, 1971).

3. Marks and Abernathy, "Toward a Sociocultural Perspective on Means of Self-Destruction," *Suicide and Life-Threatening Behavior* 4 (1974): 3–17.

4. Gastil, "Homicide and a Regional Culture of Violence," *American Sociological Review* 36 (1971): 412–27.

5. Taylor and Wicks, "The Choice of Weapons: A Study of Suicide by Sex, Race, and Region," *Suicide Life-Threatening Behav* 10 (1980): 142–49.

6. Friedman, "Suicide among Police: A Study of 93 Suicides among New York City Policemen, 1934–1940," in *Essays in Self-Destruction*, ed. E. Shneidman (New York: Science House, 1967), pp. 414–49.

7. Freud, "The Psychogenesis of a Case of Homosexuality in a Woman," in *The Standard Edition of the Complete Psychological Works*, trans. and ed. J. Strachey, vol. 18 (London: Hogarth Press, 1955; New York: Norton, 1976), pp. 147–72.

8. Furst and Ostow, "The Psychodynamics of Suicide," in *Suicide: Theory and Clinical Aspects*, ed. L. Hankoff and B. Einsidler (Littleton, Mass.: PSG Publishing Company, 1979), pp. 165–78.

9. H. De Rosis, "Supervision of the First-Year Psychiatric Resident," *Psychiatric Quarterly* 46 (1972): 292.

10. J. MacDonald, "Suicide and Homicide by Automobile," *American Journal of Psychiatry* 121 (1964): 366–70.

11. Shneidman and Farberow, "Genuine and Simulated Suicide Notes," in *Clues to Suicide*, ed E. Shneidman and N. Farberow (New York: McGraw-Hill, 1957), pp. 197–215.

12. J. Tuckman, R. Kleiner, and M. Lavell, "Emotional Content of Suicide Notes," *Am J Psychiatry* 116 (1959): 59–63.

13. S. Cohen and J. Fiedler, "Content Analysis of Multiple Messages in Suicide Notes," *Suicide Life-Threatening Behav* 4 (1974): 75–95.

14. Gottschalk and Gleser, "An Analysis of the Verbal Content of Suicide Notes," *British Journal of Medical Psychology* 33 (1960): 196.

15. Ibid., p. 203.

16. Tuckman, Kleiner, and Lavell, "Emotional Content of Suicide Notes," *Am J Psychiatry* 116 (1959): 62–63.

17. Jacobs, "A Phenomenological Study of Suicide Notes," *Social Problems* 15 (1967): 60–72.

18. Shneidman, "Suicide Notes Reconsidered," in *Suicidology: Contemporary Developments*, ed. E. Shneidman (New York: Grune & Stratton, 1976), pp. 253–78.

19. P. Marzuk, K. Tardiff, C. Hirsch, et al. "Increase in Suicide by Asphyxiation in New York City after the Publication of *Final Exit*," *New England Journal of Medicine* 329 (1993): 1508–10; B. Angelo, interview, "Assigning the Blame for a Young Man's Suicide," *Time*, November 18, 1991, p. 12.

8.   *Psychotherapy and Suicide*

1. R. Mintz, "Some Practical Procedures in the Management of Suicidal Persons," *American Journal of Orthopsychiatry* 36 (1966): 896–903; R. Mintz, "Psychotherapy of the Suicidal Patient," *American Journal of Psychotherapy* 15 (1961): 348–67; R. Mintz, "Basic Considerations in the Psychotherapy of the Depressed Suicidal Patient," *Am J Psychother* 25 (1971): 56–73; H. Shein and A. Stone, "Monitoring and Treatment of Suicidal Potential within the Context of Psychotherapy," *Comprehensive Psychiatry* 10 (1969): 59–70; H. Shein and A. Stone, "Psychotherapy Designed to Detect and Treat Suicidal Potential," *American Journal of Psychiatry* 125 (1969): 1247–51; A. Stone and H. Shein, "Psychotherapy of the Hospitalized Suicidal Patient," *Am J Psychother* 22 (1968): 15–25.

2. Mintz, "Psychotherapy of the Suicidal Patient," *Am J Psychother* 15 (1961): 348–67.

3. Wheat, "Motivational Aspects of Suicide in Patients during and after Psychiatric Treatment," *Southern Medical Journal* 53 (1960): 273–78.

4. Bloom, "An Analysis of Suicide at a Training Center," *Am J Psychiatry* 123 (1967): 918–25.

5. Lowental, "Suicide—The Other Side: The Factor of Reality among Suicidal Motivations," *Archives of General Psychiatry* 33 (1976): 838–42.

6. Alvarez, *The Savage God: A Study of Suicide* (London: Weidenfeld and Nicolson, 1972).

7. Maltsberger and Buie, "Countertransference Hate in the Treatment of Suicidal Patients," *Arch Gen Psychiatry* 30 (1974): 627.

8. D. Schwartz, D. Flinn, and P. Slawson, "Treatment of the Suicidal Character," *Am J Psychother* 28 (1974): 197.

9. Szasz, "The Ethics of Suicide," *Antioch Review* 31 (1971): 7–17.

9. Suicide Prevention

1. Informational literature of the National Save-a-Life League, 1980.

2. Varah, ed., *The Samaritans: To Help Those Tempted to Suicide or Despair* (New York: Macmillan, 1966).

3. Informational literature of the Contact Teleministries, 1980.

4. Varah, ed., *Samaritans*.

5. Yolles, "Suicide: A Public Health Problem," in *Suicidal Behaviors: Diagnosis and Management*, ed. H. Resnik (Boston: Little, Brown, 1968), pp. 50–51.

6. Shneidman and Farberow, "The Suicide Prevention Center of Los Angeles," in *Suicidal Behaviors*, pp. 367–80.

7. Varah, ed., *Samaritans*.

8. Informational literature of the American Association for Suicidology, 1980.

9. C. Bagley, "The Evaluation of a Suicide Prevention Scheme by an Ecological Method," *Social Science and Medicine* 2 (1968): 1–14; R. Fox, "The Recent Decline of Suicide in Britain: The Role of the Samaritan Suicide Prevention Movement," in *Suicidology: Contemporary Developments*, ed. E. Shneidman (New York: Grune & Stratton, 1976), pp. 499–524.

10. Weiner, "The Effectiveness of a Suicide Prevention Program," *Mental Hygiene* 53 (1969): 357–63.

11. "Directory of Suicide Prevention Facilities," *Bulletin of Suicidology* 1 (1967): 14–18; "Directory of Suicide Prevention Facilities," *Bulletin of Suicidology* 5 (1969): 47–58.

12. Lester, "Effect of Suicide Prevention Centers on Suicide Rates in the United States," *Health Services Reports* 89 (1974): 37–39.

13. C. Jennings, B. Barraclough, and J. Moss, "Have the Samaritans Lowered the Suicide Rate? A Controlled Study," *Psychological Medicine* 8 (1978): 413–22.

14. K. Whittemore, *Ten Centers: A Comparative Analysis of Incoming Calls at Ten Suicide Prevention Centers* (Atlanta: Lullwater, 1970).

15. D. Lester, "An Analysis of 'Nuisance' Calls Received by a Suicide-Prevention Center," *Crisis Intervention* 2 (1970): 48–51.

16. Maris, "The Sociology of Suicide Prevention: Policy Implications of

Differences between Suicidal Patients and Completed Suicides," *Social Problems* 17 (1969): 132–49.

17. D. Lester, "The Myth of Suicide Prevention," *Comprehensive Psychiatry* 13 (1972): 555–60.

18. Ibid.

19. Litman and C. Wold, "Beyond Crisis Intervention," in *Suicidology*, ed. Shneidman, pp. 525–46.

20. J. Sawyer, H. Sudak, and R. Hall, "A Follow-up Study of Fifty-three Suicides Known to a Suicide Prevention Center," *Suicide and Life-Threatening Behavior* 2 (1972): 227–38.

21. Litman and Wold, "Beyond Crisis Intervention," in *Suicidology*, ed. Schneidman, pp. 525–46.

22. Ibid.

23. J. Motto, "Suicide Attempts: A Longitudinal View," *Archives of General Psychiatry* 13 (1965): 516–20; T. Dorpat and H. Ripley, "The Relationship between Attempted Suicide and Committed Suicide," *Comprehensive Psychiatry* 8 (1967): 74–77.

24. Ibid. See also E. Robins et al., "The Communication of Suicidal Intent: A Study of 134 Consecutive Cases of Successful (Completed) Suicide," *American Journal of Psychiatry* 115 (1959): 724–33; T. Dorpat and H. Ripley, "A Study of Suicide in the Seattle Area," *Comp Psychi* 1 (1960): 349–59; N. Farberow and E. Shneidman, "Attempted, Threatened, and Completed Suicide," *Journal of Abnormal Social Psychiatry* 50 (1955): 230.

25. E. Cohen, J. Motto, and R. Seiden, "An Instrument for Evaluating Suicide Potential: A Preliminary Study," *Am J Psychiatry* 122 (1966): 886–91.

10. Involuntary Commitment

1. B. Ennis and T. Litwack, "Psychiatry and the Presumption of Expertise: Flipping Coins in the Courtroom," *California Law Review* 62 (1974): 693–752; B. Ennis and R. Emery, *The Rights of Mental Patients*, An American Civil Liberties Union Handbook (New York: Avon Books, 1978); D. Greenberg, "Involuntary Psychiatric Commitments to Prevent Suicide," *New York University Law Review* 49 (1974): 227–69.

2. Ennis and Emery, *Rights of Mental Patients*.

3. J. Gibbs, "Rates of Mental Hospitalization: A Study of Societal Reaction to Deviant Behavior," *American Sociological Review* 27 (1962): 782–92; J. Ordway, "Experiences in Evaluating Dangerousness in Private Practice and in a Court Clinic," in *The Clinical Evaluation of the Dangerousness of the Mentally Ill*, ed. J. Rappeport (Springfield, Ill.: C. C. Thomas, 1967), pp. 35–42.

4. D. Wenger and R. Fletcher, "The Effect of Legal Counsel on Admissions to a State Mental Hospital: A Confrontation of Professions," *Journal of Health and Social Behavior* 10 (1969): 66–72.

5. Ennis and Litwack, "Psychiatry and the Presumption of Expertise"; Greenberg, "Involuntary Psychiatric Commitments"; G. Dix, " 'Civil' Com-

mitment of the Mentally Ill and the Need for Data in Prediction of Dangerousness," *American Behavioral Scientist* 19 (1976): 318–34.

6. A. Temoche, T. Pugh, and B. MacMahon, "Suicide Rates among Current and Former Mental Institution Patients," *Journal of Nervous and Mental Disease* 138 (1964): 124–30.

7. E. Robins et al., "The Communication of Suicidal Intent: A Study of 134 Consecutive Cases of Successful (Completed) Suicide," *American Journal of Psychiatry* 115 (1959): 724–33.

8. N. Farberow and T. McEvoy, "Suicide among Patients with Diagnoses of Anxiety Reaction or Depressive Reaction in General Medical and Surgical Hospitals," *Journal of Abnormal Psychology* 71 (1966): 287–99.

9. L. Moss and D. Hamilton, "The Psychotherapy of the Suicidal Patient," *Am J Psychiatry* 112 (1956): 814–20.

10. E. Kraepelin, *Manic-Depressive Insanity and Paranoia*, ed. G. Robertson, trans. R. M. Barclay (Edinburgh: Livingstone, 1921; New York: Arno Press, 1976), p. 206.

11. R. Litman and N. Farberow, "The Hospital's Obligation toward Suicide-Prone Patients," *Hospitals* 40 (Dec. 16, 1966): 64–68, 124.

12. Farberow and McEvoy, "Suicide among Patients with Diagnoses of Anxiety Reaction," *J Ab Psych* 71 (1966): 287–99; A. Beisser and J. Blanchette, "A Study of Suicides in a Mental Hospital," *Diseases of the Nervous System* 22 (1961): 365–69; S. Levy and R. Southcombe, "Suicide in a State Hospital for the Mentally Ill," *J Nerv Ment Dis* 117 (1953): 504–13.

13. D. Schwartz, D. Flinn, and P. Slawson, "Treatment of the Suicidal Character," *American Journal of Psychotherapy* 28 (1974): 194–207.

14. Woolley and Eichert, "Notes on the Problem of Suicide and Escape," *Am J Psychiatry* 98 (1941): 110–18.

15. Mental Health Law Project, "Suggested Statute on Civil Commitment," *Mental Disability Law Reporter* 2 (1977): 131–59.

16. Alabama: ALA. CODE § 22-52-1(b) (1980 Cum. Supp.); California: CAL. WELF. & INST'NS CODE § 5260, § 5300 (West 1981); Hawaii: HAWAII REV. STAT. § 334-59 (1980 Supp.); Massachusetts: MASS. GEN. LAWS ANN. ch. 12, § 1, § 12 (West 1981); Nebraska: NEB. REV. STAT. § 83-1009 (Cum. Supp. 1980); Washington: WASH. REV. CODE ANN. § 71.05.020 (1975); Wisconsin: WIS. STAT. ANN. § 51.15, § 51.20 (West 1981).

17. *Addington v. Texas*, 441 U.S. 418 (1979).

18. See, e.g., District of Columbia: In re Ballay, 482 F.2d 648 (D.C. Cir. 1973): In re Hodges, 325 A.2d 605 (D.C. 1974); Hawaii: HAW. REV. STAT. § 334-60(b)(4)(I)(1980 Supp.); Idaho: IDAHO CODE § 66-329(i) (1980 Supp.); Kansas: KAN. STAT. ANN. § 59-2917 (1976 & 1980 Supp.); Kentucky: Denton v. Commonwealth, 383 S.W.2d 681 (Ky. 1964) (dicta); Massachusetts: *Super. of Worcester State Hospital v. Hagberg, Mass.* 372 N.E.2d 242 (1978); Minnesota: *Lausche v. Commissioner of Public Welfare*, 302 Minn. 65, 69, 225 N.W.2d 366 (1974) cert. denied, 420 U.S. 993, 95 S. Ct. 1430 (1975).

19. See, e.g., Minnesota: MINN. STAT. ANN. § 253A.07 subd. 17 (West 1971 & 1981 Supp.); Utah: UTAH CODE ANN. § 64-7-36(10) (1953 & 1979

Supp.); Hawaii: HAWAII REV. STAT. § 334-60(b)(1)(C) (1980 Supp.); Maine: ME. REV. STAT. ANN. tit. 34, § 2334 4E(2), 5(2) (1978 ed.).

20. J. Bray, "General Comments Concerning the Mental Health Law Project's Civil Commitment Section of the Model Legislative Guide," *Men Dis LR* 2 (1978): 527.

21. See, e.g., N.J. STAT. ANN. § 30:4-41 (1981), requiring notice only of the time and place of the final hearing.

22. *Lessard v. Schmidt*, 349 F. Supp. 1078, 1100–1102. (E.D. Wis. 1972) vacated and remanded on other grounds, 414 U.S. 473 (1974); on remand, 379 F. Supp. 1376 (E.D. Wis. 1974), vacated and remanded 421 U.S. 957 (1975) on remand, 413 F. Supp. 1318 (E.D. Wis. 1976): Matter of Matthews, 46 Or. App. 757, 613 P.2d 88 (1980) cert. denied 101 S. Ct. 1757 (1981). See also Suzuki v. Yuen, No. 78-1830 (9th Cir. April 16, 1980); *French v. Blackburn*, *428 F. Supp. 1351 (M.D.N.C. 1977); In re Winstead, No. 9388 (Ohio Ct. App. Jan. 9, 1980); Illinois by statute requires a Miranda warning.* ILL. REV. STAT. ch. 91½, § 3-208 (1978 Supp.); *Illinois v. Rizer*, 409 N.E.2d 383 (Ill. App. Ct. 1980).

23. Doremus v. Farrell, 407 F. Supp. 509, 515 (D. Neb. 1975).

24. See, e.g., Alaska: ALASKA STAT. § 47.30.070(h) (1962); District of Columbia D.C. CODE ENCYCL. § 21-545(a) (1967); Texas: TEX. REV. CIV. STAT. ANN. art. 5547-48 (Vernon 1958); Washington: WASH. REV. CODE ANN. § 71.05.310 (1975).

25. See note 22 above.

26. Matter of Matthews, 46, Or. App. 757, 613 P.2d 88 (1980) cert. denied 101 S. Ct. 1757 (1981).

27. *Lessard v. Schmidt*, 349 F. Supp. 1078 (E.D. Wis. 1972); *Lynch v. Baxley*, 386 F. Supp. 378 (M.D. Ala. 1974); *Doremus v. Farrell*, 407 F. Supp. 509 (D. Neb. 1975); *Suzuki v. Quisenberry*, 411 F. Supp. 1113 (D. Ha. 1976); See also State ex rel. *Hawks v. Lazaro*, 202 S.E.2d 109 (W. Va. 1974); *Stamus v. Leonhard*, 414 F. Supp. 439 (S.D. Iowa 1976); WASH. REV. CODE ANN. § 71.05.250 (1975).

28. See e.g., *Heryford v. Parker*, 396 F.2d 393 (10th Cir. 1968); Quesnell v. State, 517 P.2d 568 (Wash. 1978): State ex rel. *Hawkes v. Lazaro*, 202 S.E.2d 109 (W. Va. 1974); *Lessard v. Schmidt*, 349 F. Supp. 1078 (E.D. Wis. 1972).

29. CAL. WEL. & INST'NS CODE § 5206 (West 1972).

30. E. Andalman and D. Chambers, "Effective Counsel for Persons Facing Civil Commitment: A Survey, a Polemic, and a Proposal," *Mississippi Law Journal* 45 (1974): 43–91; T. Litwack, "The Role of Counsel in Civil Commitment Proceedings: Emerging Problems," *California Law Review* 62 (1974): 816–39; M. Blinick, "Mental Disability, Legal Ethics, and Professional Responsibility," *Albany Law Review* 33 (1968): 92–119.

31. F. Cohen, "The Function of the Attorney and the Commitment of the Mentally Ill," *Texas Law Review* 44 (1966): 424–59.

32. R. Gupta, "New York's Mental Health Information Service: An Experiment in Due Process," *Rutgers Law Review* 25 (1971): 405–50.

33. Lanterman-Petris-Short, CAL. WEL. & INST'NS CODE §§ 5000 et seq. (1972, 1981 Cum. Supp.)

34. ENKI Research Institute, A *Study of California's New Mental Health Law* (1969–1971) (Chatsworth, Calif.: ENKI, 1972).

35. Ibid.

36. ENKI Research Institute, Unpublished report, 1980.

37. N.Y. MENTAL HYG. LAW §§ 29-09 et seq. (McKinney 1978) 1981 Cum. Supp.

38. A. Broderick, "Justice in the Books or Justice in Action: An Institutional Approach to Involuntary Hospitalization for Mental Illness," *Catholic University of America Law Review* 20 (1971): 547–701; Association of the Bar of the City of New York, Special Committee to Study Commitment Procedures, *Mental Health and Due Process* (Ithaca: Cornell University Press, 1962), p. 21.

39. See notes 32, 37, and 38 above.

40. Mental Health Systems Act, 42 U.S.C.A. § 9501 (Oct. 7, 1980).

41. D. Reed, *Anna* (New York: Basic Books, 1976).

42. N.J. REV. STAT. 52: 27E–25 (1981).

43. WASH. REV. CODE ANN. § 71.05.300 (1975); N.Y. JUD. LAW § 35 (McKinney 1978, 1981 Cum. Supp.).

11. *Euthanasia and the Right to Suicide*

1. F. Nietzsche, *Human, All-Too-Human*, trans. H. Zimmern (Edinburgh: Foulis, 1909), 88.

2. T. Szasz, *The Myth of Mental Illness: Foundations of a Theory of Personal Conduct*, rev. ed. (New York: Harper & Row, 1974); Szasz, *Law, Liberty, and Psychiatry: An Inquiry into the Social Uses of Mental Health Practices* (New York: Collier Books, 1968); Szasz, *Ceremonial Chemistry: The Ritual Persecution of Drugs, Addicts, and Pushers* (Garden City, N.Y.: Anchor Books, 1974); Szasz, *The Second Sin* (Garden City, N.Y.: Anchor Books, 1974); Szasz, "The Ethics of Suicide," *Antioch Review* 31 (1971): 7–17.

3. Szasz, *The Second Sin*, 75, 76.

4. E. Robins, C. Murphy, R. Wilkenson, et al., "Some Clinical Considerations in the Prevention of Suicide Based on a Study of 134 Successful Suicides," *American Journal of Public Health* 49 (1959): 888–99.

5. E. Slater, "Choosing the Time to Die," in *Suicide: The Philosophical Issues*, ed. M. P. Battin and D. Mayo (New York: St. Martin's, 1980), 202–3.

6. M. Barrington, "Apologia for Suicide," in ibid., p. 98.

7. Slater, "Choosing the Time to Die," pp. 202–3.

8. Y. Kamisar, "Are Laws against Suicide Unconstitutional?" *Hastings Center Report* 23 (1993): 32–41.

9. D. Callahan, "When Self-Determination Runs Amok," *Hastings Center Report* 22 (1992): 52–55.

10. A. Camus, *The Myth of Sisyphus and Other Essays*, trans. Justin O'Brien (New York: Alfred Knopf, 1958).

11. H. Hendin, "New Directions in Suicide Research," *Hospital and Community Psychiatry* 37 (1986): 148–54.

12. E. Robins, G. Murphy, R. Wilkenson, et al., "Some Clinical Considerations in the Prevention of Suicide Based on a Study of 134 Successful Suicides," *American Journal of Public Health* 49 (1959): 888–99; T. L. Dorpat and H. S. Ripley, "A Study of Suicide in the Seattle Area," *Comprehensive Psychiatry* 1 (1960): 349–59; B. Barraclough, J. Bunch, B. Nelson, and P. Sainsbury, "A Hundred Cases of Suicide: Clinical Aspects," *British Journal of Psychiatry* 125 (1974): 355–73; D. C. Rich, D. Young, R. C. Fowler, "San Diego Suicide Study, I: Young vs. Old Subjects," *Archives of General Psychiatry* 43 (1986): 577–82.

13. Y. Conwell and E. D. Caine, "Rational Suicide and the Right to Die: Reality and Myth," *New England Journal of Medicine* 15 (1991): 1100–103.

14. E. Robins, G. Murphy, R. Wilkenson, et al., "Some Clinical Considerations in the Prevention of Suicide Based on a Study of 134 Successful Suicides," *Am J Pub Health* 49 (1959): 888–99; Y. Conwell and E. D. Caine, "Rational Suicide and the Right to Die: Reality and Myth," *NEJM* 15 (1991): 1100–103; B. Barraclough, J. Bunch, B. Nelson, P. Sainsbury, "A Hundred Cases of Suicide: Clinical Aspects," *Br J Psychi* 125 (1974): 355–73.

15. J. Brown, P. Henteleff, S. Barakat, and C. J. Rowe, "Is It Normal for Terminally Ill Patients to Desire Death?" *American Journal of Psychiatry* 143 (1986): 208–11.

16. Y. Conwell, E. D. Caine, and K. Olsen, "Suicide and Cancer in Later Life," *Hospital and Community Psychiatry* 41 (1990): 1334–39; T. L. Dorpat, W. F. Anderson, and H. S. Ripley, "The Relationship of Physical Illness to Suicide," in *Suicidal Behaviors: Diagnosis and Management*, ed. H. P. L. Resnick (Boston: Little, Brown, 1968).

17. S. Perry, "Suicidal Ideation and HIV Testing," *Journal of the American Medical Association* 263 (1990): 679–82.

18. Y. Conwell and E. D. Caine, "Rational Suicide and the Right to Die: Reality and Myth," *NEJM* 15 (1991): 1100–103.

19. P. J. Maas, J. J. M. van Delden, L. Pijnenborg, and C. W. H. Louwan, "Euthanasia and Other Medical Decisions Concerning the End of Life," *The Lancet* 338 (1991) 669–74.

20. K. Lebacqz and N. T. Englehardt, "Suicide and Covenant," in *Suicide: The Philosophical Issues*, ed. M. P. Battin and D. Mayo (New York: St. Martins Press, 1980), p. 85–86.

21. M. P. Battin, "Manipulated Suicide," in *Suicide: The Philosophical Issues*, ed. M. P. Battin and D. Mayo (New York: St. Martins Press, 1980).

22. "Doctor in Suicides Assails U.S. Ethics," *New York Times*, November 3, 1991, p. A14.

23. J. Kevorkian, "A Fail-Safe Model for Justifiable Medically Assisted Suicide," *American Journal of Forensic Psychiatry* 13 (1992): 7–81.

24. The Hemlock Society, *Assisted Suicide: The Compassionate Crime* (Los Angeles, 1982).

25. D. Humphry, *Final Exit* (Eugene, Ore.: Hemlock Society, 1991).

26. P. Marzuk, K. Tardiff, C. Hirsch, et al. "Increase in Suicide by Asphyxiatian in New York City after the Publication of *Final Exit*,[11] *NEJM* 329 (1993): 1508; B. Angelo, interview: "Assigning the Blame for a Young Man's Suicide," *Time*, Nov. 18, 1991, p. 12.

27. A. Wickett, *Double Exit* (National Hemlock Society, 1989); T. Gabriel, "A Fight to the Death," *New York Times Magazine*, December 8, 1991, p. 46; G. Abrams, "A Bitter Legacy—Angry Accusations Abound after the Suicide of Hemlock Society Co-Founder Ann Humphry," *Los Angeles Times*, "View" section, p. 1, October 23, 1991.

28. R. Noyes, S. Frye, and C. Hartford, "Single Case Study: Conjugal Suicide Pact," *Journal of Nervous and Mental Diseases* 165 (1977): 72–75; D. Mehta, P. Mathew, and S. Mehta, "Suicide Pact in a Depressed Elderly Couple," *Journal of the American Cancer Society* 136 (1978): 136–58.

29. A. Hoche, "Vom Sterben," in *Aus der Werkstatt* (Munich: Jehmann, 1935), pp. 210–32.

30. R. Brandt, "The Morality and Rationality of Suicide," in A *Handbook for the Study of Suicide*, ed. S. Perlin (New York: Oxford University Press, 1975), pp. 61–76.

31. H. Hendin, "Seduced by Death: Doctors, Patients and the Dutch Cure," *Issues in Law and Medicine* 10 (1994): pp. 123–68.

32. "Psychiater Vrijuit na Hulp Bij Zelfdoding," *Algemeen Dagblad*, Rotterdam, April 22, 1993, pp. 1 & 4; "Psychiater niet Gestraft voor Hulp bij Zelfdoding," *Volkskrant*, Amsterdam, April 22, 1993, pp. 1 & 3; "Dutch Seek Freer Mercy Killing," William Drozdiak, *Washington Post*, Oct. 29, 1993, pp. A29, A32.

33. P. J. van der Maas, J. J. M. van Delden, and L. Pijnenborg, *Euthanasia and Other Medical Decisions Concerning the End of Life* (New York: Elsevier, 1992).

34. L. Pijnenborg, P. J. van der Maas, J. J. van Delden, and C. W. Looman, "Life-terminating Acts without Explicit Request of Patient," *Lancet* 341 (1993): 1196–99.

35. H. W. A. Hilhorst, *Euthanasie ni het Ziekenhuis* (Lochem-Poperinge: De Tijdstroom, 1983).

36. G. F. Koerselman, "Hoemondig Zijn Moderne Patienter?" *Med Tijdseter Geneesk* 14 (1986): 156–57; H. ten Have and G. Kimsna, *Geneeskunde Tissen Droon en Drama* (Kampen: R.O.K. Agora, 1987), pp. 83–84.

37. "Psychiater Vrijuit na Hulp Bij Zelfdoding," *Algemeen Dagblad*, Rotterdam, April 22, 1993, pp. 1 & 4; "Psychiater niet Gestraft voor Hulp bij Zelfdoding," *Volkskrant*, Amsterdam, April 22, 1993, pp. 1& 3; "Dutch Seek Freer Mercy Killing," William Drozdiak, *Washington Post*, Oct. 29, 1993, pp. A29, A32.

38. "Doctor Unpunished for Dutch Suicide," *New York Times*, June 22, 1994, p. A10.

39. J. Keown, "On Regulating Death," *Hastings Center Report* 22 (1992):

39–43; A. M. Capron, "Euthanasia in the Netherlands: American Observations," *Hastings Center Report* 22 (1992): 30–33; J. Welie, "The Medical Exception: Physicians, Euthanasia, and the Dutch Criminal Law," *Journal of Medicine and Philosophy* 17 (1992): 419–37.

40. H. Brody, "Assisted Death—A Compassionate Response to a Medical Failure," *NEJM* 327 (1992): 1384–88.

41. D. Margolick, "Jury Acquits Dr. Kevorkian of Illegally Aiding a Suicide," *New York Times*, May 3, 1994, Section A, p. 1.

42. President's Commission for the Study of Ethical Problems in Medicine and Biomedical and Behavioral Research, *Decisions to Forego Life-Sustaining Treatment* (U.S. Government Printing Office, March 1983).

43. C. E. Koop, "The Challenge of Definition," *Hastings Center Report*, Special Supplement (Jan. / Feb. 1989): 2–3.

Index